THE

Ultimate
Instant Pot ®

COOKBOOK

THE
Ultimate
Instant Pot®
COOKBOOK

200 DELICIOUSLY SIMPLE
RECIPES FOR YOUR ELECTRIC
PRESSURE COOKER

Coco Morante

Photography by Jennifer Davick

TEN SPEED PRESS
California | New York

Contents

CHAPTER 4: VEGETARIAN

CHAPTER 5: SEAFOOD

CHAPTER 9: DRINKS AND DESSERTS

PANTRY

Introduction

The Instant Pot's global success seems to have come out of nowhere. We were all happily getting along with our analog pots and pans, and then, in the blink of an eye, an army of these programmable electric pressure cookers appeared on kitchen counters the world over. Instant Pots had charmed their way into the hearts of millions of home cooks seemingly overnight.

No doubt, part of the Instant Pot's immediate success is owed to its catchy name: the term "instant" makes some big promises. It sounds like you'll be able to toss some ingredients into the pot, press a button, and a complete dinner will appear in an instant, à la that space-age stove on *The Jetsons*.

Although that isn't really the case (hard-boiled eggs in the Instant Pot *do* come pretty close!), there's enormous appeal in the Instant Pot's convenience and adaptability. Any meal requires some prep on the front end, but once the Instant Pot is sealed and set to a pressure-cooking setting, you can walk out of the kitchen and not look back. It's the ultimate appliance in "set it and forget it" cooking. If you're making a dish such as Split Pea Soup (page 86) or Lamb and White Bean Tagine (page 203), it'll pressure-cook to perfection, then stay warm on the Keep Warm setting until you're ready to enjoy your home-cooked meal, for up to 10 hours.

As far as the "instant" factor goes, the recipes for which you'll see the biggest time savings include long-cooking meats, dried beans, and other ingredients that would otherwise braise in the oven or simmer on the stove for hours. In the Instant Pot, Rosemary-Dijon Pot Roast (page 224), dried chickpeas for Roasted Red Pepper Hummus (page 46),

and Pumpkin Spice Steel-Cut Oatmeal (page 17) really do cook in about half the time.

Thanks to its flexibility and ability to cook speedily, the Instant Pot allows you to incorporate wholesome home-cooked meals into your weekly routine, regardless of your schedule. Whether you like to prepare meals for the entire week on the weekends, get your cooking done in the mornings, or throw together seat-of-your-pants weeknight dinners, there are recipes in this book to suit your lifestyle.

In addition to lots and lots of recipes (two hundred!), I've included all of the information you need to start using your Instant Pot like a pro. You'll find a list of my favorite tools and accessories (page 7), an expansive FAQ (page 12), explanations for every program setting on the pot, tips for tricky ingredients (page 301), and more. Once you get to the recipes themselves, you'll see that I've included clear instructions at every step, so you never have to wonder which setting to select, when to seal the pot, or how long to wait before you can open it. In addition, there's a chapter of pantry staples that includes essentials like broths, stocks, sauces, and pickles that will make every meal more convenient and delicious.

I hope that this book becomes a new classic in your kitchen and encourages you to plug in your Instant Pot and get cooking right away. If you're new to Instant Pot cooking, welcome! The following "How to Use the Instant Pot" section will get you started.

Happy (pressure) cooking!

How to Use the Instant Pot

When you first take your Instant Pot out of the box, do yourself a favor and immediately open the manual and turn to the diagrams. They'll help you get acquainted with the different parts of the Instant Pot, including all of the buttons and light-up indicators on the front and the mechanisms of the lid.

Next, join a couple of Facebook groups if you're so inclined: Instant Pot Community and Instant Pot Recipes. The first is a lively group of participants who will answer your beginner questions in a flash. The second is my own page, where I regularly post my own recipes, as well as those from my favorite bloggers and cooking websites.

I've tested the recipes in this cookbook in four models of Instant Pot: the LUX60 V3, DUO60, DUO60 Plus, and Ultra. The DUO and Ultra models are my favorites, as they have a handy notch for resting the lid when the pot is open. They also include a setting for culturing yogurt, which the LUX models do not.

If you are primarily cooking for four people or fewer, I'd go with one of the 6-quart models. If you plan to cook larger pieces of meat (over 4 pounds) or serve a larger crowd on a regular basis, go with the DUO80, DUO80 Plus, or 8-quart Ultra, all of which have an 8-quart capacity. If you are cooking for only one or are extremely short on counter space, go for one of the 3-quart pots.

No matter which model of Instant Pot you have, the panel on the front has settings for cooking different kinds of foods, adjusting the pot to high or low pressure, regulating the temperature of certain settings, and setting the cooking time. There is also a display that lets you know when the pot is on or off and how much time is left on the program setting once the pot reaches pressure.

You'll select a function key depending on what sort of food you are cooking. In Instant Pot terminology, this translates to pressing a function key to select a cooking program, or selecting a function with the universal dial on the Ultra models. For example, you'll select the Soup/Broth function key to cook a soup, the Rice key to steam a pot of rice, and so on. Each pressure-cooking program can be adjusted to High or Low pressure, as well as Less, Normal, or More cooking time (shown in minutes on the LED display), with Normal being the default setting. You can also adjust the time up or down manually in any setting with the + and - buttons or with the dial, depending on the model. Here's a rundown of all the cooking program buttons.

Instant Pot Settings

Manual/Pressure Cook/Ultra You can cook any pressure cooker recipe on the Manual setting. If you're interested in using recipes written for stove-top pressure cookers, this setting is handy, as those recipes can easily be cooked in the Instant Pot. It opens up a whole world of recipes for you to explore, not just ones meant specifically for the Instant Pot. Stove-top cookers cook faster than the Instant Pot because they operate at slightly higher pressures, so you'll need to increase the cooking time by 15 percent. Depending on the model of Instant Pot you have, you'll use the Adjust or Pressure Level button or the universal dial to toggle between the Low Pressure and High Pressure settings.

Soup/Broth The heat ramps up a little more gently on this setting than on the previous setting, which makes it good for simmering soups and broths. Even better, broths turn out clear, not cloudy, when they're cooked under pressure. You'll find recipes for beef bone broth and chicken broth in the Pantry chapter.

Meat/Stew This one is self-explanatory. Adjust the time to Less, Normal, or More, depending on whether you like your meat cooked soft, very soft, or falling off the bone.

Bean/Chili Whether you're cooking a basic pot of beans (page 44), Indian dal, or chili, use this cooking program. Adjust the cooking time to Less for just-done beans, Normal for soft beans, or More for very soft beans. See the chart on page 302 for exact cooking times for a variety of beans.

Cake Use the Less, Normal, and More settings according to the recipe you are making, from delicate sponge cake to dense pound cake to cheesecake.

Egg When a recipe calls for eggs, use large. You can cook soft-, medium-, or hard-boiled eggs (page 21). The Less, Normal, and More settings are timed for extra-large eggs, so you'll need to adjust the cooking times up or down as needed if your eggs are a different size.

Sauté The Instant Pot allows you to simmer, sauté, and sear foods before cooking them under pressure, a feature that adds to its versatility. This is not a pressure setting, and you should never put the locking lid on when you're using it. You can use a tempered glass lid (either the one from Instant Pot or another one that fits snugly) on this setting to sweat vegetables or to get liquids to boil faster.

The Sauté setting behaves a little differently from the pressure settings on the Instant Pot, in that it doesn't display a countdown when it's on. While the pot is heating, it will display "On," and it will change to "Hot" once it is fully heated. The default Sauté level is Normal or Medium (it's labeled differently depending on your Instant Pot model), and this is the temperature level I use in these recipes, unless indicated otherwise. When I use the Sauté function in a recipe, I start cooking right away without waiting for the pot to preheat. For instance, I put garlic and oil into the pot immediately after selecting Sauté, so the oil heats up at the same time as the pot. This saves a little time.

Rice Any type of white rice can be cooked on this setting. The Less, Normal, and More settings will yield just-tender, tender, and soft rice, respectively. The Ultra models have two automatic rice program settings, for low and high pressure. Using low pressure will yield fluffier rice, while high pressure will yield grains that are softer, with a greater tendency to stick together. For full instructions, see Rice (page 51).

Multigrain The moderate, even heat of the Multigrain setting is perfect for brown rice and other long-cooking grains. The More setting includes a warm 45-minute presoak before an hour of pressure cooking and is well suited to mixtures of sturdy grains and beans.

Steam The Instant Pot comes with a wire metal steam rack that is used for raising foods off the bottom of the pot for steaming under pressure. You can also use any wire-mesh, silicone, or metal steamer basket.

Porridge Use this setting when making rice porridge, oatmeal, or a porridge made of any beans and/or other grains. Always use the natural release method when making porridge, and never fill the pot more than half full to avoid a spattered mess. Cooking porridge under pressure is perfectly safe as long as you stick to those guidelines. For a warm fall-to-winter breakfast using this setting, try Pumpkin Spice Steel-Cut Oatmeal (page 17).

Slow Cook The Instant Pot is also designed with a slow cook function. The Less, Normal, and More settings on the Instant Pot correspond to the Low, Medium, and High settings on a slow cooker, but the heating element in the Instant Pot is a focused source in the bottom of the pot, so the heat distribution is a little different from that of a slow cooker. If you come across a great new slow cooker recipe or have some old favorites that you'd like to make, you can use this setting. When using the Instant Pot for slow cooking (or any non-pressure setting), a tight seal is not required, so you can use an easy-to-clean tempered glass lid (either the one available from Instant Pot or any lid that fits on the pot), rather than the pressure cooker lid.

Yogurt This setting has two yogurt-related functions: it sterilizes milk on the More setting and then turns the milk into yogurt on the Normal setting. Homemade yogurt is easy to make and more economical than store-bought. You can even culture the yogurt right in a glass container inside the pot using my method on page 32. This is my preferred way to make yogurt, since the ingredients go from Instant Pot to fridge with zero cleanup.

Sterilize The Normal setting sterilizes at about 230°F (110°C), and the More setting sterilizes at about 240°F (115°C). This program can be used for baby bottles, canning jars, or any other heatproof items you want to sterilize.

Operation Keys

These are the buttons that adjust the pressure, cooking time, and, in certain cases, the heat level of whatever cooking program you've selected. Most Instant Pot models have an Adjust button that toggles among the Less, Normal, and More time and heat settings. For pressure settings, it adjusts the time, and for non-pressure settings, including Yogurt, Slow Cook, and Sauté, it adjusts the heat level. The + and - buttons adjust the cooking time up and down, respectively.

The DUO60 Plus has a dedicated Pressure level button instead of Adjust and/or Pressure buttons, and you press the appropriate function key more than once to toggle among the Less, Normal, and More time and heat settings. The LUX60 model pressure cooks at only High Pressure. It does not have a Low Pressure setting.

The Ultra has a universal dial that allows you to toggle between all of the Instant Pot's cooking programs, pressure settings, heat levels, and cooking times, including a highly customizable Ultra setting.

Delay Start Many Instant Pot models allow you to delay the start of the cooking time for a recipe. You won't find many uses for this function, as you typically won't want to leave perishable foods in the Instant Pot for any length of time before cooking

them. The one task I do like this function for is soaking and cooking beans and whole grains. I'll often put beans, water, and salt in the pot in the afternoon or evening; delay the time for 8 to 12 hours; and then wake up to perfectly cooked beans in the morning.

Mode and Function Indicators These are the lights that turn on to indicate what mode (low or high pressure) or function (aka cooking program) is currently selected on the Instant Pot. On Instant Pot models with a keypad interface, all of the function keys and mode indicators have a little white circle that lights up when they are selected. On models with a dial, the selected function is backlit.

Keep Warm/Cancel This multipurpose button has two separate functions: it cancels any cooking program, and it puts the pot on the Keep Warm setting, similar to the warming setting on a slow cooker. The DUO60, DUO60 Plus, and Ultra models have separate buttons for the Keep Warm and Cancel functions.

The Lid and Releasing Pressure

Now that you know the basic terminology for everything on the front panel of the pot, let's talk about the lid. The lids of the various Instant Pot models (LUX, DUO, Ultra, and SMART) all look slightly different, but they have similar mechanisms. The MAX has a wider range of pressure release modes, including an intermediate setting that allows for a gradual pressure release.

PRESSURE/STEAM RELEASE

The Pressure Release, also called Steam Release on some models, can be set to two positions, Sealing or Venting. When the pot is closed and the Pressure Release is set to Sealing, the pot can come up to pressure. When the cooking program is finished, you can move the Pressure Release to Venting to release the steam from the pot, making it safe to open. And it's okay if the Pressure Release jiggles a bit or seems as if it is not fully secured. It's supposed to feel that way. You can remove it for cleaning as well.

You can release the pressure on the Instant Pot in three different ways.

1. Quick Pressure Release (QPR) The moment the cooking program finishes, move the Pressure Release to Venting. This will cause a forceful plume of steam to issue forth, releasing the pressure from the Instant Pot. Use this method for delicate foods that require just a few minutes of cooking, like steamed vegetables.

2. Natural Pressure Release (NPR) Rather than moving the Pressure Release, do nothing. Once a cooking program finishes, the pot will gradually lose pressure on its own as it cools. This can take anywhere from a few minutes to 30 minutes or more. That's because the pot retains more or less heat and pressure depending on the volume of food inside. The pot automatically defaults to its Keep Warm setting at the end of a cooking program, and you can leave it for up to 10 hours before it will shut off completely.

3. Timed Natural Pressure Release I often wait 10 or 15 minutes after the end of a cooking program, then move the Pressure Release to Venting to release a less geyser-like amount of steam from the pot.

For each recipe in this book the pressure release (PR) is given as QPR or NPR. When a recipe requires a timed natural pressure release, it's given as a timed NPR (for example, 10 minutes NPR). This means you'll let the pressure release naturally for the listed number of minutes before moving the Pressure Release to its Venting position.

SEALING RING
The only part of the lid that you'll likely have to replace eventually is the silicone sealing ring, which is seated in a rack inside the perimeter of the lid.

It has a life of 6 to 18 months, depending on how frequently you use your Instant Pot. The sealing ring needs to be seated properly in the lid for the pot to come up to pressure, so make sure to replace it securely in the sealing ring rack after you've cleaned it. I keep separate sealing rings for sweet and savory foods because the ring can retain strong odors.

ANTI-BLOCK SHIELD
The little metal cap that fits on the inner part of the exhaust valve on the underside of the lid is the anti-block shield. It helps to keep foamy foods from blocking the valve. It's good practice to remove it and clean it after each use of the pot.

DETERMINING WHICH RELEASE METHOD TO USE
Use the quick pressure release method for:

Steamed Vegetables Release the pressure quickly (immediately after the cooking program ends) when cooking asparagus, broccoli, cauliflower, and any other vegetables you prefer lightly steamed or braised. I'll often set the cooking time to 0 (zero) minutes for these foods, so they cook only for the time it takes for the pot to come up to pressure plus the time required for a quick pressure release. It's my favorite trick for asparagus, in particular, which is so easy to overcook on the stove.

Soft- or Hard-Boiled Eggs The "set it and forget it" Instant Pot method for boiling eggs means you don't have to wait for and watch a pot of water as it heats on the stove top. A quick pressure release allows you to stop the cooking right when the cooking program ends, so the yolks never end up with a grayish ring, the telltale sign of overcooked eggs. See page 21 for how to boil eggs.

Meals in Minutes If you are cooking a recipe with minimal liquid (1 cup or less), the food won't create foam as it cooks, and the pot is less than half full, you can safely use the quick pressure release method before opening the pot immediately after the cooking program ends. The recipe for Ground Beef Tacos (page 215) is a great example of this.

Use the natural pressure release method for:

Very Full Pots of Food If you've filled the Instant Pot to its maximum capacity (half or two-thirds full, depending on the type of food you're cooking), the safest way to open the pot after cooking is with a natural pressure release. This prevents messes that can result from food or liquid sputtering out of the pressure release valve.

Foamy Foods Beans, porridge, and cooked fruits such as applesauce, jams, and compotes have a tendency to sputter and spit when using a quick release. These are all foods that tend to foam up when boiled or otherwise expand when cooked. Although quick release can work with very small batches of these foods, in general, it's safest to let the pressure release naturally, using a timed natural pressure release for at least 10 minutes.

Slow Cooker–Style Convenience The Instant Pot's convenience lies in its ability to not only cook foods fast but also hold them at temperature on the Keep Warm setting for up to 10 hours, much like a slow cooker. This means you can put the ingredients in the pot in the morning and set the cooking program. When the cooking is complete, the program will automatically switch to the Keep Warm setting, the pressure will release naturally, and you can come home to a piping-hot meal. Braises, roasts, soups, chilis, and stews hold up particularly well when left on the Keep Warm setting.

Egg Dishes and Cheesecakes Using a timed natural pressure release for at least 10 minutes allows fluffy egg dishes and cheesecakes to settle. Releasing the pressure quickly can cause these delicate foods to break apart and may make a mess inside the pot.

Seafood After experimenting with many methods for cooking fish and other types of seafood, I've determined my favorite: poach at low pressure and use a natural pressure release. This allows the seafood to cook not just while it's under pressure but also from the residual heat on the Keep Warm setting as the pot cools down. Seafood comes out evenly cooked and tender, not rubbery or tough, as it often does when the pressure is released quickly.

Use the timed natural release method for:

Pasta If you're cooking 1 pound or less of dried pasta (or 8 ounces or less in a 3-quart Instant Pot), the best way to get an al dente result is to set the cooking time for half the time recommended on the package, then let the pressure release naturally for 5 minutes before moving the Pressure Release to Venting and releasing the remaining pressure.

Half-Full Pots The time needed for the initial natural release will vary depending on the volume of food in the pot. It's difficult to come up with a hard-and-fast rule for how long you should wait before venting. In recipes where I've stated that you should let the pressure release for "at least" a given amount of time, that means you should wait that long after the cooking program ends before manually venting (a combination release), or you can leave the pot to completely release naturally. The amount of time required for a combination release varies based not only on the volume of food in the pot but whether or not it's a food that has a tendency to foam, and whether or not you're trying to make use of the carryover heat, as in poached fish and seafood recipes.

If you're cooking a half-batch of a recipe that would otherwise require a very long natural release, or if the pot is not filled to capacity, the pot will cool down and lose pressure much faster, and it will be safe to open in far less time than a very full pot. As long as you wait the minimum amount of time, you can open the pot whenever it is convenient. If you've doubled the recipe, though, it is safest to let the pressure fully release naturally.

Maximum Fill Levels

No matter what type of pressure cooker you are using, overfilling the pot can result in safety and performance issues, as food can end up clogging up the valve and pressure release mechanisms in the lid.

Depending on what you are cooking, you can safely fill your Instant Pot halfway or two-thirds full. The inner pot in most models is stamped with half and two-thirds fill lines, so make sure the food doesn't come up past the line.

Fill the pot no more than halfway full for dried beans, grains, pastas, porridges, fruit sauces, and any other foods that can foam up when boiled or that expand when cooked.

Fill the pot no more than two-thirds full for stocks, soups, stews, meaty main dishes, and steamed vegetables.

Pot-in-Pot Cooking and Steam Racks

You may have heard the term "pot-in-pot cooking" from Instant Pot aficionados—it's also referred to sometimes as PIP cooking. This simply means using an additional piece of cookware—whether it's a cake pan, soufflé dish, Pyrex container, or stacked stainless-steel pans (similar to an Indian-style tiffin)—and nesting it inside the inner pot of the Instant Pot.

This method greatly expands the categories of food that you can make in a pressure cooker. Foods that would otherwise scorch on the pot bottom due to inclusion of dairy; baked goods such as brownies and cheesecakes; and foods with too little liquid to get up to pressure can be prepared this way. With pot-in-pot cooking, the food is cooked by steam. You put a cup or two of water in the inner pot and the vessel containing the food sits on top of a steam rack.

In this book, I refer to three different kinds of steam racks: wire metal steam rack, tall steam rack, and long-handled silicone steam rack. See the following section for more information on each of these.

Tools and Accessories

You can absolutely start cooking in the Instant Pot without buying additional accessories or tools. If

you're like me, though, you'll have fun outfitting your kitchen with a few odds and ends that make Instant Pot cooking more convenient and enjoyable. Some of these items will expand your recipe repertoire, allowing you to make many dishes that couldn't otherwise be prepared in a pressure cooker, such as cheesecakes (pages 275 and 278) and two-dish, one-pot meals like Black Bean Burrito Bowls (page 125). Most of the accessories listed here are available at any well-stocked cookware store or can be purchased online.

Silicone Mini Mitts Any time I refer to "heat-resistant mitts" in this book, I mean a pair of Instant Pot–brand silicone mini mitts. They protect your hands from steam when you vent the lid, and the thin, flexible silicone allows you to easily grip bowls, pans, and steam racks so you can safely lift them out of the pot.

Extra Inner Pot If you plan on cooking two Instant Pot dishes in one night or covering the pot and storing it in the fridge, it's nice to have an extra inner pot ready to go. When storing the Instant Pot, I always make sure to leave the inner pot in the housing, in case anyone adds food or liquid to the pot without first checking if the inner pot is in place.

Extra Sealing Rings The flexible silicone sealing ring that comes with your Instant Pot will eventually wear out and need to be replaced, usually in 6 to 18 months, depending on how often you use your Instant Pot. Instant Pot's online store sells both clear and colored varieties. I like to keep a designated ring for desserts because strong odors can sometimes linger on the silicone. Using colored rings helps me remember which one to use for which purpose.

Tempered Glass Lid You can purchase a glass lid from Instant Pot or use one from another pot in your kitchen if you happen to have one that fits. I use it most often on the Sauté setting, to quickly bring a liquid to a boil or to sweat vegetables. A glass lid is also useful for the Slow Cook setting.

Fat Separator Tough cuts of meat that are well-suited for pressure cooking often render a significant amount of fat, and a fat separator is an effective way to strain the fat out of stocks and cooking liquids. My favorite models are from OXO: they make a traditional fat separator with a pouring spout, as well as an ingenious spring-loaded version with a bottom spout that has become my new favorite.

Immersion Blender An immersion blender makes quick, low-mess work of blending sauces and gravies; pureeing fruits and vegetables; and emulsifying vinaigrettes, mayonnaise, and aioli. It's an indispensable tool in my kitchen, and it's much easier to clean than a countertop blender. Just remember safety first: be sure to unplug the blender and eject the blade assembly from the motor before cleaning.

Kitchen Tongs Since everything in this book cooks in a deep pot, tongs are a helpful tool for turning and tossing ingredients. The OXO 12-inch tongs are my favorite: they're made of sturdier metal than most and have a solid, well-made spring.

Flexible Turner Using a flexible turner helps get under meat patties, chicken pieces, and other foods that can stick when seared in the pot. I'm once again partial to the OXO models, both in heat-resistant nylon and stainless steel.

Sautéing Spatula The well-loved white spatula pictured opposite is my favorite for sautéing foods in the Instant Pot. It is made by Exoglass from a composite material that's heat resistant up to 430°F. When I sauté vegetables in the Instant Pot, I use this spatula. Its slim profile also makes it great for stirring up large quantities of food without sloshing anything out of the pot.

Kitchen Thermometers Use an instant-read thermometer to check the temperature of meat or poultry to ensure it is cooked through. A probe thermometer with a remote display is useful when making yogurt, as you can set it to beep when it's time to add the culture to the cooled milk.

Bowls, Pans, and Dishes There is a wide variety of bowls, pans, and dishes that fit into the 6-quart Instant Pot for pot-in-pot cooking (see page 7). My favorites are my Vollrath-brand 1½-quart stainless-steel bowl (both their thinner and thicker ones work well), the tempered glass Pyrex 7-cup round food storage dish, and a 1½-quart ceramic soufflé dish. I use a 7-inch springform pan for cheesecakes and a 7 by 3-inch round cake pan for cakes and breads. Seven-inch Bundt pans are also useful for cake-making, and a small loaf pan (about 3¾ by 6⅓ inches, with a 3½-cup capacity) is just the right size for a meat loaf made with 1 pound of meat. Ramekins with a 4-ounce capacity are ideal for coddling eggs or making individual omelets.

Wire Metal Steam Rack This is the wire metal accessory that comes with your Instant Pot. In the manual, it is referred to simply as the "steam rack." It has arms that can be used to lift foods in and out of the pot. You can use the rack to steam vegetables and eggs, as well as ribs, whole chickens, and large roasts that would otherwise be difficult to lift out of the pan. Make sure to wear heat-resistant mitts when touching the rack, as it will be hot when you open the pot.

Tall Steam Rack This kind of rack allows you to cook two things at once. I often use one to hold a bowl of rice and water above a meat or bean dish that's cooking underneath. (I use a 1½-quart stainless-steel bowl with sloped sides to ensure all the rice is submerged in liquid. This way, the rice always cooks evenly, even amounts as small as ½ cup.) It's a great hack for cooking other grains, too.

There are many brands of tall steam racks available online. My favorite steam rack (see page 9) is 3 inches tall and 6 inches in diameter, and it has circular spaces for standing eggs upright. There are also simpler models that work well. Just make sure to purchase one that's 2¾ to 3 inches tall so that it will stand high enough to use for pot-in-pot cooking.

Long-Handled Silicone Steam Rack This is great for recipes requiring a soufflé dish, high-sided cake pan, or round heatproof glass container. I like the silicone steam rack from Instant Pot, as well as the silicone pressure cooker sling made by OXO. Both have handles long enough that you can easily lower and lift a dish into and out of the pot, and they are easy to grip.

If you don't have a long-handled silicone steam rack, you can make a sling out of aluminum foil and use it to lower and lift the dish into and out of the pot. To make an aluminum foil sling, fold a 20-inch-long sheet of aluminum foil in half lengthwise, then in half again, creating a 3-inch-wide strip. Center it underneath the pan, dish, or cooking vessel. Place the wire metal steam rack in the Instant Pot and pour in as much water as the recipe indicates. Firmly grab the ends of the foil strip and use it as a sling to lower the cooking vessel into the pot, on top of the trivet. Fold the ends of the sling so they fit into the pot. After cooking, use the sling to lift the cooking vessel out of the pot.

Steamer Basket A wire-mesh, silicone, or expandable metal steamer basket is necessary for steaming vegetables in the Instant Pot. My favorite is a wire-mesh model from the Instant Perrrt brand, as it has sturdily attached, easy-to-grab handles.

Silicone Muffin Pans and Mini Loaf Pans These small-capacity pans are great for freezing foods, including leftovers, in small portions. Having staples such as broths and sauces frozen in small portions makes for easy meal preparation, as they're quick to thaw. Plus, you can defrost only the quantity you need. Portion the food into silicone pans and freeze until solid. Unmold, transfer to ziplock plastic freezer bags, label the bags with the date and contents, and store the bags in the freezer.

Jar Lifters and Jam Funnels These are especially useful for making yogurt, and also for ladling jams, jellies, pickles, and chutneys into jars.

The Pressure Cooker Pantry

Pressure cooking is unique in that it's done in a hermetically sealed environment. A fair amount of liquid is needed for the pot to seal and come up to pressure, and very little moisture evaporates from the food as it cooks. This means that flavors don't concentrate in the same way as they would in a Dutch oven on the stove top. To compensate for this, I keep a few go-to ingredients in my pantry to amp up flavor and absorb moisture. Here are my favorites.

Broth Concentrates, Bone Broth, and Bouillon These are incredibly convenient ways to add flavor. When I don't have homemade broth on hand, I like to use the reduced-sodium broth concentrates from Better Than Bouillon and Savory Choice, bone broth concentrates from Kitchen Accomplice, and the vegetarian bouillon cubes from Edward & Sons. To recipes that call for water, I'll often add broth concentrate in a dollop, even though the label recommends reconstituting the concentrate in boiling water before use.

Curry Paste and Other Spice Pastes Red, green, and massaman Thai curry pastes; Korean gochujang; Moroccan harissa—spice pastes are used in many different cuisines, and they add instant flavor. One of my favorite tricks or flavor boosters is to add a spoonful of spice paste along with the cooking liquid (water or broth) when preparing plain rice (see page 51), quinoa, or wheat berries.

Dried Fruits and Vegetables Dehydrated foods soak up excess liquids, so they're a no-brainer in pressure cooker recipes. Add a handful of raisins to rice pudding (page 271), and it will thicken as it cools. Dried mushrooms are a great addition to soups and broths, and sun-dried tomatoes perk up pasta salads and frittatas.

Grains and Beans I make lots of one-pot dishes with chicken and grains, so I always keep a few different types on hand. Oatmeal is a morning staple, which means steel-cut oats are in my pantry at all times. Dried beans are a popular choice in my kitchen, too. I usually have chickpeas on hand for grain bowls (page 122) and hummus (page 46); black beans, white beans, and split peas for soups; and lentils for Vegan Pasta Bolognese (page 134).

Herbs and Spice Blends Spice blends are great for perking up pressure-cooked dishes. I use all types in my cooking, from common ones like chili powder and Old Bay, to herbes de Provence, North African *ras el hanout*, Jamaican jerk seasoning, and Ethiopian *berbere*. I love shopping for spices at natural food stores that sell them in bulk so I can buy only as much as I need. When I want to splurge on truly exceptional spice blends, I purchase them from Spice Hound at farmers' markets in the San Francisco Bay Area; Oaktown Spice Shop in Oakland, California; World Spice Merchants in Seattle, Washington; and Penzeys Spices, which has locations throughout the United States. All of these merchants also sell their spices online.

Tomato Paste This concentrated form of tomatoes adds body and depth of flavor to tomato-based dishes, so if you're using tomatoes (fresh or canned), double up on the flavor by adding a tablespoon of tomato paste as well. Because it can be difficult to get through a can of tomato paste before it goes bad, I like to use the variety that comes in a tube (it keeps a bit longer), or else I freeze my canned tomato paste in 1-tablespoon dollops for later use.

Worcestershire Sauce and Other Strongly Flavored Condiments These are great when you need an umami flavor bomb to enhance a recipe. They'll improve chilis, stews, and braised meat dishes, making them extra savory. Dijon mustard is another go-to flavor enhancer for me, as well as soy sauce, tamari, coconut aminos, fish sauce, miso paste, Sriracha sauce, and *sambal oelek*.

Troubleshooting and FAQ

What follows is a series of questions I get asked all the time about cooking in the Instant Pot. If I haven't answered your question or if your question isn't here, get in touch with Instant Pot directly.

Q: I have a 6-quart Instant Pot. Can I cook 6 quarts of food in it?

A: No, that 6-quart measurement refers to the capacity of the pot, but you should fill it halfway full with foods that tend to produce foam when cooked, or two-thirds full for other recipes. See Maximum Fill Levels on page 6 for more information.

Q: I selected one of the cooking programs, but nothing is happening! What's going on?

A: When you press one of the function keys, it gives you about 10 seconds of lag time so you can adjust the time, pressure, or heat setting. After that, it will beep to let you know the cooking program has started. If you're using a pressure setting, the pot will come up to pressure, then display the cooking time in minutes, counting down until the cooking program finishes. At that point, the pot will beep ten times in a row and default to its Keep Warm setting. The LED display will count up from the time the cooking program ended to indicate how long the food has been keeping warm.

Q: How do I adjust the cooking time? How do I adjust the pressure setting?

A: Once you have selected a cooking program with one of the function keys, use the + and - buttons to adjust the cooking time up or down. On most models, the Adjust button will toggle the pressure setting between the High Pressure and Low Pressure settings. The IP-DUO Plus has a Pressure Level button, and the Ultra has a central dial which is used to select and toggle between all of the pot's modes and functions. If you've selected a non-pressure setting such as Sauté, the Adjust button allows you to toggle the heat setting among Less, Normal, and More. On models without an Adjust button, press the function key itself or use the central dial.

Q: Can I cook a whole frozen chicken, a 4-pound beef roast, or other big block of rock-solid, nowhere-near-thawed meat in the Instant Pot?

A: The short answer is no, it's not a good idea. You're better off making something else for dinner and letting the frozen meat thaw for a day or two before you cook it. The long answer is plan ahead next time and cut the meat into thin slices (or shape ground meat into meatballs) before you freeze it. It will thaw a lot faster that way, and in a pinch you can cook it straight from frozen, too! Just add a few minutes to the recommended cooking time if you're using frozen meat. For more information on how to cook with frozen meat, see page 301.

Q: My Instant Pot never sealed! What happened?

A: The pot requires enough steam buildup to come up to pressure. When it comes up to pressure, the float valve lifts up and the pot seals. There are several reasons the pot may not have sealed. Here are the most likely possibilities. Did you . . .

- clean the lid well, including the sealing gasket?
- use enough liquid in the recipe (1 cup or so, for a 6-quart pot)?
- leave out any thickeners like flour or cornstarch?
- avoid layering pieces of meat on top of rice, covering it completely?
- make sure the sealing ring wasn't warped and that it was seated properly?
- set the Pressure Release to the Sealing position?
- make sure a cooking program was selected, and the LED display on the pot read "On"?
- fill the pot half full or less for starchy foods, or two-thirds full or less for soups and stews?

If you answered yes to all of these questions, then you've got me stumped! It's time to contact the Instant Pot company directly for assistance.

Q: Why won't my Instant Pot open?

A: The pot lid has a safety mechanism that prevents you from opening the pot when it is cooking under pressure. The pressure needs to be fully released before the lid can be opened. If the pot is completely quiet and steam is no longer emerging from the Pressure Release, the float valve might be slightly stuck in its raised position. This happens to me all the time. Poke the valve with a chopstick or a pen, and it'll return to its lowered position, allowing you to open the pot.

Q: Can I cook in the Instant Pot without the inner pot inside?

A: No! Never put foods directly in the Instant Pot housing. Nothing's supposed to get in there. The inner pot must always be in place before anything goes into the Instant Pot. To be safe, wash, dry, and return the inner pot as soon as you finish cooking.

Q: What is this PIP cooking I keep hearing about?

A: You can cook cakes, breads, quiches, and many other dishes in a separate pan or heatproof dish inside the Instant Pot. The pan or dish sits on top of a steam rack placed in the bottom of the inner pot, which keeps the container above the water so the food can steam under pressure. This method is referred to as PIP, or pot-in-pot, cooking.

Q: Is it normal for the Instant Pot to release steam while it comes up to pressure?

A: Yep! Depending on what's inside, the pot may release a little wisp of steam, or it may steam for a minute or two, until the valve has enough pressure behind it to pop up and seal the lid. If the pot steams at full blast for a minute or more, you may need to nudge the lid clockwise for it to seal.

Q: How do I know when the natural pressure release is complete?

A: The little round metal float valve will go down. If you're nearby, you will hear a little click when it falls. The pot may take anywhere from 10 minutes to an hour to naturally release its pressure, depending on how much food is inside.

Q: The cooking program has finished, and now the display shows "L" and a few numbers. What does this mean?

A: L stands for "lapsed time," and the numbers let you know how much time has gone by since the cooking program ended. This does not necessarily mean it's time to open the pot. For a recipe that requires a full natural pressure release, wait until the float valve goes down on its own before opening the pot. Depending on the volume of food in the pot, a natural pressure release will take anywhere from 10 minutes to an hour.

Q: Why do some Instant Pot recipes say to release the pressure for "at least" X minutes?

A: If you see this instruction, it means you should wait at least that long to open the pot, but you can also leave the pot for a full natural release. If you use a quick pressure release before the pot has sufficiently depressurized, the food could cause a splattery mess, burbling out of the Pressure Release valve. The recipes that call for at least a partial natural release tend to be more forgiving as far as "setting and forgetting," so you can leave them in the Instant Pot for a few hours on the Keep Warm setting.

Q: How do I clean that moat around the rim of the Instant Pot?

A: The Instant Pot is not submersible. So instead, take a drinking straw brush or a big pipe cleaner, wrap a paper towel around the brush end, spray it with distilled vinegar, then run it around the moat and scrub it clean, replacing the paper towel as needed. Foam paint brushes from the hardware store also work well for this purpose.

Q: How do I clean the sealing ring? It smells like the last dish I cooked.

A: You can run the sealing ring through the dishwasher, or use this nifty trick: pressure-cook 2 cups distilled white vinegar (or 2 cups water and the zest strips of 1 lemon) on the Steam setting for 2 minutes, then use a quick pressure release. This will help keep the inner pot bright and shiny, too.

Breakfast

1

This recipe uses pantry staples, so it's a great option for busy, bleary-eyed mornings when you haven't planned ahead. Get the oatmeal going at the start of your morning routine (at the same time you turn on the coffee maker), and it'll be ready in about half an hour. Raisins and cinnamon sweeten the pot, but you can leave them out or swap them for other dried fruits and spices.

OLD-FASHIONED OATMEAL WITH RAISINS AND CINNAMON

5 cups water

2 cups old-fashioned oats

½ cup raisins

¾ teaspoon ground cinnamon, plus more for serving

½ teaspoon kosher salt

Unsalted butter for serving

Brown sugar for serving

PREP	0 MINUTES
COOK	20 MINUTES
PR	15 MINUTES NPR
SERVES	4

1   Add the water, oats, raisins, cinnamon, and salt to the Instant Pot. Secure the lid and set the Pressure Release to **Sealing**. Select the **Porridge** setting and set the cooking time for 3 minutes at high pressure. (The pot will take about 15 minutes to come up to pressure before the cooking program begins.)

2   When the cooking program ends, let the pressure release naturally. This will take about 15 minutes. Open the pot and stir the oatmeal, making sure to scrape along the bottom.

3   Ladle the oatmeal into bowls and serve with butter, brown sugar, and cinnamon.

Steel-cut oats take more time to cook than the old-fashioned variety, but they're worth the wait! My favorite part of this recipe is toasting the oats in butter—the aroma is just incredible, and it fills up the whole kitchen. When the leaves start to turn, I add in pumpkin, maple syrup, and baking spices for the perfect autumn-to-winter breakfast.

PUMPKIN SPICE STEEL-CUT OATMEAL

2 tablespoons unsalted butter, plus more for serving

1½ cups steel-cut oats

4½ cups water

1 cup pumpkin puree (fresh or canned)

¼ cup maple syrup, plus more for serving

¾ teaspoon pumpkin pie spice

¾ teaspoon kosher salt

½ cup chopped pecans or walnuts

PREP	0 MINUTES
COOK	30 MINUTES
PR	10 MINUTES NPR
SERVES	6

1   Select the **Sauté** setting on the Instant Pot and melt the butter. Add the oats and cook, stirring often, for about 5 minutes, until the oats are aromatic and lightly toasted. Stir in the water, pumpkin puree, maple syrup, pumpkin pie spice, and salt, making sure all of the oats are submerged in the liquid.

2   Secure the lid and set the Pressure Release to **Sealing**. Press the **Cancel** button to reset the cooking program, then select the **Porridge** setting and set the cooking time for 12 minutes at high pressure. (The pot will take about 10 minutes to come up to pressure before the cooking program begins.)

3   When the cooking program ends, let the pressure release naturally for 10 minutes, then move the Pressure Release to **Venting** to release any remaining steam. Open the pot and stir the oatmeal to incorporate any extra liquid.

4   Ladle the oatmeal into bowls and serve with butter, maple syrup, and the chopped nuts.

Variation: To make this dairy-free and vegan, use coconut oil in place of the unsalted butter when cooking the oatmeal, and serve with coconut butter.

A bowl of cheesy, silky grits is breakfast by itself, or you can serve it alongside a pile of lightly dressed mixed greens at brunch. In this extra-thick version of a Southern classic, the corn flavor really shines through. Any variety of coarse grits will work well, and my favorites are produced by Anson Mills and Bob's Red Mill.

CHEDDAR–BLACK PEPPER BREAKFAST GRITS

4 cups water

2 tablespoons unsalted butter

¾ teaspoon kosher salt

1 cup coarse grits (not instant)

1 tightly packed cup shredded sharp Cheddar cheese, plus more for serving

¼ cup grated Parmesan cheese

1 teaspoon freshly ground black pepper

2 green onions, white and tender green parts, thinly sliced

PREP	0 MINUTES
COOK	40 MINUTES
PR	15 MINUTES NPR
SERVES	4

1   Select the **Sauté** setting on the Instant Pot and add the water, butter, and salt. Cover the pot with the glass lid and bring to a simmer.

2   Uncover the pot. While whisking continuously, slowly pour the grits into the simmering water. Continue to whisk until the mixture returns to a simmer.

3   Secure the pressure cooker lid and set the Pressure Release to **Sealing**. Press the **Cancel** button to reset the cooking program, then select the **Porridge** setting and set the cooking time for 20 minutes at high pressure (if using fine grits, shorten the cooking time to 10 minutes). (The pot will take about 5 minutes to come up to pressure before the cooking program begins.)

4   When the cooking program ends, let the pressure release naturally for 15 minutes, then move the Pressure Release to **Venting** to release any remaining steam. Open the pot and add the Cheddar, Parmesan, and pepper, whisking vigorously to smooth out any lumps.

5   Ladle the grits into bowls and serve sprinkled with additional Cheddar and the green onions.

Variation: For sweet grits, omit the cheeses, pepper, and green onions. Serve the grits topped with a pat of butter or a splash of cream, along with a drizzle of maple syrup or a spoonful of brown sugar.

There's a Porridge setting on the Instant Pot that's tailor-made for foods like oatmeal, cream of wheat, and savory rice porridges. Known by many names, including *jook* or *congee*, this restorative breakfast has been enjoyed for thousands of years in China and many other East Asian countries. Leave off the *sambal oelek* (chile paste) on this Taiwanese-style congee if you need something gentle on your stomach, or top with extra sambal for a sinus-clearing bowl.

SAVORY RICE PORRIDGE

4 cups chicken broth (page 286) or vegetable broth (page 284)

1 cup water

½ cup short-grain or medium-grain white rice

1-inch knob fresh ginger, cut into ¼-inch slices

1 green onion, white and tender green parts, thinly sliced

Soy sauce, toasted sesame oil, and/or sambal oelek or Sriracha for serving

PREP	0 MINUTES
COOK	50 MINUTES
PR	25 MINUTES NPR
REST	5 MINUTES
SERVES	2 OR 3

1   Add the chicken broth, water, rice, and ginger to the Instant Pot.

2   Secure the lid and set the Pressure Release to **Sealing**. Select the **Porridge** setting and set the cooking time for 25 minutes at high pressure. (The pot will take about 20 minutes to come up to pressure before the cooking program begins.)

3   When the cooking program ends, let the pressure release naturally; this will take about 25 minutes. Open the pot and stir the congee. It will be quite thin at first but will thicken up as it sits. Remove and discard the ginger slices, then let the congee stand and thicken for 5 minutes.

4   Ladle the congee into bowls and sprinkle with the green onion. Serve with soy sauce, sesame oil, and sambal oelek on the side.

Notes: This recipe uses my preferred liquid-to-rice ratio of 10:1, and it yields a medium-thick porridge, but you can use less or more liquid to suit your taste. If you like, you can use all water or all broth instead of a combination of the two.

The possibilities for add-ins and toppings are endless. For a more filling meal, I sometimes whisk in a beaten egg or two after releasing the pressure naturally, with the pot on the low Sauté setting, for about 2 minutes.

This recipe is easily doubled. Allow extra time for the pot to come up to pressure and for the natural pressure release.

Soft- or hard-boiled eggs turn out evenly cooked and are easy to peel when they're steamed under pressure in the Instant Pot. This recipe works if you are boiling only an egg or two or up to a dozen. You'll need a steamer rack or basket to keep the eggs out of the water as they cook or, for just an egg or two, you can use the wire metal steam rack that comes with the Instant Pot. I prefer to use stackable steamer racks made especially for eggs because they hold the eggs upright, allowing the yolks to remain centered. Do not be tempted to use a solid bowl, as the eggs will not cook as quickly or evenly.

SOFT- OR HARD-BOILED EGGS

Up to 12 large eggs, straight from the refrigerator

PREP	5 MINUTES
COOK	15 MINUTES
PR	QPR

1   Pour 1 cup water into the Instant Pot and place the wire metal steam rack or steamer basket in the pot. Gently place the eggs on the rack or in the basket, taking care not to crack the eggs as you add them.

2   Secure the lid and set the Pressure Release to **Sealing**. Select the **Steam** setting and set the cooking time for 3 minutes at high pressure for soft-boiled eggs or 6 minutes at high pressure for hard-boiled eggs. (For extra-large eggs, increase the cooking time to 4 minutes for soft-boiled or 7 minutes for hard-boiled. For jumbo eggs, increase the cooking time to 5 minutes for soft-boiled or 8 minutes for hard-boiled.) (The pot will take about 10 minutes to come up to pressure before the cooking program begins. This will vary by a few minutes, depending on how many eggs you are cooking.)

3   While the eggs are cooking, prepare an ice bath.

4   When the cooking program ends, perform a quick release by moving the Pressure Release to **Venting**.

5   Open the pot and transfer the eggs to the ice bath to cool. The eggs will keep, refrigerated, for up to 1 week.

Coddled eggs are easier to make than poached eggs, and they look so darn cute! Steamed in individual ramekins (or coddling cups if you have them) with ham and cheese, they're also more flavorful. These eggs turn out with firm whites and golden, runny yolks. Serve them with toast alongside.

CODDLED EGGS WITH HAM AND GRUYÈRE

⅓ cup chopped ham

½ cup tightly packed shredded Gruyère cheese

Freshly ground black pepper

4 eggs

1 tablespoon chopped fresh flat-leaf parsley or fresh chives

PREP	10 MINUTES
COOK	10 MINUTES
PR	5 MINUTES NPR
SERVES	4

1   Pour 1 cup water into the Instant Pot and place the wire metal steam rack in the pot.

2   Lightly butter four 4-ounce ramekins or coat with nonstick cooking spray. Sprinkle 1 tablespoon of the ham and 1 tablespoon of the cheese into each ramekin. Make a well in the center, then add a grind of pepper on top of the cheese. Crack an egg into each ramekin. Top the eggs with the remaining ham, dividing it evenly, and another grind of pepper. Cover each ramekin tightly with aluminum foil.

3   Place the ramekins on the steam rack in the pot. Secure the lid and set the Pressure Release to **Sealing**. Select the **Steam** setting and set the cooking time for 3 minutes at high pressure. (The pot will take about 5 minutes to come up to pressure before the cooking program begins.)

4   When the cooking program ends, let the pressure release naturally for 5 minutes, then move the Pressure Release to **Venting** to release any remaining steam. Open the pot and, wearing heat-resistant mitts, grab the handles of the steam rack and carefully lift it out of the pot and transfer it to the countertop. Uncover the ramekins, taking care to avoid getting burned by the steam.

5   Sprinkle the eggs with the remaining ¼ cup cheese and the parsley. Serve warm.

Assemble this Italian-inspired strata before you go to bed, then pop it in the Instant Pot in the morning for a hands-off one-pot breakfast meal. A base of egg whites and vegetable broth keeps it on the lighter side, and add-ins of spinach, mushrooms, and sun-dried tomatoes contribute plenty of flavor. It's my go-to vegetarian option for breakfast or brunch. If you like, substitute 4 whole eggs for the egg whites.

EGG WHITE STRATA FLORENTINE

1 cup egg whites

1 cup vegetable broth (page 284)

1 teaspoon Italian seasoning

½ teaspoon freshly ground black pepper

¼ teaspoon kosher salt

4 cups cubed ciabatta or sourdough bread

2 cups baby spinach

1 cup sliced cremini or button mushrooms

½ cup grated Parmesan cheese

¼ cup chopped oil-packed sun-dried tomatoes

1 garlic clove, minced or pressed

2 tablespoons chopped fresh basil

PREP	10 MINUTES
CHILL	4 HOURS
COOK	40 MINUTES
PR	10 MINUTES NPR
REST	10 MINUTES
SERVES	4

1   Lightly coat a 1½-quart soufflé dish or a 7-cup round heatproof glass ontainer with olive oil or nonstick cooking spray.

2   In a bowl, whisk together the egg whites, vegetable broth, Italian seasoning, pepper, and salt. Stir in the bread, spinach, mushrooms, Parmesan, tomatoes, and garlic, making sure all of the bread is coated with the egg mixture. Pour the mixture into the prepared dish, cover tightly with aluminum foil, and refrigerate at least 4 hours or up to overnight.

3   When you are ready to cook the strata, pour 1½ cups water into the Instant Pot. Place the dish on a long-handled silicone steam rack. Holding the handles of the steam rack, lower it into the pot.

4   Secure the lid and set the Pressure Release to **Sealing**. Select the **Pressure Cook** or **Manual** setting and set the cooking time for 25 minutes at high pressure. (The pot will take about 15 minutes to come up to pressure before the cooking program begins.)

5   When the cooking program ends, let the pressure release naturally for 10 minutes, then move the Pressure Release to **Venting** to release any remaining steam. Open the pot and, wearing heat-resistant mitts, grab the handles of the steam rack and lift the dish out of the pot. Uncover the dish, taking care to avoid getting burned by the steam.

6   Let the strata rest for 10 minutes, then sprinkle with the basil and slice. Serve warm.

Start with a combination of eggs, milk, salt, and pepper, and you've got a base for any type of quiche you like. This is my take on quiche Lorraine, and it's on the lighter side as far as quiches go. It contains all of the classic elements but skips the heavy cream and butter-laden crust. Have a wedge on its own for breakfast or serve it with some lightly dressed greens for lunch.

CRUSTLESS QUICHE LORRAINE

6 eggs

½ cup whole milk

½ teaspoon kosher salt

½ teaspoon freshly ground black pepper

¼ teaspoon ground nutmeg

1 small yellow onion, finely diced

4 slices cooked bacon, crumbled

1 cup tightly packed shredded Gruyère cheese

PREP	5 MINUTES
COOK	40 MINUTES
PR	10 MINUTES NPR
REST	5 MINUTES
SERVES	4

1   Butter a 1½-quart soufflé dish or a 7-cup round heatproof glass container. Pour 1½ cups water into the Instant Pot.

2   In a bowl, whisk together the eggs, milk, salt, pepper, and nutmeg until well blended, then stir in the onion, bacon, and cheese.

3   Pour the egg mixture into the prepared dish and cover tightly with aluminum foil. Place the dish on a long-handled silicone steam rack. Holding the handles of the steam rack, lower it into the pot.

4   Secure the lid and set the Pressure Release to **Sealing**. Select the **Pressure Cook** or **Manual** setting and set the cooking time for 25 minutes at high pressure. (The pot will take about 15 minutes to come up to pressure before the cooking program begins.)

5   When the program ends, let the pressure release naturally for 10 minutes, then move the Pressure Release to **Venting** to release any remaining steam. Open the pot and, wearing heat-resistant mitts, grab the handles of the steam rack and lift the quiche out of the pot. Uncover the quiche, taking care to avoid getting burned by the steam. Let the quiche cool for 5 minutes, giving it time to reabsorb any liquid and set up.

6   Slice the quiche into wedges and serve warm or at room temperature.

Take a classic omelet and make it into a family-size brunch dish. Cooked in a Pyrex dish, this omelet rises beautifully, ready to be sliced into impressively tall single-serving wedges. The combination of onion, bell pepper, ham, and cheese is always a crowd-pleaser. Serve the omelet with whole wheat toast and a side of orange wedges for an easy, generous breakfast or brunch.

DENVER OMELET

12 eggs

½ cup whole milk or water

1 teaspoon kosher salt

½ teaspoon freshly ground black pepper

1 small yellow onion, diced

1 small red bell pepper, seeded and diced

4 ounces ham, diced

1 cup tightly packed shredded Cheddar cheese

2 tablespoons chopped fresh chives

PREP	5 MINUTES
COOK	40 MINUTES
PR	10 MINUTES NPR
SERVES	4 TO 6

1   Lightly butter a 7-cup round heatproof glass container or coat with nonstick cooking spray. Pour 2 cups water into the Instant Pot.

2   In a bowl, whisk together the eggs, milk, salt, and pepper until well blended, then stir in the onion, bell pepper, ham, and ½ cup of the cheese.

3   Pour the egg mixture into the prepared glass container and cover tightly with aluminum foil. Place the container on a long-handled silicone steam rack. Holding the handles of the steam rack, lower it into the pot.

4   Secure the lid and set the Pressure Release to **Sealing**. Select the **Pressure Cook** or **Manual** setting and set the cooking time for 25 minutes at high pressure. (The pot will take about 15 minutes to come up to pressure before the cooking program begins.)

5   When the cooking program ends, let the pressure release naturally for 10 minutes, then move the Pressure Release to **Venting** to release any remaining steam. Open the pot and let the omelet sit for a minute or two, until it deflates and settles into its container. Then, wearing heat-resistant mitts, grab the handles of the steam rack and lift the container out of the pot. Uncover the omelet, taking care to avoid getting burned by the steam.

6   Cut the omelet into wedges, sprinkle with the remaining ½ cup cheese and the chives, and serve warm.

With the Instant Pot and a 7-cup round heatproof glass container, you can easily whip up an omelet large enough to serve a small crowd. This recipe is great for busy mornings when you don't have time to cook individual omelets in a frying pan. Feel free to replace the Cheddar and green onions with whatever toppings you like.

BASIC 12-EGG OMELET

12 eggs

½ cup whole milk or water

1 teaspoon kosher salt

½ teaspoon freshly ground black pepper

½ cup grated Cheddar cheese

2 green onions, tender green parts only, thinly sliced

PREP	5 MINUTES
COOK	35 MINUTES
PR	10 MINUTES NPR
SERVES	4 TO 6

1   Lightly butter a 7-cup round heatproof glass container or coat with nonstick cooking spray. Pour 2 cups water into the Instant Pot.

2   In a bowl, whisk together the eggs, milk, salt, and pepper until well blended.

3   Pour the egg mixture into the prepared glass container and cover tightly with aluminum foil. Place the container on a long-handled silicone steam rack. Holding the handles of the steam rack, lower it into the pot.

4   Secure the lid and set the Pressure Release to **Sealing**. Select the **Pressure Cook** or **Manual** setting and set the cooking time for 25 minutes at high pressure. (The pot will take about 10 minutes to come up to pressure before the cooking program begins.)

5   When the cooking program ends, let the pressure release naturally for 10 minutes, then move the Pressure Release to **Venting** to release any remaining steam. Open the pot and let the omelet sit for a minute or two, until it deflates and settles into its container. Then, wearing heat-resistant mitts, grab the handles of the steam rack and lift the container out of the pot. Uncover the omelet, taking care to avoid getting burned by the steam.

6   Sprinkle the omelet with the cheese and green onions. Cut into wedges and serve warm.

This recipe makes an impressive 12-egg frittata studded with creamy goat cheese, silky strips of roasted red pepper, and baby greens. If a dozen eggs is too much for your morning routine, don't worry—the recipe is easily halved. Just shorten the cooking time to 20 minutes and you're good to go.

ROASTED RED PEPPER AND GOAT CHEESE FRITTATA

12 eggs

½ cup whole milk or water

Kosher salt

Freshly ground black pepper

2 cups baby kale or baby arugula

One 12-ounce jar roasted red bell peppers, drained and cut into ¼ inch by 2-inch strips

1 cup crumbled fresh goat cheese (chèvre)

6 cups mixed baby greens for serving

¾ cup cherry or grape tomatoes, halved, for serving

2 tablespoons extra-virgin olive oil for serving

PREP	5 MINUTES
COOK	40 MINUTES
PR	10 MINUTES NPR
SERVES	4 TO 6

1   Lightly butter a 7-cup round heatproof glass container or coat with nonstick cooking spray. Pour 2 cups water into the Instant Pot.

2   In a bowl, whisk together the eggs, milk, ¾ teaspoon salt, and ½ teaspoon pepper until well blended, then stir in the kale, roasted peppers, and goat cheese.

3   Pour the egg mixture into the prepared glass container and cover tightly with aluminum foil. Place the container on a long-handled silicone steam rack. Holding the handles of the steam rack, lower it into the Instant Pot.

4   Secure the lid and set the Pressure Release to **Sealing**. Select the **Pressure Cook** or **Manual** setting and set the cooking time for 25 minutes at high pressure. (The pot will take about 15 minutes to come up to pressure before the cooking program begins.)

5   When the cooking program ends, let the pressure release naturally for 10 minutes, then move the Pressure Release to **Venting** to release any remaining steam. Open the pot and let the frittata sit for a minute or two, until it deflates and settles into its container. Then, wearing heat-resistant mitts, grab the handles of the steam rack and lift the container out of the pot. Uncover the frittata, taking care to avoid getting burned by the steam.

6   In a medium bowl, toss together the mixed greens, tomatoes, and olive oil, and season with salt and pepper.

7   Cut the frittata into wedges and serve warm, with the mixed greens salad alongside.

It takes just two ingredients to whip up a batch of full-fat yogurt in the DUO, DUO Plus, Ultra, and SMART models of the Instant Pot. All you need are whole milk and a starter culture (a spoonful of fresh plain yogurt or an envelope of dried starter culture will work). You can make yogurt either right in the inner pot or, my favorite way, in a glass container that fits inside the inner pot—this way, the container goes straight from Instant Pot to refrigerator with practically zero cleanup. See Variations for instructions on how to make Greek yogurt and dairy-free coconut milk yogurt.

PLAIN YOGURT

4 cups whole milk

2 tablespoons plain yogurt with live active cultures or one 5-gram envelope freeze-dried yogurt starter

PREP	5 MINUTES
COOK	8½ TO 12 HOURS
PR	10 MINUTES NPR
MAKES	4 CUPS

1   Pour 1 cup water into the Instant Pot and place the wire metal steam rack in the pot. Place a 7-cup round heatproof glass container on the steam rack. Pour the milk into the container. Secure the lid and set the Pressure Release to **Sealing**. Select the **Steam** setting and set the cooking time for 1 minute at high pressure. (The pot will take about 10 minutes to come up to pressure before the cooking program begins.)

2   Let the pressure release naturally. This will take about 10 minutes. Open the pot and press the **Cancel** button to turn off the Instant Pot.

3   Let the milk cool to 115°F. (A probe thermometer with a remote display is ideal for this step because you can leave the thermometer in the milk and set it to alert you when the milk has cooled to the proper temperature. Alternatively, you can test the milk periodically with an instant-read thermometer. If you don't have a thermometer, let the milk cool until lukewarm to the touch.) Add the plain yogurt or yogurt starter to the cooled milk and whisk gently until fully incorporated.

4   Secure the lid on the pot and set the Pressure Release to **Sealing** or **Venting** (either is fine), then select the **Yogurt** setting. The yogurt will begin to thicken after about 3 hours but the flavor will be very mild at this point. For a moderately tart yogurt, let it culture for the full 8 hours of the default **Yogurt** program. If you like your yogurt more tart or very tart, adjust the program time to 10 or 12 hours, respectively.

5   Open the pot and remove the yogurt container. Cover and refrigerate for 6 hours before serving. The yogurt will keep, refrigerated, for up to 2 weeks.

Note: To speed up the milk's cooling process, carefully lower the glass container of heated milk into a large bowl, then carefully pour a few inches of cold tap water into the bowl. Do not use ice water, as the thermal shock could cause the container to break.

Variations:

Greek Yogurt: Place a 4-cup or larger fine-mesh strainer over a bowl. Line the strainer with cheesecloth, a paper towel, or a clean tea towel. Pour the just-made yogurt into the prepared strainer, transfer the bowl to the refrigerator, and allow the yogurt to drain until it reaches the desired thickness. This will take from 2 hours for a lightly drained yogurt to overnight for a very thick, spreadable consistency.

Dairy-Free Coconut Yogurt: Whisk together one 13½-ounce can coconut cream, one 13½-ounce can coconut milk, 2 tablespoons sugar, and one ¼-ounce envelope unflavored powdered gelatin; use this mixture in place of dairy milk. Use 2 tablespoons nondairy yogurt with live active cultures or two probiotic capsules for a starter culture. Let the yogurt culture for 8 hours on the default **Yogurt** program, then chill for 6 hours before serving. A thin layer of gelatin may settle at the bottom; for a homogenous, creamy consistency, blend the yogurt on low speed for about 15 seconds.

With homemade or store-bought yogurt and jam on hand, along with a few jam jars or other tightly lidded containers, you can make your own single-serving yogurt cups. Assemble them on a Sunday and they'll be ready to pack into lunches all week long.

FRUIT-ON-THE-BOTTOM YOGURT CUPS

6 tablespoons Mixed Berry Jam (page 293), Stone Fruit Jam (page 292), or your favorite store-bought jam

4 cups Plain Yogurt (opposite)

1   Spoon 1 tablespoon of the jam into each of six jam jars with tight-fitting lids. Spoon the yogurt into the jars on top of the jam, dividing it evenly.

2   Secure lids on the jars and refrigerate for up to 1 week.

PREP	5 MINUTES
COOK	0 MINUTES
PR	N/A
SERVES	6

Once you've made a batch of Greek yogurt with your Instant Pot, the possibilities for breakfast are endless! I enjoy my yogurt with fresh fruit (such as berries or chopped melon in the spring and summer, or chopped apples or pears in fall and winter), homemade granola, and honey. When I'm feeling fancy, I'll layer everything in jam jars for pretty parfaits. This granola is also great as a breakfast cereal, served in a bowl with milk and fresh berries or sliced bananas.

GREEK YOGURT PARFAITS WITH GRANOLA AND FRESH FRUIT

Granola

¼ cup honey or agave nectar

¼ cup unsalted butter or coconut oil

1 teaspoon vanilla extract

½ teaspoon kosher salt

3 cups old-fashioned oats

1 cup pecans, chopped

1 cup raisins, coconut flakes, or chopped dried fruit (optional)

Parfaits

2 cups Greek yogurt (page 33)

1 cup granola

2 cups fresh fruit (such as berries, seeded and diced melon, or cored and diced apples or pears)

4 teaspoons honey

1   To make the granola: Preheat the oven to 300°F. Line a rimmed baking sheet with parchment paper or a silicone baking mat.

2   Select the low **Sauté** setting on the Instant Pot and heat the honey and butter for about 3 minutes, stirring once or twice, until the butter has completely melted. Stir in the vanilla and salt. Select **Cancel** to turn off the pot, then stir in the oats and pecans.

3   Use a silicone spatula to transfer the mixture to the prepared baking sheet, spreading it out in an even layer. Bake for about 30 minutes, stirring every 10 minutes, until the granola is evenly golden brown. Let the granola cool to room temperature on the baking sheet, then sprinkle with the raisins. Transfer to an airtight container and store at room temperature for up to 2 weeks.

4   Spoon ¼ cup of the yogurt into each of four jam jars or drinking glasses, followed by 2 tablespoons granola and ¼ cup of the fruit. Repeat the layers, then drizzle each parfait with 1 teaspoon of the honey. Serve immediately.

PREP	0 MINUTES
COOK	45 MINUTES
PR	N/A
COOL	30 MINUTES
SERVES	4

Everyone needs a simple go-to smoothie recipe for a quick breakfast or snack, and this one is mine. Tangy homemade yogurt is tempered by sweet banana, berries, and orange juice. Keep the recipe basic, or add in a handful of baby spinach, a scoop of protein powder, or a drizzle of honey.

MIXED BERRY AND YOGURT SMOOTHIES

1 cup frozen strawberries

½ cup frozen blueberries

½ cup frozen raspberries

1 banana, broken into 1-inch pieces

1 cup fresh orange juice

1 cup Plain Yogurt (page 32)

In a blender jar, combine the strawberries, blueberries, raspberries, banana, orange juice, and yogurt. Blend at high speed until smooth, about 30 seconds. Pour into glasses and serve right away.

PREP	5 MINUTES
COOK	0 MINUTES
PR	N/A
SERVES	2

When you combine the ingredients for blueberry pancakes, mix the batter in a blender, and cook the berry-studded mixture in the Instant Pot, you get a breakfast clafoutis. This dish traditionally includes cherries and is served as a dessert, but I've lightened up on the sugar to serve it as a morning treat. The texture is custardy and creamy but also sliceable, and the buttermilk's tang offsets the sweetness of the berries.

BLUEBERRY-BUTTERMILK BREAKFAST CLAFOUTIS

1 cup buttermilk

4 eggs

2 tablespoons unsalted butter, melted and cooled

1 teaspoon finely grated lemon zest

¾ cup all-purpose flour

⅓ cup granulated sugar

½ teaspoon kosher salt

⅔ cup fresh blueberries

Confectioners' sugar for dusting

PREP	10 MINUTES
COOK	45 MINUTES
PR	QPR
REST	10 MINUTES
SERVES	4

1   Grease a 1½-quart soufflé dish or a 7 by 3-inch round cake pan with butter or nonstick cooking spray, then set the dish on a long-handled silicone steam rack. Pour 1½ cups water into the Instant Pot.

2   In a blender or mixing bowl, combine the buttermilk, eggs, melted butter, and lemon zest. Blend on low speed or whisk by hand until smooth. Add the flour, granulated sugar, and salt. Blend on low speed or whisk just until the flour is incorporated, scraping down the sides of the blender or bowl as needed.

3   Pour the batter into the prepared dish, then sprinkle evenly with the blueberries; they shouldn't sink too much. Cover the dish tightly with aluminum foil. Holding the handles of the steam rack, lower the dish into the Instant Pot.

4   Secure the lid and set the Pressure Release to **Sealing**. Select the **Cake**, **Manual**, or **Pressure Cooker** program and set the cooking time for 30 minutes at high pressure. (The pot will take about 15 minutes to come up to pressure before the cooking program begins.)

5   When the cooking program ends, perform a quick pressure release by moving the Pressure Release to **Venting**, or let the pressure release naturally. Open the pot and, wearing heat-resistant mitts, grab the handles of the steam rack to lift the dish out of the pot. Uncover the dish, taking care to avoid getting burned by the steam. Let cool for about 10 minutes, allowing the clafoutis to absorb any liquid released by the berries.

6   Slice the clafoutis into wedges and dust with confectioners' sugar. Serve warm.

This breakfast dish has all of the deliciousness of French toast, but in an easy-to-make multi-serving casserole! It comes together like a bread pudding, and is lightly sweetened with maple syrup and cinnamon. Assemble the ingredients in the morning and let it rest on the counter for a few minutes to let the bread absorb the egg mixture, or assemble it the evening before and refrigerate overnight. This recipe works equally well with fresh and day-old bread.

FRENCH TOAST CASSEROLE

4 eggs

1 cup whole milk

2 tablespoons maple syrup, plus more for drizzling

1 teaspoon ground cinnamon

¼ teaspoon kosher salt

4 cups cubed baguette, batard, or other crusty bread

Confectioners' sugar for dusting

PREP	15 MINUTES
COOK	35 MINUTES
PR	10 MINUTES NPR
SERVES	4

1   Grease a 1½-quart soufflé dish or a 7-cup round heatproof glass container with butter or nonstick cooking spray.

2   In a medium bowl, whisk together the eggs, milk, maple syrup, cinnamon, and salt. Stir in the bread, pressing it down into the egg mixture and making sure all of it is coated. Pour the mixture into the prepared dish, cover tightly with aluminum foil, and let stand at room temperature for 10 minutes or refrigerate up to overnight.

3   Pour 1½ cups water into the Instant Pot. Place the dish on a long-handled silicone steam rack. Holding the handles of the steam rack, lower the dish into the pot.

4   Secure the lid and set the Pressure Release to **Sealing**. Select the **Pressure Cook** or **Manual** setting and set the cooking time for 25 minutes at high pressure. (The pot will take 10 to 15 minutes to come up to pressure, depending on whether the casserole is at room temperature or chilled, before the cooking program begins.)

5   When the cooking program ends, let the pressure release naturally for 10 minutes, then move the Pressure Release to **Venting** to release any remaining steam. Open the pot and, wearing heat-resistant mitts, grab the handles of the steam rack and lift the dish out of the pot. Uncover the dish, taking care to avoid getting burned by the steam.

6   Dust the casserole with confectioners' sugar. Cut into wedges and serve warm, drizzled with maple syrup.

With a sweet topping of cream cheese icing and a swirl of cinnamon sugar running through the middle, this cake is like an oversize cinnamon roll. It's best served warm, either right after baking or after a few seconds in a microwave.

CINNAMON SWIRL BUNDT CAKE

Cinnamon Sugar

2 tablespoons granulated sugar

½ teaspoon ground cinnamon

Cake

2 cups all-purpose flour

⅔ cup granulated sugar

2 teaspoons baking powder

½ teaspoon kosher salt

½ cup whole milk, at room temperature

½ cup unsalted butter, melted and cooled

2 eggs, at room temperature

2 teaspoons vanilla extract

Icing

¼ cup cream cheese, at room temperature

½ cup confectioners' sugar

½ teaspoon vanilla extract

PREP	10 MINUTES
COOK	45 MINUTES
PR	10 MINUTES NPR
REST	5 MINUTES
SERVES	8

1   Butter a 1-quart Bundt or ring-mold pan and dust with flour, tapping out the excess. Pour 1½ cups water into the Instant Pot.

2   To make the cinnamon sugar: In a small bowl, stir together the granulated sugar and cinnamon. Set aside.

3   To make the cake: In a medium bowl, whisk together the flour, granulated sugar, baking powder, and salt. In another bowl, whisk the milk, melted butter, eggs, and vanilla until well combined. Add the wet ingredients to the dry ingredients and whisk until fully incorporated.

4   Spoon half of the batter into the prepared pan, spread it in an even layer, and sprinkle with the cinnamon sugar. Run a silicone spatula through the batter in a zigzag motion to swirl the cinnamon sugar throughout the cake. Spoon the remaining batter on top. Run the spatula through the batter once more, then smooth the surface of the batter. Tap the pan on the counter a few times to remove any air pockets. Place the pan on a long-handled silicone steam rack. Holding the handles of the steam rack, lower the pan into the pot.

5   Secure the lid and set the Pressure Release to **Sealing**. Select the **Cake**, **Manual**, or **Pressure Cook** setting and set the cooking time for 35 minutes at high pressure. (The pot will take about 10 minutes to come up to pressure before the cooking program begins.)

6   To make the icing: While the cake is cooking, in a small bowl, whisk together the cream cheese, confectioners' sugar, and vanilla until smooth. Transfer to a 1-quart ziplock plastic bag, seal the bag, and set aside.

7 When the cooking program ends, let the pressure release naturally for 10 minutes, then move the Pressure Release to **Venting** to release any remaining steam. Open the pot and, wearing heat-resistant mitts, grab the handles of the steam rack and lift the pan out of the pot. Let the cake cool in the pan for 5 minutes, then invert the pan onto a cooling rack and lift off the pan.

8 Set the rack with the cake over a large plate, to catch drips when you glaze the cake. Cut off a small corner of the ziplock bag, squeeze the glaze all over the cake, and transfer to a serving plate.

9 While the cake is still warm, cut into wedges and serve.

2

Beans, Grains, and Pastas

With cooked beans on hand, quick meals are within easy reach. Dried beans are more economical than their canned counterparts, they require less storage space in the pantry, and cooking them yourself allows you to control the amount of salt that goes into the pot. Plus, in my opinion, beans cooked from the dried state taste much better than beans from a can. After combining the beans, water, and salt in the Instant Pot, the Timer function allows you to soak the beans and then cook them at the touch of a few buttons.

Soaked beans tend to hold their shape better during cooking, while unsoaked beans have a tendency to split their skins a bit. If you're short on time or making a last-minute meal, cooking unsoaked beans is fine in a pinch. Both methods are outlined here.

BASIC BEANS

1 pound dried beans (any variety)

8 cups water

2 teaspoons kosher salt

MAKES   ABOUT 6 CUPS

1   Add the beans, water, and salt to the Instant Pot and stir to dissolve the salt.

2   Secure the lid and set the Pressure Release to **Sealing**.

3   If soaking the beans, select the **Bean/Chili**, **Pressure Cook**, or **Manual** setting, then refer to the Soaked Cooking Time in the table on page 302 for setting the cooking time; use high pressure. Next, select the **Timer** or **Delay** function and set the time delay for 8 to 12 hours. (When the soaking time is complete, the pot will take about 20 minutes to come up to pressure before the cooking program begins.)

4   If cooking the beans right away, select the **Bean/Chili**, **Pressure Cook**, or **Manual** setting, then refer to the Unsoaked Cooking Time in the table on page 302 for setting the cooking time; use high pressure. (The pot will take about 20 minutes to come up to pressure before the cooking program begins.)

5   When the cooking program ends, let the pressure release naturally; this will take about 30 minutes. Open the pot and, wearing heat-resistant mitts, lift out the inner pot. If using the beans immediately, drain them in a colander. To refrigerate, ladle the beans and their cooking liquid into airtight containers, let cool for about 1 hour, then cover and refrigerate for up to 5 days. To freeze, drain the beans in a colander, portion them into 1-quart ziplock plastic freezer bags, seal well, and freeze for up to 6 months.

Pungent rosemary, fresh garlic, and tangy lemon juice give this white bean dip Mediterranean flair. Serve it as a snack or appetizer with pita chips and fresh vegetables, such as carrot sticks, halved radishes, and bite-size broccoli florets.

WHITE BEAN DIP

1 cup dried navy, great Northern, or cannellini beans

4 cups water

Kosher salt

3 tablespoons fresh lemon juice

¼ cup extra-virgin olive oil, plus more for drizzling

1¼ teaspoons chopped fresh rosemary

1 garlic clove, minced

Freshly ground black pepper

PREP	0 MINUTES
COOK	1 HOUR, 5 MINUTES
PR	15 MINUTES NPR
MAKES	ABOUT 3 CUPS

1   Add the beans, water, and 1 teaspoon salt to the Instant Pot and stir to dissolve the salt.

2   Secure the lid and set the Pressure Release to **Sealing**. Select the **Bean/Chili**, **Pressure Cook**, or **Manual** setting and set the cooking time for 30 minutes if using navy or great Northern beans, or 40 minutes if using cannellini beans; use high pressure. (The pot will take about 15 minutes to come up to pressure before the cooking program begins.)

3   When the cooking program ends, let the pressure release naturally for 15 minutes, then move the Pressure Release to **Venting** to release any remaining steam. Open the pot, then ladle out and reserve ½ cup of the cooking liquid. Wearing heat-resistant mitts, lift out the inner pot and drain the beans in a colander.

4   In a food processor or blender, combine the reserved cooking liquid, beans, lemon juice, olive oil, rosemary, garlic, 1 teaspoon salt, and ½ teaspoon pepper. Process or blend on medium speed for about 1 minute, scraping down the sides of the container as needed, until the mixture is smooth. Taste and adjust the seasoning with salt if needed.

5   Transfer the dip to a serving bowl. Drizzle with olive oil and sprinkle with a few grinds of pepper. Serve warm or at room temperature.

When you blend warm just-cooked chickpeas into hummus like they do in Israel, the texture of the dip is silky smooth and creamy. I add roasted red peppers for a West Coast twist. Serve the hummus with wedges of pita and carrot sticks, or spread it thickly in a pita pocket, then load the bread with crunchy vegetables.

ROASTED RED PEPPER HUMMUS

4 cups water

1 cup dried chickpeas

2 teaspoons kosher salt

One 12-ounce jar roasted red bell peppers, drained (see Note)

½ cup tahini

3 tablespoons fresh lemon juice

2 garlic cloves, minced

¼ teaspoon ground cumin

¼ teaspoon smoked paprika

¼ teaspoon sweet paprika

1 tablespoon extra-virgin olive oil

PREP	0 MINUTES
COOK	1 HOUR
PR	15 MINUTES NPR
MAKES	ABOUT 3½ CUPS

1   Add the water, chickpeas, and 1 teaspoon of the salt to the Instant Pot.

2   Secure the lid and set the Pressure Release to **Sealing**. Select the **Bean/Chili**, **Pressure Cook**, or **Manual** setting and set the cooking time for 40 minutes at high pressure. (The pot will take about 15 minutes to come up to pressure before the cooking program begins.)

3   When the cooking program ends, let the pressure release naturally for 15 minutes, then move the Pressure Release to **Venting** to release any remaining steam. Open the pot, then ladle out and reserve ¾ cup of the cooking liquid. Wearing heat-resistant mitts, lift out the inner pot and drain the chickpeas in a colander.

4   Transfer the warm drained chickpeas to a food processor or blender. Add the reserved cooking liquid, the roasted red peppers, tahini, lemon juice, garlic, cumin, smoked paprika, and remaining 1 teaspoon salt. Process at medium speed for about 1 minute, until the mixture is smooth and creamy.

5   Spoon the hummus into the center of a wide, shallow serving bowl and spread it out into a thick circle. Sprinkle with the sweet paprika, then drizzle with the olive oil. Serve immediately.

Note: If you prefer, you can roast two fresh red bell peppers instead of using store-bought roasted peppers. Wearing heat-resistant mitts and using tongs, hold each bell pepper over a medium flame for a few minutes, turning the pepper when the skin blisters and blackens, until charred on all sides. Alternatively, put the bell peppers on an aluminum foil–lined baking sheet and broil for 15 to 20 minutes, turning every few minutes, until they are charred on all sides. Transfer the just-charred peppers to a bowl and cover tightly with plastic wrap. Let stand for 15 minutes, then scrape off the skins and remove the stems and seeds. You can do this while the chickpeas are cooking.

With sweet onion, smoky bacon, and tangy barbecue sauce in the mix, it's hard to go wrong with a pot of these baked beans. Rather than mix up a concoction of molasses, ketchup, sugar, and spices, I rely on store-bought sauce to get the job done. Use your favorite; I happen to like Sweet Baby Ray's. The beans do need to be soaked overnight so that they become tender without losing their shape, so don't skip that step. You'll end up with gorgeous dark-brown beans in a thick, rich sauce, with lots of bacon throughout. Serve them with Smoky Brisket (page 220) or with any grilled meats, seafood, or veggies.

BARBECUE BAKED BEANS

7¾ cups water

1 tablespoon kosher salt

2½ cups dried great Northern beans

1 cup barbecue sauce

¼ cup yellow mustard

2 tablespoons maple syrup

1 teaspoon freshly ground black pepper

6 slices thick-cut bacon, cut into ½-inch pieces

1 large yellow onion, diced

2 garlic cloves, minced

1 bay leaf

PREP	8 HOUR SOAK
COOK	1 HOUR, 10 MINUTES
PR	35 MINUTES NPR
SERVES	8 TO 10

1   In a large bowl, stir together 6 cups of the water and the salt. Add the beans and let soak for at least 8 hours or up to overnight. Drain the beans and set aside.

2   In a liquid measuring cup or small bowl, stir together the remaining 1¾ cups water, the barbecue sauce, mustard, maple syrup, and pepper.

3   Select the **Sauté** setting on the Instant Pot and add the bacon. Sauté for about 7 minutes, stirring occasionally, until the bacon is just beginning to brown. Add the onion and garlic and sauté for about 3 minutes more, until the onion is slightly softened. Add the barbecue sauce mixture, drained beans, and bay leaf. Stir to combine.

4   Secure the lid and set the Pressure Release to **Sealing**. Press the **Cancel** button to reset the cooking program, then select the **Bean/Chili**, **Pressure Cook**, or **Manual** setting and set the cooking time for 40 minutes at high pressure. (The pot will take about 20 minutes to come up to pressure before the cooking program begins.)

5   When the cooking program ends, let the pressure release naturally for 35 minutes, then move the Pressure Release to **Venting** to release any remaining steam. Open the pot, stir the beans, and discard the bay leaf.

6   Ladle the beans into bowls and serve hot.

Make a batch of refried beans to tuck into bean-and-cheese burritos or to serve with any Mexican or Tex-Mex main dish, such as Ground Beef Tacos (page 215) or Chile Colorado (page 113). Cook the beans right away or let them soak overnight: you'll find instructions for both methods here.

REFRIED BEANS

2¼ cups dried pinto beans

8 cups water

Kosher salt

3 tablespoons olive oil

4 garlic cloves

1 medium yellow onion, diced

One 4-ounce can diced green chiles and their liquid (mild or hot)

1 teaspoon ground cumin

Shredded Monterey Jack or Cheddar cheese for serving

Hot sauce (such as Cholula or Tapatío) for serving

PREP	0 MINUTES
COOK	1 HOUR
PR	15 MINUTES NPR
SERVES	6 TO 8

1   Combine the beans, water, and 2 teaspoons salt in the Instant Pot and stir to dissolve the salt.

2   Secure the lid and set the Pressure Release to **Sealing**.

3   If soaking the beans, select the **Bean/Chili**, **Pressure Cook**, or **Manual** setting and set the cooking time for 25 minutes at high pressure. Next, select the **Timer** or **Delay** function and set the time delay for 8 to 12 hours. (When the soaking time is complete, the pot will take about 20 minutes to come up to pressure before the cooking program begins.)

4   If cooking the beans right away, select the **Bean/Chili**, **Pressure Cook**, or **Manual** setting and set the cooking time for 30 minutes at high pressure. (The pot will take about 20 minutes to come up to pressure before the cooking program begins.) Set a colander in a large bowl.

5   When the cooking program ends, let the pressure release naturally for 15 minutes, then move the Pressure Release to **Venting** to release any remaining steam. Open the pot and, wearing heat-resistant mitts, lift out the inner pot and strain the beans in the colander; reserve the cooking liquid. Rinse out the inner pot and return it to the housing.

6   Add the olive oil and garlic to the Instant Pot. Press the **Cancel** button to reset the cooking program, then select the **Sauté** setting and sauté until the garlic begins to bubble, about 1 minute. Add the onion and sauté for about 4 minutes, until the onion begins to soften. Add the green chiles and their liquid and the cumin and sauté for about 1 minute more, until the cumin is fragrant and the chiles are heated through. Add the beans and 1 cup of the reserved cooking liquid to the pot and stir to combine. Press the **Cancel** button to turn off the pot. Using an immersion blender, puree the beans, adding more cooking liquid if you like your refried beans with a looser consistency. Taste and adjust the seasoning with salt if needed.

7   Scoop the beans into serving bowls or onto plates, top with shredded cheese, and serve warm with hot sauce on the side.

Once you've discovered how simple it is to make rice in the Instant Pot, you'll never go back to cooking it on the stove top. The method is straightforward, and there are no tricky ratios to remember: every type of rice can be cooked with a 1:1 ratio of rice to liquid. Whether you're cooking brown, white, long-grain, or short-grain rice, that ratio works perfectly. It results in firm-textured, separate grains, so if you like your rice to have a softer consistency, use a bit more liquid. (When making risotto [see page 52] you'll use even more liquid to achieve a looser consistency.)

BASIC RICE

Rules for Perfect Rice

- Because it's difficult to cook small amounts of rice evenly, use 1 cup in the 3-quart pot, 1½ cups in the 6-quart pot, or 2 cups in the 8-quart pot. (For a smaller amount, see the Note.)

- Rinse your rice before cooking. In a wire-mesh strainer, swish it around under running water to rinse off any extra starch, then drain well. This step ensures that you won't end up with gummy, goopy rice, and the grains will come out separate and fluffy.

- Don't fill the pot more than half full of liquid. Grains and beans can foam and spatter when they cook. Keeping the pot no more than half full prevents clogging the pressure valve.

- Letting the rice rest on the Keep Warm setting for 10 minutes once it finishes cooking ensures that the grains are evenly cooked and the moisture redistributes, with no sticking or burning on the bottom of the pot.

1   Measure the rice into a wire-mesh strainer, then rinse under running water for 10 seconds, swishing the grains around. Set the strainer over a bowl and let the rice drain well, which should take about 1 minute. Remove the inner pot from the Instant Pot housing and pour the rice and your chosen liquid into the inner pot. Jiggle the pot back and forth on the countertop so the rice settles in an even layer, then return the inner pot to the housing. Secure the lid in the **Sealing** position.

2   For white rice, select the **Rice** setting. The pot will adjust the cooking time automatically. For brown rice, select the **Multigrain** setting and set the cooking time for 25 minutes. When the cooking program ends, leave on the **Keep Warm** setting for 10 minutes, then move the Pressure Release to **Venting** to release any remaining steam. Open the pot and, wearing heat-resistant mitts, lift out the inner pot. Use a rice paddle to scoop the rice out of the pot. Serve warm or freeze for later use.

3   To freeze individual portions of rice, spread the hot rice in a thin layer on a rimmed baking sheet, then let cool for about 20 minutes, until room temperature. Scoop the cooled rice into small plastic bags in single or double portions and seal closed. Slip the bags into 1-quart or 1-gallon ziplock freezer bags, seal them closed, and freeze them flat. Rice will keep in the freezer for up to 2 months. When you're ready to eat the rice, transfer it, still frozen, to a bowl, cover the bowl with a reusable silicone lid or plastic wrap, and heat in the microwave for 2 to 3 minutes, until piping hot.

Note: To cook a smaller amount of rice, use the pot-in-pot method explained on page 7 and used in Thai Green Curry Tofu with Rice on page 124.

Risotto is rich and creamy, yet it contains no cream. It owes its texture to the starch that comes out of the rice during cooking. Of course, butter, olive oil, and Parmesan cheese don't hurt, either! Pressure cooking helps the grains release their starch, so unlike making risotto on the stove top, there's zero stirring required when making risotto in the Instant Pot. For best results, use Italian rice such as Arborio, Carnaroli, or Vialone Nano, or if those aren't available, a short- or medium-grain Japanese-style rice.

RISOTTO

2 tablespoons olive oil

2 tablespoons unsalted butter

1 large shallot, minced

1½ cups Arborio, Carnaroli, or Vialone Nano rice

⅓ cup dry white wine

3 cups chicken broth (page 286) or vegetable broth (page 284)

½ cup grated Parmesan cheese

¼ teaspoon freshly ground black pepper

Kosher salt

PREP	0 MINUTES
COOK	25 MINUTES
PR	10 MINUTES NPR
SERVES	4 TO 6

Note: If you like your risotto with a looser texture, stir in an additional ¼ cup broth just before serving.

1   Select the **Sauté** setting on the Instant Pot and heat the olive oil and butter. When the butter has melted, add the shallot and sauté for about 4 minutes, until slightly softened and just beginning to brown. Stir in the rice and sauté for about 1 minute more. Pour in the wine and cook for about 2 minutes, until the liquid has evaporated and the rice begins to sizzle. Stir in the chicken broth, then scrape down the sides of the pot to make sure all the grains are submerged in the broth.

2   Secure the lid and set the Pressure Release to **Sealing**. Select the **Pressure Cook** or **Manual** setting and set the cooking time for 5 minutes at high pressure. (The pot will take about 10 minutes to come up to pressure before the cooking program begins.)

3   When the cooking program ends, let the pressure release naturally for 10 minutes, then move the Pressure Release to **Venting** to release any remaining steam. Open the pot and stir in the Parmesan and pepper. Taste and adjust the seasoning with salt if needed.

4   Spoon the risotto into bowls and serve immediately.

Variations:

Butternut Squash Risotto: Omit the wine. Add 1 pound peeled, seeded, and diced butternut squash with the broth. Add ¼ teaspoon grated nutmeg and ⅛ teaspoon ground cinnamon along with the Parmesan and pepper.

Lemon-Shrimp Risotto: Heat 2 garlic cloves, minced; ¼ teaspoon red pepper flakes; and ¼ teaspoon kosher salt along with the oil and butter. When the butter has melted, add 1 pound small (51/60 size) or medium (41/50 size) shrimp, peeled and deveined. Sauté for 2 to 3 minutes, until the shrimp are fully cooked. Spoon the shrimp onto a plate and set aside. Add the shallot to the fat remaining in the pot and proceed as directed, omitting the Parmesan and stirring the shrimp and 2 tablespoons fresh lemon juice into the risotto after opening the pot. Serve topped with fresh chopped parsley.

This Indian-style rice gets its vibrant color from ground turmeric. Luxe add-ins of ghee-toasted cashews and currants make it an extra-special side dish, but it only takes a couple minutes more to put together than a basic pot of rice.

INDIAN-STYLE RICE WITH TURMERIC AND CASHEWS

2 tablespoons ghee (page 291) or coconut oil

½ cup raw cashews

¾ teaspoon kosher salt

½ teaspoon ground coriander

½ teaspoon ground cumin

½ teaspoon ground turmeric

2 cups chicken broth (page 286) or vegetable broth (page 284)

1½ cups basmati or long-grain white rice, rinsed and drained

⅓ cup currants or raisins

1 cup frozen peas

PREP	0 MINUTES
COOK	30 MINUTES
PR	10 MINUTES NPR
SERVES	4

1   Select the **Sauté** setting on the Instant Pot and melt the ghee. Add the cashews and sauté for about 3 minutes, until lightly toasted. Add the salt, coriander, cumin, and turmeric and sauté for 1 minute more. Stir in the chicken broth and rice, using a wooden spoon to nudge loose any browned bits from the bottom of the pot. Scrape down any grains of rice stuck to the sides of the pot, making sure the rice is fully submerged in the broth. Sprinkle in the currants.

2   Secure the lid and set the Pressure Release to **Sealing**. Press the **Cancel** button to reset the cooking program, then select the **Pressure Cooker** or **Manual** setting and set the cooking time for 15 minutes at low pressure. (The pot will take about 10 minutes to come up to pressure before the cooking program begins.)

3   When the cooking program ends, let the pressure release naturally for 10 minutes, then move the Pressure Release to **Venting** to release any remaining steam. Open the pot and, wearing heat-resistant mitts, lift out the inner pot. Add the peas, then, using a fork, fluff the rice and incorporate the peas. Let stand for about 3 minutes, until the peas have warmed through, then fluff once more.

4   Transfer the rice to a serving bowl or spoon into individual bowls and serve warm.

Serve this tomatoey, fragrantly spiced rice with any Mexican main dish. It goes great with Ground Beef Tacos (page 215), burritos, or tostada salads.

MEXICAN-STYLE RICE

2 tablespoons olive oil

2 garlic cloves, minced

1½ cups long-grain white rice, rinsed and drained

1 tablespoon chili powder

1 teaspoon ground coriander

1 teaspoon ground cumin

1 teaspoon kosher salt

1½ cups vegetable broth (page 284)

2 tablespoons tomato paste

1 tablespoon fresh lime juice

PREP	0 MINUTES
COOK	25 MINUTES
PR	10 MINUTES NPR
SERVES	6

1   Select the **Sauté** setting on the Instant Pot, heat the olive oil and garlic, and sauté for about 2 minutes, until the garlic is bubbling. Stir in the rice, chili powder, coriander, cumin, salt, and broth, using a wooden spoon to nudge loose any browned bits from the bottom of the pot. Scrape down any grains of rice stuck to the sides of the pot, making sure the rice is fully submerged in the broth. Add the tomato paste in a dollop on top of the rice. Do not stir.

2   Secure the lid and set the Pressure Release to **Sealing**. Press the **Cancel** button to reset the cooking program, then select the **Pressure Cook** or **Manual** setting and set the cooking time for 15 minutes at low pressure. (The pot will take about 5 minutes to come up to pressure before the cooking program begins.)

3   When the cooking program ends, let the pressure release naturally for 10 minutes, then move the Pressure Release to **Venting** to release any remaining steam. Open the pot and, wearing heat-resistant mitts, lift out the inner pot. Add the lime juice, then use a fork to fluff the rice.

4   Spoon the rice onto plates and serve warm.

Note: The ratio of rice to broth in this recipe produces chewy, separate grains. For a softer texture, add an extra ¼ to ½ cup of broth.

You can cook any type of whole grain in the Instant Pot. While pearl barley, kasha, and quinoa are not technically whole grains, the cooking method is the same, so they are found in this table. Use the Multigrain setting when cooking 1½ cups or more; for smaller amounts, use the Steam setting and the pot-in-pot (PIP) method (see page 7). After adding the grain and water to the pot, make sure the pot is no more than half full to prevent excessive foaming and/or bubbling and blocking of the mechanisms in the lid. If the grain-to-water ratio in the table contains a range for the amount of water, use less if you like your grains with firmer texture or more if you prefer them softer and more tender. The shorter cooking time will result in firmer grains, while the longer cooking time will result in softer grains.

BASIC WHOLE GRAINS

Grain	Grain:Water Ratio	Cooking Time (in minutes)	Pressure
Barley, pearl	1:1½ to 2	25 to 30	High
Barley, pot	1:3 to 4	25 to 30	High
Brown rice (short-, medium-, or long-grain)	1:1 to 1¼	20 to 25	High
Bulgur (coarse)	1:1½	10 to 15	Low
Freekeh (cracked)	1:1½	10 to 15	Low
Kasha (roasted buckwheat)	1:1½	10 to 15	Low
Millet	1:1⅔	10 to 12	High
Oats (whole groats)	1:3	25 to 30	High
Oats (steel-cut)	1:3	15 to 20	High
Quinoa (rinsed and drained)	1:1¼ to 1½	12 to 15	Low
Wheat berries, rye berries, spelt, farro, and kamut	1:1½ to 2	25 to 30	High
Wild rice	1: 1⅓ to 1½	25 to 30	High

1   For less than 1½ cups of uncooked grain, use the grain-to-water ratio, cooking time, and pressure indicated in the preceding table and cook according to the PIP method.

2   For 1½ cups or more of uncooked grain, combine the grain and water in the Instant Pot. Season with salt (optional).

3   Secure the lid and set the Pressure Release to **Sealing**, then refer to the table for setting the cooking time and pressure.

4   When the cooking program ends, let the pressure release naturally for 10 minutes, then move the Pressure Release to **Venting** to release any remaining steam. Open the pot and fluff the grains with a fork if desired.

5   Serve or use immediately, or let cool to room temperature (to cool the grains quickly, spread them on a rimmed baking sheet), then transfer to an airtight container and refrigerate for up to 4 days or freeze for up to 2 months.

There are lots of versions of tabbouleh, and my favorites are spiced, contain a modest amount of bulgur, and are full of fresh parsley and mint. I like the bouncy chew of coarse bulgur wheat, which cooks in the Instant Pot in about 15 minutes. For tomatoes, I use cherry or grape varieties because they're reliably sweet and flavorful no matter the time of the year. Go with in-season tomatoes if you have them.

TABBOULEH

½ cup water

½ cup coarse bulgur wheat

¼ teaspoon freshly ground black pepper

¼ teaspoon ground allspice

¼ teaspoon ground cinnamon

Kosher salt

1 pint cherry or grape tomatoes, halved

2 Persian cucumbers or 1 small English cucumber, diced

2 green onions, white and tender green parts, thinly sliced

¼ cup chopped fresh mint

2 large bunches flat-leaf parsley, stems removed, chopped

¼ cup extra-virgin olive oil

2 tablespoons fresh lemon juice

1 head butter lettuce, leaves separated, optional

PREP	5 MINUTES
COOK	15 MINUTES
PR	QPR
COOL	5 MINUTES
SERVES	6

1   Add 1 cup water to the Instant Pot.

2   In a 1½-quart stainless-steel bowl, combine the ½ cup water, bulgur, pepper, allspice, cinnamon, and ¼ teaspoon salt. Place the bowl on the wire metal steam rack and, holding the arms of the steam rack, lower the bowl into the pot.

3   Secure the lid and set the Pressure Release to **Sealing**. Select the **Steam** setting and set the cooking time for 4 minutes at high pressure. (The pot will take about 10 minutes to come up to pressure before the cooking program begins.)

4   When the cooking program ends, perform a quick pressure release by moving the Pressure Release to **Venting**. Open the pot and, wearing heat-resistant mitts, grab the arms of the steam rack and lift the bowl out of the pot. Using a fork, fluff the bulgur, then let it cool for 5 minutes.

5   In a large bowl, combine the tomatoes, cucumber, green onions, mint, and parsley. Add the bulgur, followed by the olive oil, lemon juice, and ¼ teaspoon salt. Toss until the ingredients are evenly distributed. Taste for seasoning and add more salt if needed. (At this point, you can refrigerate for up to 1 day, if desired.)

6   Serve in individual bowls, or arrange the lettuce leaves on individual serving plates and spoon the tabbouleh into the leaves.

This super-fast side cooks entirely on the Sauté setting. Dried apricots, slivered almonds, and a hint of cinnamon add a special something to an easy weeknight grain dish. I often make this to go with a rotisserie chicken and a big salad. It's also great with Lamb and White Bean Tagine (page 203).

COUSCOUS WITH APRICOTS AND ALMONDS

1 tablespoon unsalted butter

½ cup slivered almonds

1 pinch ground cinnamon

2 cups chicken broth (page 286) or vegetable broth (page 284)

1½ cups couscous

½ cup dried Turkish apricots, diced

½ teaspoon kosher salt

PREP	0 MINUTES
COOK	15 MINUTES
PR	N/A
SERVES	4 TO 6

1   Select the **Sauté** setting on the Instant Pot and melt the butter. Add the almonds and sauté for about 5 minutes, until light golden brown. Add the cinnamon and stir for a few seconds, until fragrant. Add the chicken broth, couscous, apricots, and salt and stir to combine. Bring to a simmer (this will take about 3 minutes), then cover the pot with the glass lid. Press the **Cancel** button to turn off the pot. Let stand, covered, for 5 minutes. Uncover the pot and fluff the couscous with a fork.

2   Transfer the couscous to a serving bowl or spoon onto individual serving plates. Serve warm.

Switch up your grain side dish from the usual steamed rice to this fluffy, flavorful quinoa pilaf. It's full of sweet currants and rich, mellow pine nuts, with a good amount of toasty garlic, too. Serve it on a weeknight with pan-seared fish fillets, or double the recipe for the holiday table.

QUINOA WITH CURRANTS AND PINE NUTS

1 tablespoon olive oil

2 garlic cloves, minced

⅓ cup pine nuts

2 cups chicken broth (page 286) or vegetable broth (page 284)

1½ cups quinoa, rinsed and drained

Kosher salt

⅓ cup dried currants

PREP	0 MINUTES
COOK	25 MINUTES
PR	10 MINUTES NPR
SERVES	4 TO 6

1   Add the olive oil, garlic, and pine nuts to the Instant Pot and select the **Sauté** setting. Sauté for about 4 minutes, until the garlic is golden brown and the pine nuts are lightly toasted. Stir in the chicken broth, quinoa, and ¾ teaspoon salt, using a wooden spoon to nudge loose any browned bits from the bottom of the pot. Sprinkle in the currants.

2   Secure the lid and set the Pressure Release to **Sealing**. Press the **Cancel** button to reset the cooking program, then select the **Pressure Cooker** or **Manual** setting and set the cooking time for 12 minutes at low pressure. (The pot will take about 10 minutes to come up to pressure before the cooking program begins.)

3   When the cooking program ends, let the pressure release naturally for 10 minutes, then move the Pressure Release to **Venting** to release any remaining steam. Open the pot and, wearing heat-resistant mitts, lift out the inner pot. Fluff the quinoa with a fork. Taste and adjust the seasoning with salt if needed.

4   Spoon the quinoa onto plates and serve warm.

Notes: You can substitute coarse bulgur for the quinoa, or use a mixture of the two.

If you like, use chopped dried Turkish apricots, sweetened dried cranberries, or golden raisins in place of the currants.

Polenta is one of my favorite things to cook in the Instant Pot, because it's faster, mostly hands off, and it turns out just as good as when I make it in a double-boiler on the stove. Rich with creamy mascarpone and salty, savory Parmesan cheese, this is such a comforting side dish for cold nights. To turn it into a main course, top it with marinara (page 287) or Bolognese (page 288). Once you make it this way, you'll never want to stir a scary pot of burbling polenta on the stove again.

CREAMY POLENTA WITH PARMESAN

4 cups chicken broth (page 286) or vegetable broth (page 284)

2 tablespoons unsalted butter

1 cup coarse polenta (not an instant or quick-cooking variety)

½ cup grated Parmesan cheese

½ cup mascarpone or cream cheese, at room temperature

¼ teaspoon freshly ground black pepper

Kosher salt

PREP	0 MINUTES
COOK	25 MINUTES
PR	15 MINUTES NPR
SERVES	4

1   Select the **Sauté** setting on the Instant Pot. Add the chicken broth and butter, then cover the pot with the glass lid and cook until it just begins to simmer, 8 to 10 minutes. Then, while whisking constantly, pour the polenta into the broth in a thin stream. Press the **Cancel** button to reset the cooking program.

2   Secure the lid and set the Pressure Release to **Sealing**. Select the **Porridge** setting and set the cooking time for 10 minutes at high pressure. (The pot will take about 5 minutes to come up to pressure before the cooking program begins.)

3   When the cooking program ends, let the pressure release naturally for 15 minutes, then move the Pressure Release to **Venting** to release any remaining steam. Open the pot, and wearing heat-resistant mitts, lift out the inner pot. The polenta will have some liquid on the top; this is normal. Stir to incorporate the liquid, scraping along the bottom of the pot to loosen any stuck polenta. If there are any lumps, break them up with a whisk. Stir in the Parmesan, mascarpone, pepper, and ¼ teaspoon salt. Taste for seasoning and add more salt if needed.

4   Spoon polenta into bowls and serve piping hot.

Note: Wash the Instant Pot lid and inner pot immediately after use. They're much easier to clean before the polenta has had a chance to become dry.

You can make homemade marinara according to this recipe, or take a shortcut and use a jar of store-bought pasta sauce (see Variations). Short, sturdy pastas such as penne, ziti, and rigatoni work best in the pressure cooker; feel free to use your favorite.

PENNE ALLA MARINARA

¼ cup olive oil

3 garlic cloves, chopped

One 28-ounce can whole San Marzano tomatoes and their liquid

2 teaspoons Italian seasoning

1½ teaspoons kosher salt

½ teaspoon red pepper flakes (optional)

1 pound penne pasta

3½ cups water

Grated Parmesan cheese for sprinkling

PREP	0 MINUTES
COOK	35 MINUTES
PR	5 MINUTES NPR
REST	3 MINUTES
SERVES	4 TO 6

1   Select the **Sauté** setting on the Instant Pot and heat the olive oil and garlic for about 3 minutes, until the garlic is bubbling and beginning to turn blond. Add the tomatoes and their liquid, crushing the tomatoes with your hands as you add them to the pot. Stir in the Italian seasoning, salt, and red pepper flakes. Cook, stirring occasionally, for about 10 minutes, until the sauce has thickened slightly. Stir in the pasta and water and spread the pasta in an even layer, making sure it is all submerged in the cooking liquid.

2   Secure the lid and set the Pressure Release to **Sealing**. Press the **Cancel** button to reset the cooking program, then select the **Pressure Cook** or **Manual** setting and set the cooking time for 5 minutes at high pressure. (The pot will take about 15 minutes to come up to pressure before the cooking program begins.)

3   When the cooking program ends, let the pressure release naturally for 5 minutes, then move the Pressure Release to **Venting** to release any remaining steam. Open the pot and give the pasta and sauce a good stir. Let stand, uncovered, for 3 minutes; the mixture will appear watery at first, but the pasta will absorb the excess moisture as it stands.

4   Spoon the pasta into bowls and serve immediately, sprinkled with Parmesan.

Variations:

Rigatoni with Meat Sauce: Cook 1 pound lean Italian sausage (casings removed) or ground beef (93 percent lean) with the olive oil and garlic for about 6 minutes, breaking up the meat with a wooden spoon, until no traces of pink remain. Continue as directed, substituting rigatoni for the penne.

Jarred Sauce Variation: Omit the olive oil, garlic, tomatoes, Italian seasoning, salt, and red pepper flakes. Select the **Sauté** setting on the Instant Pot and pour in one 24-ounce jar of your favorite store-bought pasta sauce. Let the sauce come up to a simmer, stirring occasionally, then add the pasta and water and continue as directed.

Pesto is one of my favorite sauces. The classic combination of raw garlic, savory Parmesan, mellow pine nuts, and fresh herbs is hard to beat; using both basil and parsley gives this pesto a fresh and vibrant flavor that sets it apart from all-basil versions. It comes together in minutes in the food processor, there's no cooking required, and it's kid-friendly! Plus, pesto freezes very well. This recipe makes a double batch so you can use half now and freeze the other half for another meal.

MACARONI WITH PEAS AND PESTO

1 pound elbow macaroni

4 cups water

Kosher salt

Pesto

1 large bunch basil, leaves only

1 large bunch flat-leaf parsley, bottom 4 inches of stems discarded

½ cup pine nuts, slivered almonds, or cashew pieces, toasted

½ cup grated Parmesan cheese

2 garlic cloves, minced

1 teaspoon kosher salt

1 teaspoon freshly ground black pepper

½ cup extra-virgin olive oil

One 10-ounce bag frozen peas

Freshly ground black pepper

Grated Parmesan cheese for serving

PREP	0 MINUTES
COOK	20 MINUTES
PR	5 MINUTES NPR
REST	5 MINUTES
SERVES	6

1   Add the pasta, water, and 1 teaspoon salt to the Instant Pot. Use a spoon or spatula to spread the pasta in an even layer, making sure it is all submerged in the water.

2   Secure the lid and set the Pressure Release to **Sealing**. Select the **Pressure Cook** or **Manual** setting and set the cooking time for 6 minutes at high pressure. (The pot will take about 15 minutes to come up to pressure before the cooking program begins.)

3   To make the pesto: While the pasta is cooking, in a food processor, combine the basil, parsley, pine nuts, Parmesan, garlic, salt, pepper, and olive oil. Process for ten 1-second pulses, scraping down the sides as needed, until the pesto has a fairly coarse texture. Transfer half of the pesto to a freezer-safe container and freeze for up to 6 months.

4   When the cooking program ends, let the pressure release naturally for 5 minutes, then move the Pressure Release to **Venting** to release any remaining steam. Open the pot and stir in the peas and reserved pesto. Let stand for about 5 minutes, then stir again. Taste and adjust the seasoning with salt and/or pepper if needed.

5   Spoon the pasta into bowls and serve immediately, with Parmesan on the side.

Variation: For a vegan version, substitute vegan "Parmesan" (page 36) for the regular Parmesan.

Mac 'n' cheese gets an upgrade with browned onions and Gouda cheese. It's still kid-friendly, but a nice change of pace from the usual versions made with Cheddar. Serve it right out of the pot or broil it in a baking dish just before serving, with some bread crumbs sprinkled on top (see Note).

MACARONI AND CHEESE WITH GOUDA AND CARAMELIZED ONIONS

3 tablespoons unsalted butter

1 yellow onion, diced

1 pound elbow macaroni

4 cups chicken broth (page 286) or vegetable broth (page 284)

3 cups tightly packed shredded Gouda cheese

½ cup grated Parmesan cheese

½ cup half-and-half

2 teaspoons Dijon mustard

½ teaspoon freshly ground black pepper

PREP	0 MINUTES
COOK	30 MINUTES
PR	QPR
SERVES	8

1   Select the high **Sauté** setting on the Instant Pot and melt the butter. Add the onion and sauté for about 10 minutes, until the onion begins to brown. Add the macaroni and broth. Stir to combine, using a wooden spoon to nudge loose any browned bits from the bottom of the pot.

2   Secure the lid and set the Pressure Release to **Sealing**. Press the **Cancel** button to reset the cooking program, then select the **Pressure Cook** or **Manual** setting and set the cooking time for 6 minutes at high pressure. (The pot will take about 10 minutes to come up to pressure before the cooking program begins.)

3   When the cooking program ends, perform a quick pressure release by moving the Pressure Release to **Venting**. Open the pot and stir in the Gouda, Parmesan, half-and-half, mustard, and pepper. Let stand for 5 minutes, until thickened, then stir again.

4   Spoon the macaroni and cheese into bowls and serve hot.

Note: If you like a crisp topping, transfer the macaroni and cheese to a 3-quart broiler-safe baking dish, sprinkle evenly with 1 cup panko bread crumbs, then broil for a few minutes, until the bread crumbs are golden brown, before serving.

This pasta salad is packed with a confetti assortment of my favorite antipasto nibbles, such as olives, sun-dried tomatoes, and sliced salami. Bring it for your weekday lunches, or make a double batch and take it to a potluck or picnic. See Variations for vegetarian and vegan options.

ANTIPASTO PASTA SALAD

8 ounces rotini or fusilli pasta

2 cups water

½ teaspoon kosher salt

Italian Vinaigrette

¼ cup extra-virgin olive oil

2 tablespoons red wine vinegar

¾ teaspoon sugar

½ teaspoon dried oregano

¼ teaspoon kosher salt

¼ teaspoon freshly ground black pepper

1 small garlic clove, minced

1 cup frozen peas

½ cup diced red onion

½ cup drained sliced black olives

⅓ cup sliced drained pepperoncini

¼ cup drained oil-packed sun-dried tomato halves, cut into thin strips

1½ ounces hot or sweet salami, quartered lengthwise and cut into ⅛-inch-thick slices

1 small green bell pepper, seeded and diced

2 tablespoons fresh chopped basil

1   Add the pasta, water, and salt to the Instant Pot, spreading the pasta in as even a layer as possible. It's fine if a few pieces are sticking up out of the water.

2   Secure the lid and set the Pressure Release to **Sealing**. Select the **Pressure Cook** or **Manual** setting and set the cooking time for 6 minutes at high pressure. (The pot will take about 10 minutes to come up to pressure before the cooking program begins.)

3   To make the Italian vinaigrette: While the pasta cooks, in a jar with a tight-fitting lid or other leakproof container, combine the olive oil, vinegar, sugar, oregano, salt, pepper, and garlic. Cover tightly and shake vigorously to combine. Set aside.

4   When the cooking program ends, perform a quick pressure release by moving the Pressure Release to **Venting**. Open the pot and, wearing heat-resistant mitts, lift out the inner pot. Stir the peas into the pasta, then let stand for 5 minutes. Stir again, then let sit for 5 minutes more.

5   Pour the vinaigrette over the pasta and peas, then add the onion, olives, pepperoncini, tomatoes, salami, bell pepper, and basil. Stir to combine and coat all of the ingredients with vinaigrette.

6   Spoon the salad into bowls and serve.

Variations:

Vegetarian Antipasto Pasta Salad: Substitute ½ cup shaved Parmesan cheese for the salami.

Vegan Antipasto Pasta Salad: Substitute one 6-ounce jar marinated artichoke hearts, drained and sliced ¼-inch thick, for the salami.

PREP	0 MINUTES
COOK	30 MINUTES
PR	QPR
SERVES	6

3

Soups and Chilis

This minestrone strikes the perfect balance between nutritious and hearty—it's chock-full of vegetables, with enough substance to make for a filling meal when paired with a slice of crusty bread. It's made with diced potatoes instead of the usual pasta, so it will keep for several days in the fridge, and it freezes well, too.

MINESTRONE

2 tablespoons olive oil

1 medium yellow onion, diced

1 carrot, diced

2 celery stalks, diced

½ teaspoon kosher salt

¼ teaspoon freshly ground black pepper

¼ head green cabbage, cored and chopped

2 medium zucchini, diced

1 pound russet potatoes, peeled and diced

1½ cups cooked cannellini or kidney beans (page 44), or one 15-ounce can cannellini or kidney beans, rinsed and drained

One 14½-ounce can diced tomatoes and their liquid

4 cups vegetable broth (page 284)

1½ teaspoons Italian seasoning

1 bay leaf

Grated Parmesan cheese for serving (optional)

Chopped fresh flat-leaf parsley for serving (optional)

1   Select the **Sauté** setting on the Instant Pot and heat the olive oil for 1 minute. Add the onion, carrot, celery, salt, and pepper and sauté for about 5 minutes, until the onion has softened but not browned. Add the cabbage, zucchini, potatoes, beans, tomatoes and their liquid, vegetable broth, Italian seasoning, and bay leaf and stir well. It's fine if the vegetables aren't fully submerged, as they will release their own liquid as they cook.

2   Secure the lid and set the Pressure Release to **Sealing**. Press the **Cancel** button to reset the cooking program, then select the **Pressure Cook** or **Manual** setting and set the cooking time for 5 minutes at high pressure. (The pot will take about 20 minutes to come up to pressure before the cooking program begins.)

3   When the cooking program ends, let the pressure release naturally for 15 minutes, then move the Pressure Release to **Venting** to release any remaining steam. Open the pot and remove and discard the bay leaf.

4   Ladle the soup into bowls and top with Parmesan and parsley. Serve piping hot.

PREP	0 MINUTES
COOK	30 MINUTES
PR	15 MINUTES NPR
SERVES	8

This soup is a weeknight lifesaver, as it's a one-pot meal made with mostly refrigerator and pantry staples. A hearty mix of macaroni and kidney beans makes for a filling bowl, and it's vegan-friendly when made with vegetable broth. Serve the soup right away, before the noodles have a chance to soften too much in the broth.

PASTA E FAGIOLI

2 tablespoons olive oil

1 yellow onion, diced

1 carrot, peeled and diced

1 celery stalk, diced

2 garlic cloves, minced

1½ teaspoons Italian seasoning

Kosher salt

½ teaspoon freshly ground black pepper

¼ teaspoon red pepper flakes

One 14½-ounce can diced tomatoes and their liquid

4 cups vegetable broth (page 284) or chicken broth (page 286)

1½ cups cooked kidney beans (see page 44), or one 15-ounce can kidney beans, rinsed and drained

1 cup elbow macaroni

3 tablespoons chopped fresh flat-leaf parsley

Extra-virgin olive oil for drizzling

Sliced crusty bread for serving

1   Select the **Sauté** setting on the Instant Pot and heat the olive oil for 1 minute. Add the onion, carrot, celery, and garlic, and sauté for about 5 minutes, until the onion is softened. Add the Italian seasoning, ½ teaspoon salt, black pepper, and red pepper flakes and sauté for about 1 minute more. Add the tomatoes and their liquid, vegetable broth, beans, and macaroni. Stir to combine, making sure all of the pasta is submerged in the liquid.

2   Secure the lid and set the Pressure Release to **Sealing**. Press the **Cancel** button to reset the cooking program, then select the **Pressure Cook** or **Manual** setting and set the cooking time for 3 minutes at high pressure. (The pot will take about 15 minutes to come up to pressure before the cooking program begins.)

3   When the cooking program ends, let the pressure release naturally for 10 minutes, then move the Pressure Release to **Venting** to release any remaining steam. Open the pot, then taste the soup and adjust the seasoning with salt if needed. Stir in the parsley.

4   Ladle the soup into bowls and drizzle with extra-virgin olive oil. Serve piping hot, with crusty bread alongside.

PREP	0 MINUTES
COOK	25 MINUTES
PR	10 MINUTES NPR
SERVES	4

A hearty Portuguese soup filled with dark leafy greens, *caldo verde* is my idea of nourishing comfort food. Potatoes add body to the broth, and rounds of garlicky paprika-red sausage give up their flavor to the soup during cooking. Like a lot of simmered and braised dishes, it's even better the next day. If you're in a hurry, substitute a 10-ounce bag of chopped lacinato or curly kale for the bunched kale and collards.

CALDO VERDE

2 tablespoons olive oil

8 ounces Portuguese linguiça or Spanish chorizo sausage, casing removed, cut into ¼-inch rounds

1 yellow onion, diced

3 garlic cloves, minced

1 bunch lacinato kale, stems discarded and leaves sliced into ¼-inch ribbons

1 bunch collard greens, stems discarded and leaves sliced into ¼-inch ribbons

2 large russet potatoes, peeled and diced

4 cups chicken broth (page 286)

Kosher salt

Freshly ground black pepper

PREP	0 MINUTES
COOK	35 MINUTES
PR	10 MINUTES NPR
SERVES	6

1   Select the **Sauté** setting on the Instant Pot and heat the olive oil for 1 minute. Add the linguiça and sauté for about 3 minutes, until it begins to brown. Add the onion and garlic and sauté for about 3 minutes more, until the onion is beginning to soften. Add the kale and collards and sauté for about 2 minutes, until the greens are wilted. Add the potatoes and chicken broth and stir to combine.

2   Secure the lid and set the Pressure Release to **Sealing**. Press the **Cancel** button to reset the cooking program, then select the **Soup/ Broth** setting and set the cooking time for 5 minutes at high pressure. (The pot will take about 20 minutes to come up to pressure before the cooking program begins.)

3   When the cooking program ends, let the pressure release naturally for 10 minutes, then move the Pressure Release to **Venting** to release any remaining steam. Open the pot and, if desired, thicken the soup a bit by using the back of a spoon or ladle to gently mash some of the potatoes. Taste and adjust the seasoning with salt if needed.

4   Ladle the soup into bowls and top with a few grinds of pepper. Serve piping hot.

In this recipe, tender chunks of pork and chewy hominy corn are simmered in a vibrant red soup. I like that this broth is a bit richer and more velvety than the usual pozole broth. It gets its deep flavor and ruddy hue from guajillo and ancho chiles, which are available in Mexican grocery stores, in the international food aisle of many supermarkets, and, of course, online. Though a lot of chiles are used here, the soup is not very spicy. If you like, add red pepper flakes at the table for extra kick.

POZOLE ROJO

6 guajillo chiles, stemmed and seeded

3 ancho chiles, stemmed and seeded

3 cups water

4 cups chicken broth (page 286)

4 garlic cloves, minced

1 small yellow onion, diced

1 teaspoon dried oregano

½ teaspoon ground cumin

Kosher salt

2 tablespoons olive oil

1½ pounds pork stew meat or boneless pork shoulder, trimmed of excess fat and cut into 1-inch pieces

One 30-ounce can hominy, drained

3 cups shredded green cabbage

1 bunch radishes, sliced

2 limes, cut into wedges for serving

Red pepper flakes for serving

PREP	0 MINUTES
COOK	1 HOUR, 20 MINUTES
PR	15 MINUTES NPR
SERVES	6

1   Place the guajillo and ancho chiles in the Instant Pot, then pour in the water. Cover the pot with the glass lid, then select the **Sauté** setting and set the cooking time for 8 minutes. When the timer goes off, let the chiles soak in the water for an additional 20 minutes to soften.

2   Open the pot and, using tongs, transfer the soaked chiles to a blender; discard the soaking water and wipe out the pot. To the blender, add 1 cup of the chicken broth, along with the garlic, onion, oregano, cumin, and 1 teaspoon salt. Blend on medium speed for about 1 minute, until smooth.

3   Select the **Sauté** setting on the Instant Pot and heat the olive oil. Pour in the chile puree and bring to a simmer (this will take about 3 minutes). Stir in the remaining 3 cups chicken broth, the pork, and hominy.

4   Secure the pressure cooking lid and set the Pressure Release to **Sealing**. Press the **Cancel** button to reset the cooking program, then select the **Meat/Stew** setting and set the cooking time for 30 minutes at high pressure. (The pot will take about 15 minutes to come up to pressure before the cooking program begins.)

5   When the cooking program ends, let the pressure release naturally for 15 minutes, then move the Pressure Release to **Venting** to release any remaining steam. Open the pot; if a lot of fat has collected on the surface, use a ladle or spoon to skim it off. Taste for seasoning and add more salt if needed.

6   Ladle the pozole into bowls. Top each bowl with ½ cup shredded cabbage and sliced radishes. Serve piping hot, with lime wedges and red pepper flakes alongside.

This is an adaptation of a fantastic recipe from *The Pho Cookbook* by my friend Andrea Nguyen. She's *the* authority on Vietnamese home cooking, and this recipe yields a light yet flavorful beef broth. Classic pho condiments of Sriracha and hoisin sauce are included here, but see Notes for my favorite fresh toppings, the ones commonly served in restaurants. You can go as simple or as complicated as you like.

BEEF PHO

Broth

2½ star anise pods

One 3-inch cinnamon stick

3 whole cloves

2-inch knob fresh ginger, peeled, smashed, and sliced into ⅛-inch-thick rounds

1 large yellow onion, cut into wedges

8 cups water, plus more as needed

2½ teaspoons kosher salt

3 pounds beef knuckle bones and marrow bones (a combination is best), rinsed

1 pound beef brisket or boneless beef chuck roast, rinsed

1 Fuji, Gala, or Braeburn apple, peeled, quartered, cored, and cut into ½-inch pieces

1 tablespoon fish sauce

1 teaspoon sugar

8 to 10 ounces dried flat rice noodles (aka rice sticks)

½ small yellow onion, thinly sliced, rinsed under cold water, and drained

2 green onions, tender green parts only, thinly sliced

Leaves from 8 sprigs cilantro

Sriracha and/or hoisin sauce for serving

1   To make the broth: Select the **Sauté** setting on the Instant Pot and add the star anise pods, cinnamon, and cloves, scooting them to the edges of the pot. Toast the spices for about 4 minutes, until aromatic, stirring them once halfway through. Add the ginger and onion and sear for about 1 minute, until aromatic and lightly browned.

2   Add 4 cups of the water and the salt, using a wooden spoon to nudge loose any browned bits from the bottom of the pot. Add the bones, placing them in a layer, followed by the brisket, then sprinkle the apple pieces around the beef. Add the remaining 4 cups water, pouring slowly to prevent splashing. Make sure the pot is no more than two-thirds full; you can add a little more water if you haven't reached the max fill line.

3   Secure the lid and set the Pressure Release to **Sealing**. Press the **Cancel** button to reset the cooking program, then select the **Soup/Broth** setting and set the cooking time for 25 minutes at high pressure. (The pot will take about 30 minutes to come up to pressure before the cooking program begins.)

4   When the cooking program ends, let the pressure release naturally for 45 minutes, then move the Pressure Release to **Venting** to release any remaining steam. Open the pot and, using tongs, transfer the brisket to a bowl and cover with cold water. Let soak for about 10 minutes (this will prevent the meat from drying out and discoloring). Drain off the water, partially cover the bowl with a reusable lid or plastic wrap, and set the brisket aside to cool.

5   While the brisket soaks, use tongs to remove the bones from the pot; discard them or rinse and reserve for another batch of broth.

6   Place a fine-mesh strainer over a large bowl or pitcher and line it with a double layer of cheesecloth. Wearing heat-resistant mitts, lift out the

Notes: Andrea Nguyen recommends using boiling water instead of tap water to jumpstart the cooking process for the broth.

If you're not able to find beef knuckle bones or marrow bones, use 2 pounds of beef shanks or oxtails in place of the bones *and* the brisket. To serve the beef shanks, slice as the brisket. Serve oxtails directly in the soup.

Brisket will hold together in one piece for slicing, while chuck roast may not hold together as well. Just do your best to slice it thinly, and don't worry if it falls apart a bit.

If you like, prepare additional toppings of Thai basil, mung bean sprouts, thinly sliced jalapeños, and wedges of lime to serve alongside.

PREP	0 MINUTES
COOK	1 HOUR, 45 MINUTES
PR	45 MINUTES NPR
SERVES	4

inner pot and pour the liquid through the strainer. Discard the solids. Rinse the inner pot, scrubbing off any particles clinging to the pot, then return to the Instant Pot housing.

7   Working in batches, pour the liquid into a fat separator, then pour from the fat separator back into the pot. If you do not have a fat separator, skim off the fat with a ladle or spoon, then pour the liquid back into the pot. You may discard the fat or add a tablespoon or two back to the pot for a richer soup. Leave on the **Keep Warm** setting until you are ready to serve, up to 10 hours.

8   Stir the fish sauce and sugar into the liquid. Taste and adjust the seasoning with salt if needed. Once again secure the lid, but set the Pressure Release to **Venting**.

9   Carve the brisket against the grain into ⅛-inch-thick slices. Cover and set aside.

10   Have ready four serving bowls and divide the noodles into four even portions.

11   Fill a large (6-quart) pot with 5 quarts water and bring to a boil over high heat. When the water is boiling, place one portion of the noodles in a long-handled steamer basket, and lower it into the pot by its handle (to distance your hand from the boiling water, you can use tongs to grip the handle). Hold the basket in the water for about 2 minutes, until the noodles are soft; the timing depends on the noodles' thickness. Lift out the basket, shake to drain excess water back into the pot, then transfer the noodles to a serving bowl. Repeat with the remaining portions of noodles.

12   Open the Instant Pot and ladle the hot broth over the noodles in the serving bowls. Top each bowl with sliced beef, yellow onion, green onions, and cilantro. Serve piping hot, with Sriracha and hoisin sauce on the side.

Yellow lentils, also known as split mung beans or moong dal, are simmered with onion and spices in this deeply savory and flavorful vegetarian dish. Don't mistake split yellow peas for the mung beans—mung beans are much smaller and cook in about a quarter of the time. You can buy them in Indian grocery stores and well-stocked supermarkets, at health food stores, or online.

YELLOW LENTIL CURRY (MOONG DAL)

3½ cups water

1 cup yellow lentils (moong dal), rinsed and drained

Kosher salt

3 tablespoons ghee (page 291) or coconut oil

1 teaspoon cumin seeds

1 yellow onion, thinly sliced

1 large jalapeño chile, seeded and diced

3 garlic cloves, thinly sliced

1 large Roma tomato, diced

1 teaspoon ground coriander

½ teaspoon ground turmeric

¼ teaspoon cayenne pepper

¼ cup chopped fresh cilantro

Steamed rice (see page 51) or warmed naan for serving

PREP	0 MINUTES
COOK	15 MINUTES
PR	10 MINUTES NPR
SERVES	4

1   Add the water, lentils, and 1½ teaspoons salt to the Instant Pot and stir to combine.

2   Secure the lid and set the Pressure Release to **Sealing**. Select the **Bean/Chili**, **Pressure Cook**, or **Manual** setting and set the cooking time for 5 minutes at high pressure. (The pot will take about 10 minutes to come up to pressure before the cooking program begins.)

3   While the lentils are cooking, in a large skillet over medium-high heat, melt the ghee. Add the cumin seeds and cook, stirring, until toasty and fragrant, about 1 minute. Add the onion and jalapeño and sauté for about 4 minutes, until the onion is softened. Nudge the mixture to the sides of the skillet. Add the garlic to the center of the skillet and sauté for about 2 minutes, until the garlic is browned but not burnt. Add the tomato and sauté for about 3 minutes, mixing in the ingredients from the sides of the skillet and scraping up any browned bits from the bottom of the skillet. Remove the skillet from the heat, then stir in the coriander, turmeric, and cayenne. Set aside.

4   When the cooking program ends, let the pressure release naturally for 10 minutes, then move the Pressure Release to **Venting** to release any remaining steam. Open the pot and add the mixture from the skillet along with the cilantro, then stir to combine. Taste and adjust the seasoning with salt if needed.

5   Ladle the curry into bowls and serve piping hot, with rice or naan.

Notes: If you prefer your dal with a thinner consistency, stir in more water after cooking, along with the spices and cilantro.

If you want to get your greens, add a 6-ounce bag of baby spinach to the dal after cooking, along with the spices and cilantro. As you stir in the spinach, the heat will wilt the leaves.

I like to use small green lentils, Puy lentils, or beluga lentils in this soup, since these types retain their texture better than larger green lentils. The soup itself is very simple, but it gets a bold punch of flavor when you stir in the garlicky, lemony gremolata.

LENTIL SOUP WITH GREMOLATA

Soup

2 tablespoons olive oil

1 large yellow onion, diced

2 medium carrots, peeled and diced

2 celery stalks, diced

2 garlic cloves, minced

Kosher salt

1 cup small green lentils, Puy lentils, or beluga lentils

4 cups vegetable broth (page 284)

Gremolata

1 cup loosely packed fresh flat-leaf parsley leaves

1 garlic clove, peeled

Finely grated zest of 1 lemon

2 tablespoons fresh lemon juice

Extra-virgin olive oil for drizzling

PREP	0 MINUTES
COOK	30 MINUTES
PR	10 MINUTES NPR
SERVES	4 TO 6

1   To make the soup: Select the **Sauté** setting on the Instant Pot and heat the olive oil. Add the onion, carrots, celery, garlic, and 1 teaspoon salt and sauté for about 5 minutes, until the onion is softened. Add the lentils and vegetable broth and stir to combine.

2   Secure the lid and set the Pressure Release to **Sealing**. Press the **Cancel** button to reset the cooking program, then select the **Soup/Broth** setting and set the cooking time for 15 minutes at high pressure. (The pot will take about 10 minutes to come up to pressure before the cooking program begins.)

3   To make the gremolata: While the soup is cooking, pile the parsley onto a cutting board, along with the garlic. Chop them together until the parsley is finely chopped and there are no large bits of garlic. Add the lemon zest and chop a little more, until the mixture is combined.

4   When the cooking program ends, let the pressure release naturally for 10 minutes, then move the Pressure Release to **Venting** to release any remaining steam. Open the pot, then stir in the gremolata and lemon juice. Taste and adjust the seasoning with salt if needed.

5   Ladle the soup into bowls and drizzle with extra-virgin olive oil. Serve piping hot.

You can do all of the steps up to searing the tofu ahead of time, and the soup will wait for you on the Keep Warm setting until dinnertime. This is a vegetarian version of the Chinese restaurant classic.

HOT AND SOUR SOUP

2 tablespoons neutral vegetable oil

1-inch knob fresh ginger, peeled and finely grated

3 garlic cloves, minced

1 teaspoon ground white pepper

6 cups mushroom broth (page 284)

8 ounces cremini or button mushrooms, sliced

8 dried shiitake mushrooms, rehydrated in boiling water for 30 minutes (or leftover from the mushroom broth), stems removed, sliced thinly

One 8-ounce can sliced bamboo shoots, rinsed and drained

One 14-ounce block firm tofu

2 tablespoons cornstarch

2 tablespoons rice vinegar

1 tablespoon water

1 tablespoon soy sauce, tamari, or coconut aminos

1 tablespoon sugar

2 eggs, well beaten (optional)

4 green onions, white and tender green parts, thinly sliced

¼ cup chopped fresh cilantro

PREP	0 MINUTES
COOK	20 MINUTES
PR	15 MINUTES NPR
SERVES	6 TO 8

1   Select the **Sauté** setting on the Instant Pot and add 1 tablespoon of the vegetable oil, ginger, and garlic. Sauté for about 2 minutes, until the mixture is bubbling and fragrant but not browned. Add the white pepper and sauté for about 1 minute more. Add the mushroom broth, cremini and shiitake mushrooms, and bamboo shoots and stir to combine, using a wooden spoon to nudge loose any browned bits from the bottom of the pot.

2   Secure the lid and set the Pressure Release to **Sealing**. Press the **Cancel** button to reset the cooking program, then select the **Pressure Cook** or **Manual** setting and set the cooking time for 5 minutes at high pressure. (The pot will take about 15 minutes to come up to pressure before the cooking program begins.)

3   While the soup is cooking, cut the tofu into ½-inch slices. Sandwich the slices in a single layer between double layers of paper towels, or a folded tea towel, and press firmly to wick away as much moisture as possible. Cut the slices into ½-inch cubes.

4   In a large skillet over medium-high heat, warm the remaining 1 tablespoon oil. Add the cubed tofu in a single layer and cook without stirring for about 3 minutes, or until lightly browned. Using a spatula, turn the cubes and cook for about 3 minutes more, until lightly browned on their second sides. Turn off the heat and set aside.

5   In a small bowl, combine the cornstarch, vinegar, water, soy sauce, and sugar and stir until the sugar dissolves. Set aside.

6   When the cooking program ends, let the pressure release naturally for 15 minutes, then move the Pressure Release to **Venting** to release any remaining steam. Open the pot, then stir in the seared tofu. Stir the cornstarch mixture to recombine, then stir it into the soup. Press the **Cancel** button to reset the cooking program, then select the **Sauté** setting. Bring the soup to a simmer and cook for about 4 minutes, stirring occasionally, until the soup thickens. If using the eggs, pour them into the simmering soup in a thin stream while stirring constantly. Press the **Cancel** button to turn off the pot. Stir in the green onions and cilantro.

7   Ladle the soup into bowls and serve piping hot.

Start by making a batch of 30-Minute Caramelized Onions for this decadent, comforting soup. (You can also make the caramelized onions in advance and freeze them.) I like to use homemade beef broth when I can, but if I don't have any on hand, the Reduced Sodium Roasted Beef Base from Better Than Bouillon tastes nearly as good as homemade when diluted according to the package directions. With the cheese, onions, bread, and Worcestershire sauce, there are so many layers of savory flavor in this soup. My favorite thing is when they all come together in one bite.

FRENCH ONION SOUP

Soup

1 recipe 30-Minute Caramelized Onions (page 290), still in the pot

¼ cup dry sherry

3 cups beef broth (page 285)

1 teaspoon Worcestershire sauce

¼ teaspoon freshly ground black pepper

¼ teaspoon dried thyme

1 bay leaf

Gruyère Toasts

2 teaspoons Dijon mustard

Eight ½-inch-thick baguette slices

½ cup tightly packed shredded Gruyère cheese

Freshly ground black pepper

PREP	0 MINUTES
COOK	15 MINUTES
PR	10 MINUTES NPR
SERVES	4

1   To make the soup: When the caramelized onions have finished cooking, the **Sauté** program will end and the Instant Pot will turn off. Pour in the sherry and, using a wooden spoon, nudge loose any browned bits from the bottom of the pot. Add the beef broth, Worcestershire, pepper, thyme, and bay leaf.

2   Secure the lid and set the Pressure Release to **Sealing**. Select the **Pressure Cook** or **Manual** setting and set the cooking time for 5 minutes at high pressure. (The pot will take about 10 minutes to come up to pressure before the cooking program begins.)

3   When the cooking program ends, let the pressure release naturally for 10 minutes, then move the Pressure Release to **Venting** to release any remaining steam.

4   To make the Gruyère toasts: Preheat the broiler.

5   A few minutes before you are ready to serve the soup, spread ¼ teaspoon of the mustard onto one side of each baguette slice, then sprinkle with 1 tablespoon of the cheese and a grind of pepper. Place cheese-side up on a baking sheet and toast under the broiler (or in a toaster oven) for about 5 minutes, until the cheese is bubbly and beginning to brown. Watch carefully so the toasts do not burn.

6   Open the pot and remove and discard the bay leaf.

7   Ladle the soup into bowls, then top each bowl with two slices of toast. Serve piping hot.

Hearty, chewy grains and mushrooms give substance to this vegan dish. Most mushroom-barley soups include beef, but this is an equally satisfying version for nonmeat eaters to enjoy. It's savory and filling, so you can serve a bowlful as a complete meal, with some crusty bread on the side, or offer just a cupful alongside a sandwich or salad. See Note for a gluten-free variation.

MUSHROOM-BARLEY SOUP

2 tablespoons olive oil

2 garlic cloves, minced

1 yellow onion, diced

2 carrots, peeled and diced

2 celery stalks, diced

Kosher salt

1 teaspoon dried thyme

½ teaspoon freshly ground black pepper

2 tablespoons tomato paste

1 pound cremini or button mushrooms, halved and sliced

½ cup pearl barley

1 bay leaf

5 cups mushroom broth or vegetable broth (page 284)

1 tablespoon fresh lemon juice

PREP	0 MINUTES
COOK	55 MINUTES
PR	20 MINUTES NPR
SERVES	8

1   Select the **Sauté** setting on the Instant Pot and heat the olive oil and garlic for about 2 minutes, until the garlic is bubbling. Add the onion, carrots, celery, and 1½ teaspoons salt and sauté for about 5 minutes more, until the onion is softened. Add the thyme, pepper, and tomato paste, then sauté for about 1 minute more. Stir in the mushrooms, barley, bay leaf, and mushroom broth, using a wooden spoon to nudge loose any browned bits from the bottom of the pot.

2   Secure the lid and set the Pressure Release to **Sealing**. Press the **Cancel** button to reset the cooking program, then select the **Pressure Cook** or **Manual** setting and set the cooking time for 30 minutes at high pressure. (The pot will take about 15 minutes to come up to pressure before the cooking program begins.)

3   When the cooking program ends, let the pressure release for 20 minutes, then move the Pressure Release to **Venting** to release any remaining steam. Open the pot, then remove and discard the bay leaf and stir in the lemon juice. Taste and adjust the seasoning with salt if needed.

4   Ladle the soup into bowls and serve piping hot.

Note: To make the soup gluten free, substitute medium-grain brown rice for the barley.

A brothy soup packed with spinach, this is a nice option for lunch or a light dinner. The tortellini cook right in the broth, so there's no need to bring a separate pot of water to a boil. You can double the amount of pasta if you want a heartier, more pasta-filled bowl.

TORTELLINI AND SPINACH SOUP

1 tablespoon olive oil

1 medium yellow onion, diced

2 garlic cloves, diced

1 celery stalk, diced

1 medium carrot, peeled and diced

Kosher salt

½ teaspoon freshly ground black pepper

1 teaspoon Italian seasoning

4 cups chicken broth (page 286) or vegetable broth (page 284)

One 14½-ounce can diced tomatoes with their liquid

8 ounces dried tortellini

One 6-ounce bag baby spinach

Grated Parmesan cheese for sprinkling

Extra-virgin olive oil for drizzling

1   Select the **Sauté** setting on the Instant Pot and heat the olive oil. Add the onion, garlic, celery, carrot, ½ teaspoon salt, pepper, and Italian seasoning and sauté for about 5 minutes, until the onion is softened. Add the chicken broth, tomatoes with their liquid, and tortellini.

2   Secure the lid and set the Pressure Release to **Sealing**. Press the **Cancel** button to reset the cooking program, then select the **Pressure Cook** or **Manual** setting and set the cooking time for 5 minutes at high pressure. (The pot will take about 15 minutes to come up to pressure before the cooking program begins.)

3   When the cooking program ends, let the pressure release naturally for 10 minutes, then move the Pressure Release to **Venting** to release any remaining steam. Open the pot, then stir in the spinach. Let stand for 2 minutes, until the spinach wilts. Taste and adjust the seasoning with salt if needed.

4   Ladle the soup into bowls, sprinkle with Parmesan, and drizzle with extra-virgin olive oil. Serve piping hot.

PREP	0 MINUTES
COOK	30 MINUTES
PR	10 MINUTES NPR
SERVES	4 TO 6

There's no such thing as a senate bean, but there is a bean-and-ham soup that's been served in the United States Senate dining room since the early twentieth century. This recipe is my Instant Pot adaptation of that soup. It's hearty and filling, and studded with tender navy beans and smoky ham.

SENATE BEAN SOUP

1 bay leaf, broken in half

3 whole cloves

1 teaspoon black peppercorns

2 tablespoons olive oil

1 yellow onion, diced

2 celery stalks, diced

2 carrots, peeled and diced

1 teaspoon kosher salt

1 pound dried navy beans

One 1½-pound smoked ham hock, cut in half (ask the butcher to cut it)

8 cups water

Freshly ground black pepper

PREP	5 MINUTES
COOK	1 HOUR, 5 MINUTES
PR	45 MINUTES NPR
SERVES	8 TO 10

1   Enclose the bay leaf, cloves, and peppercorns in a piece of cheese-cloth; gather the edges to make a bundle; and tie it with kitchen twine. Set aside.

2   Select the **Sauté** setting on the Instant Pot and heat the olive oil. Add the onion, celery, carrots, and salt and sauté for about 5 minutes, until the onion is softened. Add the beans, ham hock, water, and spice pouch.

3   Secure the lid and set the Pressure Release to **Sealing**. Press the **Cancel** button to reset the cooking program, then select the **Pressure Cook** or **Manual** setting and set the cooking time for 35 minutes at high pressure. (The pot will take about 25 minutes to come up to pressure before the cooking program begins.)

4   When the cooking program ends, let the pressure release naturally (this will take about 45 minutes). Open the pot, then remove and discard the spice pouch. Using tongs, carefully transfer the ham hock to a cutting board (the meat will be falling off the bone). Holding the ham bone steady with the tongs, use a fork to pull off the meat. Remove and discard the skin and bone. Chop the meat and add it back to the pot.

5   Ladle the soup into bowls and top with a few grinds of pepper. Serve piping hot.

You don't have to soak the black beans before making this smoky Cuban-style soup. It takes a while to cook, but most of that time is unattended. Put the ingredients together in the morning for lunch, or in the afternoon for dinner. My version gets its smokiness from a smoked turkey drumstick, but if you're unable to find one at the grocery store, you can substitute 8 ounces chopped smoked turkey.

BLACK BEAN AND SMOKED TURKEY SOUP

3 tablespoons olive oil

1 medium yellow onion, diced

1 medium green bell pepper, seeded and diced

2 medium celery stalks, diced

2 garlic cloves, minced

Kosher salt

1¼ cups dried black beans

One 12-ounce smoked turkey drumstick

4 cups water

1 tablespoon apple cider vinegar, plus more as needed

PREP	0 MINUTES
COOK	1 HOUR, 40 MINUTES
PR	25 MINUTES NPR
SERVES	6

1   Select the **Sauté** setting on the Instant Pot and heat the olive oil. Add the onion, bell pepper, celery, garlic, and 1 teaspoon salt and sauté for about 5 minutes, until the onion is softened but not browned. Add the black beans, turkey, and water.

2   Secure the lid and set the Pressure Release to **Sealing**. Press the **Cancel** button to reset the cooking program, then select the **Bean/Chili**, **Pressure Cook**, or **Manual** setting and set the cooking time for 1 hour and 15 minutes at high pressure. (The pot will take about 15 minutes to come up to pressure before the cooking program begins.)

3   Let the pressure release naturally for 25 minutes, then move the Pressure Release to **Venting** to release any remaining steam. Open the pot and, using tongs or a slotted spoon, transfer the turkey drumstick to a plate or cutting board. Remove the meat from the bone and shred or chop the meat into bite-size pieces. Discard the bone, skin, and cartilage.

4   Return the turkey to the pot and stir in the vinegar. Taste and adjust the seasoning with salt and vinegar if needed.

5   Ladle the soup into bowls and serve piping hot.

Every year at the Outside Lands music festival in San Francisco, I seek out the booth that sells split pea soup. It's kind of a weird thing to order at a music festival, but split pea soup is perfect for sipping in the city's famous fog. My version is thick and hearty, with smoked ham shank and Old Bay seasoning for lots of flavor. Pea soup of any sort will thicken as it cools. When reheating leftovers, add a splash of broth or water if needed to thin the consistency. See Variations for how to make a faster soup and a vegan option.

SPLIT PEA SOUP

2 tablespoons olive oil

1 yellow onion, diced

2 carrots, peeled and diced

2 celery stalks, diced

1 tablespoon Old Bay seasoning, or 1½ teaspoons sweet paprika plus 1½ teaspoons kosher salt

½ teaspoon freshly ground black pepper

1 pound green split peas

8 cups water

One 1½-pound smoked ham hock, cut in half (ask the butcher to cut it)

1 bay leaf

PREP	5 MINUTES
COOK	1 HOUR, 5 MINUTES
PR	45 MINUTES NPR
SERVES	8 TO 10

1   Select the **Sauté** setting on the Instant Pot and heat the olive oil. Add the onion, carrots, and celery and sauté for 5 minutes, until the onion is softened. Add the Old Bay, pepper, split peas, water, ham hock pieces, and bay leaf. Stir to combine.

2   Secure the lid and set the Pressure Release to **Sealing**. Press the **Cancel** button to reset the cooking program, then select the **Pressure Cook** or **Manual** setting and set the cooking time for 35 minutes on high pressure. (The pot will take about 25 minutes to come up to pressure before the cooking program begins.)

3   When the cooking program ends, let the pressure release naturally (this will take about 45 minutes). Open the pot, then remove and discard the bay leaf. Using tongs, carefully transfer the ham hock to a cutting board (the meat will be falling off the bone). Holding the ham bone steady with the tongs, use a fork to pull off the meat. Remove and discard the skin and bone. Chop the meat and add it back to the pot.

4   Ladle the soup into bowls and serve piping hot.

Variations:

Quick Split Pea Soup: For a fast version, substitute 8 ounces chopped ham steak for the ham hock and decrease the cooking time to 20 minutes.

Vegan Split Pea Soup: Omit the ham hock. Add 1 teaspoon smoked paprika and 1 teaspoon kosher salt along with the split peas. Decrease the cooking time to 20 minutes.

This vegetarian soup is creamy and comforting, with cubes of silky potato and bright kernels of corn throughout. It's thickened with a little masa harina for even more corn flavor, but you can use cornstarch if you don't have masa harina on hand.

HEARTY CORN AND POTATO SOUP

½ cup heavy cream or half-and-half

3 tablespoons masa harina or 1 tablespoon cornstarch

1 tablespoon unsalted butter

2 celery stalks, diced

1 small yellow onion, diced

Kosher salt

3 cups vegetable broth (page 284)

2 medium russet potatoes, peeled and diced

One 1-pound bag frozen corn kernels, thawed

1 bay leaf

Chopped fresh chives for sprinkling

Freshly ground black pepper

PREP	5 MINUTES
COOK	25 MINUTES
PR	10 MINUTES NPR
SERVES	6

1   In a widemouthed 1-pint jar, stir together the cream and masa harina. Set aside.

2   Select the **Sauté** setting on the Instant Pot and melt the butter. Add the celery, onion, and 1 teaspoon salt and sauté for 4 minutes, until the onion is softened. Stir in the vegetable broth, potatoes, corn kernels, and bay leaf.

3   Secure the lid and set the Pressure Release to **Sealing**. Press the **Cancel** button to reset the cooking program, then select the **Pressure Cook** or **Manual** setting and set the cooking time for 5 minutes at low pressure. (The pot will take about 15 minutes to come up to pressure before the cooking program begins.)

4   When the cooking program ends, let the pressure release naturally for 10 minutes, then move the Pressure Release to **Venting** to release any remaining steam. Open the pot, then remove and discard the bay leaf. Ladle about ½ cup of the soup into the masa harina mixture and use an immersion blender to blend until smooth. Stir the mixture into the soup. Press the **Cancel** button to reset the cooking program, then select the **Sauté** setting. Bring the soup to a simmer and cook for 2 minutes, stirring occasionally, to thicken the soup. Stir once more, then taste and adjust the seasoning with salt if needed.

5   Ladle the soup into bowls, sprinkle with chives and a few grinds of pepper, and serve piping hot.

Note: In the summertime, you can replace the frozen corn with fresh in-season corn. Cut the kernels from 4 large shucked ears. For extra flavor, add the cobs to the pot along with the kernels. After opening the pot, use tongs to remove and discard the cobs before thickening the soup with the masa harina mixture.

This tomato soup is silky and smooth, even if you decide to forgo the final swirl of heavy cream. It owes its texture to the addition of a little bit of rice, which thickens the soup as it cooks. Sip it out of a mug as a snack, or enjoy it with garlic bread or a grilled cheese sandwich for lunch or dinner. This vegetarian soup is gluten-free, and it can be made vegan by leaving out the heavy cream.

CREAM OF TOMATO SOUP

2 tablespoons unsalted butter or olive oil

1 small yellow onion, diced

2 medium carrots, peeled and diced

1 garlic clove, minced

Kosher salt

One 28-ounce can diced tomatoes and their liquid

2 cups vegetable broth (page 284)

¼ cup uncooked long-grain white rice

1½ teaspoons Italian seasoning

¼ cup heavy cream (optional)

Freshly ground black pepper for serving

PREP	0 MINUTES
COOK	25 MINUTES
PR	10 MINUTES NPR
SERVES	4 TO 6

1   Select the **Sauté** setting on the Instant Pot and melt the butter. Add the onion, carrots, garlic, and ¼ teaspoon salt and sauté for 5 minutes, until the onion is softened but not browned. Add the tomatoes and their liquid, vegetable broth, rice, and Italian seasoning.

2   Secure the lid and set the Pressure Release to **Sealing**. Press the **Cancel** button to reset the cooking program, then select the **Soup/Broth** setting and set the cooking time for 5 minutes at high pressure. (The pot will take about 15 minutes to come up to pressure before the cooking program begins.)

3   When the cooking program ends, let the pressure release naturally for 10 minutes, then move the Pressure Release to **Venting** to release any remaining steam. Open the pot, add the cream, and use an immersion blender to puree the soup until smooth. Taste and adjust the seasoning with salt if needed.

4   Ladle the soup into mugs or bowls, sprinkle with pepper, and serve piping hot.

Sandwich shops often serve a version of this hearty soup. This one's got tons of Cheddar and a generous amount of broccoli—and it happens to be both vegetarian and gluten-free. Enjoy it in a bowl with a hunk of rustic bread alongside for dunking, or in a sourdough bread bowl just like you might find at your favorite café.

BROCCOLI-CHEDDAR SOUP

2 tablespoons unsalted butter

1 medium yellow onion, finely diced

1 large carrot, shredded

1 celery stalk, finely diced

2 garlic cloves, minced

Kosher salt

1 pound broccoli florets, chopped

3 cups vegetable broth (page 284)

1 cup half-and-half

2 tablespoons cornstarch

1 tablespoon hot sauce (such as Frank's RedHot or Crystal), plus more as needed

2 cups tightly packed shredded Cheddar cheese

PREP	0 MINUTES
COOK	20 MINUTES
PR	5 MINUTES NPR
SERVES	6

1   Select the **Sauté** setting on the Instant Pot and melt the butter. Add the onion, carrot, celery, garlic, and ½ teaspoon salt and sauté for about 5 minutes, until the onion is softened but not browned. Add the broccoli and vegetable broth.

2   Secure the lid and set the Pressure Release to **Sealing**. Press the **Cancel** button to reset the cooking program, then select the **Pressure Cook** or **Manual** setting and set the cooking time for 1 minute at high pressure. (The pot will take about 10 minutes to come up to pressure before the cooking program begins.)

3   While the soup is cooking, in a liquid measuring cup, stir together the half-and-half, cornstarch, and hot sauce.

4   When the cooking program ends, let the pressure release naturally for 5 minutes, then move the Pressure Release to **Venting** to release any remaining steam. Open the pot, press the **Cancel** button to reset the cooking program, then select the **Sauté** setting. Stir the half-and-half mixture to recombine, then pour it into the pot. Stir in the cheese. Let the soup come up to a simmer and cook for 1 to 2 minutes, stirring occasionally, until it has thickened slightly. Press the **Cancel** button to turn off the Instant Pot. Taste and adjust the seasoning with salt and hot sauce if needed.

5   Ladle the soup into bowls and serve piping hot.

For this soup, you can peel and dice a whole butternut squash or use the pre-cut squash sold in most grocery stores. Alternatively, you can quarter and steam the squash in the Instant Pot before making the soup; see Note. Finished with heavy cream, the soup is vegetarian; with coconut cream, it's vegan. If you like, you can forgo the cream for a lighter puree. I switch up the spice in this recipe all the time—any savory blend works well, from mild yellow curry powder to a spicy, fragrant *berbere* to *ras el hanout*.

BUTTERNUT SQUASH SOUP

2 tablespoons olive oil

1 medium yellow onion, diced

2 large carrots, diced

2 garlic cloves, chopped

One 2½- to 3-pound butternut squash, peeled, seeded, and diced

4 cups vegetable broth (page 284)

1 teaspoon curry powder, or your favorite spice blend

Kosher salt

¼ cup heavy cream or coconut cream (optional)

2 tablespoons chopped fresh flat-leaf parsley or fresh chives

Croutons for serving

PREP	0 MINUTES
COOK	25 MINUTES
PR	10 MINUTES NPR
SERVES	8

1   Select the **Sauté** setting on the Instant Pot and heat the olive oil. Add the onion, carrots, and garlic and sauté for about 5 minutes, until the onion has softened but not browned. Add the squash, vegetable broth, curry powder, and ½ teaspoon salt.

2   Secure the lid and set the Pressure Release to **Sealing**. Press the **Cancel** button to reset the cooking program, then select the **Pressure Cook** or **Manual** setting and set the cooking time for 5 minutes at high pressure. (The pot will take about 15 minutes to come up to pressure before the cooking program begins.)

3   When the cooking program ends, let the pressure release naturally for 10 minutes, then move the Pressure Release to **Venting** to release any remaining steam. Open the pot and use an immersion blender to puree the soup until smooth. Stir in the cream, then taste and adjust the seasoning with salt if needed.

4   Ladle the soup into bowls or cups. Top with chopped fresh herbs and serve with croutons.

Note: If you find it difficult to peel and dice raw butternut squash, see page 252 for instructions on how to precook the squash before preparing the soup. After scooping the flesh from the skin, prepare the soup, adding the squash along with the broth, curry powder, and salt.

Inspired by the Russian Cabbage Soup at Max's Opera Café in San Francisco, this Eastern European–style soup has a fairly light sweet-and-sour broth. Serve it with some crusty rye bread and pickles on the side for a great cold-weather meal.

BEEF AND CABBAGE SOUP

1 pound beef stew meat, boneless chuck roast, or brisket, cut into ½-inch pieces

Kosher salt

½ teaspoon freshly ground black pepper

1 tablespoon olive oil

1 yellow onion, diced

2 carrots, peeled and sliced into ¼-inch-thick rounds

2 tablespoons brown sugar

2 tablespoons white wine vinegar

2 cups beef broth (page 285)

1 cup water

¼ cup golden raisins

1 bay leaf

One 8-ounce can tomato sauce

½ head green cabbage, cored and chopped into 1-inch pieces

Sour cream for serving (optional)

Chopped fresh flat-leaf parsley for sprinkling

PREP	5 MINUTES
COOK	1 HOUR, 5 MINUTES
PR	25 MINUTES NPR
SERVES	6

1   Sprinkle the beef all over with 1 teaspoon salt and the pepper.

2   Select the **Sauté** setting on the Instant Pot and heat the olive oil. Add the onion and carrots and sauté for about 5 minutes, until the onion is softened and translucent. Add the beef and sauté for about 3 minutes more, until the beef is browned but not cooked through. Stir in the brown sugar, vinegar, beef broth, water, raisins, and bay leaf. Pour in the tomato sauce and stir to combine.

3   Secure the lid and set the Pressure Release to **Sealing**. Press the **Cancel** button to reset the cooking program, then select the **Pressure Cook** or **Manual** setting and set the cooking time for 30 minutes at high pressure. (The pot will take about 15 minutes to come up to pressure before the cooking program begins.)

4   When the cooking program ends, let the pressure release naturally for 15 minutes, then move the Pressure Release to **Venting** to release any remaining steam. Open the pot, remove and discard the bay leaf, and sprinkle the cabbage onto the soup. Secure the lid and set the Pressure Release to **Sealing**. Press the **Cancel** button to reset the cooking program, then select the **Pressure Cook** or **Manual** setting and set the cooking time for 0 (zero) minutes at low pressure. (The pot will take about 10 minutes to come up to pressure before the cooking program begins.)

5   When the cooking program ends, let the pressure release naturally for 10 minutes, then move the Pressure Release to **Venting** to release any remaining steam. Open the pot, taste the soup, and adjust the seasoning with salt if needed.

6   Ladle the soup into bowls, dollop with sour cream, and sprinkle with parsley. Serve piping hot.

When you're feeling under the weather, or even when it's just a little chilly outside, cook up a pot of this simple Greek chicken-and-rice soup. Made with boneless chicken breasts, it's light and bright, and weeknight-friendly, too. Additions of lemon, dill, and peppery extra-virgin olive oil perk up the bowl.

AVGOLEMONO

1 pound boneless, skinless chicken breasts

4 cups chicken broth (page 286)

½ teaspoon dried oregano

¼ teaspoon freshly ground black pepper

⅔ cup long-grain white rice

⅔ cup water

⅓ cup fresh lemon juice

2 egg yolks

Kosher salt

1 tablespoon chopped fresh dill

Extra-virgin olive oil for drizzling

PREP	0 MINUTES
COOK	35 MINUTES
PR	QPR
SERVES	4

1   Add the chicken breasts, chicken broth, oregano, and pepper to the Instant Pot. Place a tall steam rack in the pot, making sure all of its legs are resting firmly on the bottom.

2   Combine the rice and water in a 1½-quart stainless-steel bowl and place the bowl on top of the steam rack.

3   Secure the lid and set the Pressure Release to **Sealing**. Select the **Pressure Cook** or **Manual** setting and set the cooking time for 10 minutes at high pressure. (The pot will take about 20 minutes to come up to pressure before the cooking program begins.)

4   When the cooking program ends, perform a quick pressure release by moving the Pressure Release to **Venting**. Open the pot and, wearing heat-resistant mitts, remove the bowl and the steam rack from the pot. Using tongs, transfer the chicken breasts to a plate, then use two forks to shred the chicken.

5   In a blender, combine the lemon juice and egg yolks with 1 cup of the hot broth from the pot and ½ cup of the cooked rice. Blend on medium speed until smooth, then stir the mixture along with the rest of the rice and the shredded chicken into the pot. Press the **Cancel** button to reset the cooking program, then select the low **Sauté** setting for 5 minutes. Cook, stirring occasionally, until the soup is simmering and thickened and the cooking program ends. Stir the soup once more. Taste and adjust the seasoning with salt if needed.

6   Ladle the soup into bowls, sprinkle with the dill, and drizzle with olive oil. Serve piping hot.

Notes: For this soup, I like to cook the chicken and rice separately because the grains better retain their texture that way, but you can simplify the recipe by cooking the chicken and rice together, then letting the pressure release naturally. Prepared this way, the soup has a thicker, more porridge-like texture; you can thin it out with water or additional broth if needed.

For a dose of greens, add a 5- to 6-ounce bag of baby spinach or kale at the end of cooking and stir until the leaves are wilted.

The combination of lemongrass, coconut milk, fish sauce, and lime juice makes this soup taste distinctly Thai. It's light enough to serve as a first course, but you can make a meal of it, especially with a bowl of jasmine rice served alongside. Fresh galangal is sold in some well-stocked supermarkets and most Asian grocery stores, but if you can't find any, just leave it out rather than substituting ginger, which looks similar but tastes very different.

COCONUT-CHICKEN SOUP WITH LEMONGRASS

8 ounces button or cremini mushrooms, sliced

1 pound boneless, skinless chicken breasts, tenders, or thighs, cut into bite-size pieces

2-inch piece fresh galangal, cut into ⅛-inch slices

1 lemongrass stalk, trimmed to bottom 6 inches, dry outer layers discarded, gently smashed, and cut into 3-inch lengths

5 fresh Thai chiles; 4 gently smashed, 1 thinly sliced on the diagonal for serving

4 cups chicken broth (page 286)

One 13½-ounce can coconut milk

3 tablespoons fresh lime juice, plus more as needed

2 tablespoons fish sauce, plus more as needed

¼ cup fresh cilantro leaves

PREP	0 MINUTES
COOK	25 MINUTES
PR	QPR
SERVES	4

1   Add the mushrooms to the Instant Pot in an even layer, followed by the chicken, galangal, lemongrass, and smashed chiles. Pour in 2 cups of the chicken broth.

2   Secure the lid and set the Pressure Release to the **Sealing**. Select the **Pressure Cook** or **Manual** setting and set the cooking time for 3 minutes at high pressure. (The pot will take about 15 minutes to come up to pressure before the cooking program begins.)

3   When the cooking program ends, perform a quick pressure release by moving the Pressure Release to **Venting**. Open the pot, press the **Cancel** button to reset the cooking program, and select the **Sauté** setting. Stir in the remaining 2 cups chicken broth and the coconut milk and bring the soup to a simmer (this will take about 7 minutes). Press the **Cancel** button to turn off the Instant Pot. Using a slotted spoon or a pair of tongs, remove the galangal, lemongrass, and smashed chiles. Stir in the lime juice and fish sauce. Taste for seasoning and add more lime juice or fish sauce if needed.

4   Ladle the soup into bowls and garnish with the sliced chile and cilantro leaves. Serve piping hot.

When I'm in the mood for Mexican food and I want something light and fresh, I make a batch of this quick and easy tortilla soup. It's brothy, tomatoey, and full of black beans, corn, and shredded chicken. Sprinkle a handful of tortilla chips on top just before serving—the crunchy contrast really makes the dish!

CHICKEN TORTILLA SOUP

1½ to 2 pounds boneless, skinless chicken breasts

4 cups chicken broth (page 286)

One 28-ounce can diced tomatoes and their liquid

1½ cups cooked black beans (page 44), or one 15-ounce can black beans, rinsed and drained

1½ cups frozen corn kernels

1 medium yellow onion, diced

3 garlic cloves, minced

1 chipotle chile in adobo sauce, minced

1 tablespoon chili powder

1 teaspoon ground cumin

1 teaspoon dried oregano

¼ cup chopped fresh cilantro, plus more for serving

Tortilla chips for serving

1 avocado, halved, pitted, peeled, and diced

Lime wedges for serving

PREP	0 MINUTES
COOK	45 MINUTES
PR	10 MINUTES NPR
SERVES	6

1   Put the chicken breasts in the Instant Pot and pour in 1 cup of the chicken broth. Secure the lid and set the Pressure Release to **Sealing**. Select the **Pressure Cook** or **Manual** setting and set the cooking time for 10 minutes at high pressure. (The pot will take about 10 minutes to come up to pressure before the cooking program begins.)

2   When the cooking program ends, perform a quick pressure release by moving the Pressure Release to **Venting**. Open the pot and, using tongs or a slotted spoon, transfer the chicken to a plate or cutting board. Use two forks to shred the chicken into bite-size pieces.

3   Return the chicken to the pot and add the remaining 3 cups chicken broth, the tomatoes and their liquid, black beans, corn, onion, garlic, chipotle, chili powder, cumin, and oregano. Press the **Cancel** button to reset the cooking program, then select the **Soup** setting and set the cooking time for 5 minutes at high pressure. (The pot will take about 20 minutes to come up to pressure before the cooking program begins.)

4   When the cooking program ends, let the pressure release naturally for 10 minutes, then move the Pressure Release to **Venting** to release any remaining steam. Open the pot and stir in the cilantro.

5   Ladle the soup into bowls and sprinkle with tortilla chips. Serve piping hot topped with the avocado and cilantro, with lime wedges alongside.

Some gumbos simmer on the stove all day, but this one takes only about an hour from start to finish. It's full of tender chicken and spicy andouille sausage (I like using chicken andouille because it's a bit leaner than the traditional pork version, and the gumbo already has plenty of richness). I use fat rendered while crisping up the chicken skins to make the roux, then top the finished gumbo with the crackly skins.

CHICKEN AND ANDOUILLE GUMBO

2 pounds bone-in, skin-on chicken thighs

Kosher salt

2 to 3 tablespoons neutral vegetable oil, if needed (see Notes)

¼ cup all-purpose flour

1 medium yellow onion, diced

1 medium green bell pepper, seeded and diced

1 celery stalk, diced

2 garlic cloves, minced

¼ teaspoon cayenne pepper

2 cups chicken broth (page 286)

12 ounces fully cooked andouille sausage, sliced into ¼-inch rounds

2 bay leaves

4½ cups cooked long-grain white rice (page 51) for serving

Sliced green onions for serving

Hot sauce (such as Crystal or Tabasco) for serving

PREP	5 MINUTES
COOK	1 HOUR
PR	10 MINUTES NPR
SERVES	6

1   Line a plate with a double layer of paper towels. Remove the skin from the chicken thighs and cut the skin into 1-inch pieces. Set the thighs aside.

2   Select the **Sauté** setting on the Instant Pot and add the chicken skins, spreading the pieces in an even layer. Sprinkle with ½ teaspoon salt and cook without stirring for 10 minutes to render the fat. Stir, then continue to cook for about 5 minutes more. Using a slotted spoon, transfer the chicken skin to the prepared plate.

3   Make sure there is at least ¼ cup of rendered chicken fat in the pot. If necessary, add enough of the vegetable oil to make up the difference (see Notes). Add the flour to the rendered fat in the Instant Pot and cook, stirring often, for about 7 minutes, until the roux is toasty and brown. If you like, you may cook the roux for a few minutes longer, until it's a few shades darker.

4   Add the onion, bell pepper, celery, garlic, and cayenne to the pot. Sauté for about 4 minutes, until the onion is softened. Pour in the chicken broth and, using a wooden spoon, nudge loose any browned bits from the bottom of the pot. Add the chicken thighs, sausage, and bay leaves.

5   Secure the lid and set the Pressure Release to **Sealing**. Press the **Cancel** button to reset the cooking program, then select the **Pressure Cook** or **Manual** setting and set the cooking time for 20 minutes at high pressure. (The pot will take about 15 minutes to come up to pressure before the cooking program begins.)

Notes: The gumbo is thickened with roux, which increases the chance of a "burn" error message due to scorching on the pot bottom. To lessen the likelihood of this happening, make sure to use a 1:1 ratio of fat to flour, cook the roux for at least 7 minutes, and after adding the broth, make sure to thoroughly scrape up any browned bits off the bottom of the pot.

For a faster gumbo, you can substitute 1½ pounds boneless, skinless chicken thighs for the bone-in, skin-on thighs. Skip the fat-rendering step and use ¼ cup neutral-flavored oil in place of the chicken fat. Add the salt along with the vegetables.

6   When the cooking program ends, let the pressure release naturally for 10 minutes, then move the Pressure Release to **Venting** to release any remaining steam. Open the pot and remove and discard the bay leaves. Using tongs, transfer the chicken thighs to a plate. Remove the meat from the bones and return the meat to the pot; discard the bones. Give the gumbo a stir to break up the chicken meat and mix everything together. Taste for seasoning and add more salt if needed.

7   Spoon the rice into bowls, then ladle in the gumbo. Top with green onions and crispy chicken skins. Serve piping hot, with hot sauce alongside.

This chicken noodle soup with a made-from-scratch broth is much speedier than its stove-top counterpart—there's no hours-long cooking time, need to take apart a whole chicken, or straining involved. Start with bone-in, dark-meat chicken pieces for the most flavorful soup.

CHICKEN NOODLE SOUP

1½ to 2 pounds bone-in chicken drumsticks or thighs, skin removed

2 celery stalks, diced

1 yellow onion, diced

2 bay leaves

½ teaspoon dried oregano

Kosher salt

Freshly ground black pepper

6 cups water

2 carrots, peeled and diced

8 ounces linguine, broken into 2-inch lengths

Lemon wedges for serving

PREP	0 MINUTES
COOK	1 HOUR
PR	25 MINUTES NPR
SERVES	4 TO 6

1   Add the chicken, celery, onion, bay leaves, oregano, 1½ teaspoons salt, and ½ teaspoon pepper to the Instant Pot. Pour in 4 cups of the water.

2   Secure the lid and set the Pressure Release to **Sealing**. Select the **Soup/Broth** setting and set the cooking time for 20 minutes at high pressure. (The pot will take about 25 minutes to come up to pressure before the cooking program begins.)

3   When the cooking program ends, let the pressure release naturally for 15 minutes, then move the Pressure Release to **Venting** to release any remaining steam. Open the pot and, using tongs, transfer the chicken to a plate.

4   Add the carrots, linguine, and remaining 2 cups water to the pot. Stir to combine. Secure the lid and set the Pressure Release to **Sealing**. Press the **Cancel** button to reset the cooking program, then select the **Pressure Cook** or **Manual** setting and set the cooking time for 5 minutes at high pressure. (The pot will take about 10 minutes to come up to pressure before the cooking program begins.)

5   While the carrots and pasta are cooking, remove the chicken meat from the bones; discard the bones. Shred or dice the meat and set aside.

6   When the cooking program ends, let the pressure release naturally for 10 minutes, then move the Pressure Release to **Venting** to release any remaining steam. Open the pot, remove and discard the bay leaves, then stir the meat into the soup. Taste and adjust the seasoning with salt and pepper if needed.

7   Ladle the soup into bowls and serve piping hot with lemon wedges on the side.

Notes: Feel free to add more vegetables. I often include diced parsnip and rutabaga along with the carrots.

You can omit the noodles and cook the soup in one step. Add the chicken, aromatics, carrots, and 4 cups water, and cook on the **Soup/Broth** setting for 20 minutes at high pressure. You won't need the remaining 2 cups water. After opening the pot, remove the chicken meat from the bones, shred the meat, and immediately return the meat to the pot.

Manhattan-style clam chowder is a totally different soup from the creamy New England–style chowder most people are familiar with. It's lighter, tomato-based, and dairy-free. This version is loaded with vegetables, and bacon adds a nice smoky flavor as well as a little richness to the broth.

MANHATTAN CLAM CHOWDER

3 slices thick-cut bacon, cut into ¼-inch pieces

2 garlic cloves, minced

1 yellow onion, diced

2 carrots, peeled and diced

1 green bell pepper, seeded and diced

2 celery stalks, diced

2 teaspoons Old Bay seasoning

1 teaspoon dried thyme

1 teaspoon freshly ground black pepper

Two 10-ounce cans baby clams and their liquid

One 8-ounce bottle clam juice

One 14½-ounce can diced tomatoes and their liquid

1 cup chicken broth (page 286) or vegetable broth (page 284)

2 bay leaves

1 large russet potato, peeled and diced

3 tablespoons tomato paste

Kosher salt

¼ cup chopped fresh flat-leaf parsley

1   Select the **Sauté** setting on the Instant Pot, add the bacon, and sauté for about 5 minutes, until the bacon has rendered some of its fat and has begun to brown. Add the garlic, onion, carrots, bell pepper, and celery and sauté for about 4 minutes more, until the onion is softened. Add the Old Bay, thyme, and black pepper and sauté for about 1 minute more. Add the clams and their liquid, clam juice, diced tomatoes and their liquid, chicken broth, and bay leaves. Stir to combine, using a wooden spoon to nudge loose any browned bits from the bottom of the pot. Add the potatoes and dollop the tomato paste on top. Do not stir.

2   Secure the lid and set the Pressure Release to **Sealing**. Press the **Cancel** button to reset the cooking program, then select the **Pressure Cook** or **Manual** setting and set the cooking time for 5 minutes at low pressure. (The pot will take about 15 minutes to come up to pressure before the cooking program begins.)

3   When the cooking program ends, let the pressure release naturally for 10 minutes, then move the Pressure Release to **Venting** to release any remaining steam. Open the pot, then remove and discard the bay leaves. Taste and adjust the seasoning with salt if needed. Stir in the parsley.

4   Ladle the chowder into bowls and serve piping hot.

PREP	0 MINUTES
COOK	30 MINUTES
PR	10 MINUTES NPR
SERVES	6

Don't be intimidated by the long ingredient list for this light and flavorful chili. It's made with a few pantry staples and easy-to-find produce, and it's gluten-free and vegan (if you leave out the cheese). If you've got garden-fresh bell peppers, tomatoes, zucchini, and corn, by all means use them. But in the wintertime, when you're craving a little bit of summer flavor, there's nothing wrong with using frozen or canned veggies. Serve the chili on its own, over steamed rice, or with cornbread or tortilla chips.

SUMMER VEGETABLE CHILI

2 tablespoons olive oil

1 poblano chile or green bell pepper, seeded and diced

1 jalapeño chile, seeded and diced

1 medium yellow onion, diced

1 celery stalk, diced

2 garlic cloves, minced

Kosher salt

2 tablespoons chili powder

1 teaspoon dried oregano

½ teaspoon ground cumin

¼ teaspoon cayenne pepper

2 medium zucchini, diced

One 12-ounce bag frozen corn, or kernels cut from 3 ears fresh corn

One 14½-ounce can diced fire-roasted tomatoes and their liquid

1½ cups cooked pinto or peruano beans (page 44), or one 15-ounce can pinto beans, rinsed and drained

1 cup vegetable broth (page 284)

¼ cup chopped fresh cilantro

2 green onions, white and tender green parts, thinly sliced

1 cup tightly packed shredded Cheddar cheese (optional)

1   Select the **Sauté** setting on the Instant Pot and heat the olive oil. Add both chiles, the onion, celery, garlic, and ½ teaspoon salt and sauté for about 5 minutes, until the vegetables are softened. Add the chili powder, oregano, cumin, and cayenne and sauté for about 1 minute more. Add the zucchini, corn, tomatoes and their liquid, beans, and vegetable broth and stir to combine.

2   Secure the lid and set the Pressure Release to **Sealing**. Press the **Cancel** button to reset the cooking program, then select the **Bean/Chili** setting and set the cooking time for 5 minutes at high pressure. (The pot will take about 15 minutes to come up to pressure before the cooking program begins.)

3   When the cooking program ends, perform a quick pressure release by moving the Pressure Release to **Venting**. Open the pot and give the chili a final stir. Taste for seasoning and add more salt if needed.

4   Ladle the chili into bowls and sprinkle with the cilantro, green onions, and cheese. Serve piping hot.

PREP	0 MINUTES
COOK	25 MINUTES
PR	QPR
SERVES	6

Hardy winter vegetables cook in minutes in this vegan-friendly chili. You can substitute any type of beans for the black beans, use a large onion instead of the leeks, and/or replace the jalapeños with spicier or milder chiles. The chili gets its smoky heat from a canned chipotle chile in adobo sauce, one of my favorite ingredients for amping up the flavor in vegan and vegetarian dishes. Serve on its own or over steamed rice.

WINTER VEGETABLE CHILI

3 tablespoons olive oil

2 garlic cloves, minced

2 leeks, dark green parts discarded, halved lengthwise, thinly sliced, washed, and drained

2 jalapeño chiles, seeded and diced

Kosher salt

1 chipotle chile in adobo sauce (see Notes), minced

3 tablespoons chili powder

1 cup vegetable broth (page 284)

2 carrots, peeled and diced

1½ cups cooked black beans (page 44), or one 15-ounce can black beans, rinsed and drained

One 1-pound delicata squash (see Notes), unpeeled, seeded, and diced

One 14½-ounce can diced fire-roasted tomatoes and their liquid

Chopped fresh cilantro for sprinkling

PREP	0 MINUTES
COOK	30 MINUTES
PR	QPR
SERVES	4 TO 6

1   Select the **Sauté** setting on the Instant Pot and heat the olive oil and garlic for about 2 minutes, until the garlic is bubbling. Add the leeks, jalapeños, and 1 teaspoon salt and sauté for about 5 minutes, until the leeks are wilted and beginning to release their moisture. Add the chipotle chile and chili powder and sauté for about 1 minute more. Stir in the vegetable broth, using a wooden spoon to nudge loose any browned bits from the bottom of the pot. In fairly even layers, add the carrots to the pot, followed by the beans and the squash. Pour the tomatoes and their liquid over the top. Do not stir.

2   Secure the lid and set the Pressure Release to **Sealing**. Press the **Cancel** button to reset the cooking program, then select the **Pressure Cook** or **Manual** setting and set the cooking time for 5 minutes at high pressure. (The pot will take about 15 minutes to come up to pressure before the cooking program begins.)

3   When the cooking program ends, perform a quick pressure release by moving the Pressure Release to **Venting**. Open the pot, then taste the chili and adjust the seasoning with salt if needed.

4   Ladle the chili into bowls and sprinkle with cilantro. Serve piping hot.

Notes: Chipotle chiles come about a dozen to a small can, and since I only use a few at a time, I like to freeze them individually so I always have some on hand. Spoon the chiles with some of their sauce into a silicone muffin pan or onto a plastic wrap–lined tray or baking sheet, freeze them until solid, transfer to a ziplock plastic freezer bag, and store in the freezer for up to 6 months. The chiles are easy to mince in their frozen state.

You can substitute any variety of winter squash for the delicata squash. If the skin is thick, bumpy, or blemished, or if the squash has been coated with wax for storage, make sure to peel before use.

This spicy chili is Texan through and through—it's my adaptation of a recipe from my good friend Chris Hamje, an Austin native and founder of 4th Tap Brewing Co-op. The base is made mostly with dried chiles, and there are no beans or tomatoes to be found. The recipe calls for a long list of spices, but you can substitute 3½ tablespoons store-bought chili powder if you want to simplify things.

FIVE-ALARM TEXAS-STYLE CHILI

10 guajillo chiles, stemmed and seeded

2 ancho chiles, stemmed and seeded

3 cups water

2 cups vegetable broth (page 284) or beef broth (page 285)

2 chipotle chiles in adobo sauce

1 tablespoon neutral vegetable oil

1 large yellow onion, diced, plus chopped onion for serving

4 garlic cloves, minced

2 jalapeño chiles, diced, plus sliced jalapeño for serving

1½ tablespoons ground cumin

1 teaspoon ground coriander

1 teaspoon ground black pepper

1 teaspoon ground white pepper

1 teaspoon dried oregano

1 teaspoon dried thyme

¾ teaspoon sweet paprika

¼ teaspoon ground cinnamon

¼ teaspoon ground cloves

Kosher salt

1 cup American pale ale

PREP	0 MINUTES
COOK	1 HOUR, 40 MINUTES
PR	30 MINUTES NPR
SERVES	8 TO 10

1   Place the guajillo and ancho chiles in the Instant Pot, then pour in the water. Cover the pot with the glass lid, then select the **Sauté** setting and set the cooking time for 8 minutes. When the timer goes off, let the chiles soak in the water for an additional 20 minutes to soften.

2   Open the pot and, using tongs, transfer the soaked chiles to a blender; discard the soaking water and wipe out the pot. To the blender, add the vegetable broth and chipotles. Blend on medium speed for about 1 minute, until smooth.

3   Select the high **Sauté** setting on the Instant Pot and heat the vegetable oil. Add the diced onion, garlic, and diced jalapeños and sauté for about 5 minutes, until the onion is softened. Add the cumin, coriander, black pepper, white pepper, oregano, thyme, paprika, cinnamon, cloves, and 2 teaspoons salt and sauté for about 2 minutes more. Pour in the ale and, using a wooden spoon, nudge loose any browned bits from the bottom of the pot. Bring to a boil and cook for 5 minutes, until most of the liquid has evaporated. Stir in the chile-broth puree, along with the beef, coffee, and bay leaves.

4   Secure the pressure cooking lid and set the Pressure Release to **Sealing**. Press the **Cancel** button to reset the cooking program, then select the **Meat/Stew** setting and set the cooking time for 45 minutes at high pressure. (The pot will take about 15 minutes to come up to pressure before the cooking program begins.)

5   When the cooking program ends, let the pressure release naturally for 30 minutes, then move the Pressure Release to **Venting** to release any remaining steam. Open the pot; if a lot of fat has collected on the surface, use a ladle or spoon to skim it off. Remove and discard the bay leaves, then taste for seasoning and add more salt if needed.

4 pounds beef chuck roast or brisket, cut into 1-inch pieces

1 teaspoon finely ground coffee or instant coffee crystals (optional)

2 bay leaves

2 tablespoons masa harina (optional)

Shredded Cheddar cheese for serving

Cornbread or tortillas for serving

6   At this point, you may either serve the chili as is or thicken it with masa harina. To thicken, press the **Cancel** button to reset the cooking program and select the medium **Sauté** setting. Stir in the masa harina and cook for about 5 minutes, stirring often, until thickened.

7   Ladle the chili into bowls. Serve piping hot with chopped onion, sliced jalapeño, Cheddar, and cornbread or tortillas.

If you like beans in your beef chili, this recipe is for you! Ground beef and kidney beans are the base of this hearty one-pot meal. It takes less than an hour to make, but the chili tastes like it simmered all day long. Serve it over steamed rice (see page 51) or Cauliflower "Rice" (page 233), or with a hunk of cornbread alongside.

BEEF, BEAN, AND TOMATO CHILI

2 tablespoons neutral vegetable oil

1 medium yellow onion, diced

2 garlic cloves, diced

1 green bell pepper, seeded and diced

2 celery stalks, diced

1 pound lean ground beef (93% lean)

3 tablespoons chili powder

1 teaspoon dried oregano

Kosher salt

1 cup water

One 14½-ounce can diced tomatoes and their liquid

1½ cups cooked kidney beans (see page 44), or one 15-ounce can kidney beans, rinsed and drained

2 tablespoons tomato paste

1½ cups shredded Mexican cheese blend for serving

3 green onions, white and tender green parts, sliced thinly, for serving

PREP	0 MINUTES
COOK	45 MINUTES
PR	QPR
REST	5 MINUTES
SERVES	4 TO 6

1   Select the **Sauté** setting on the Instant Pot and heat the vegetable oil. Add the onion, garlic, bell pepper, and celery and sauté for about 5 minutes, until the onion is softened. Add the ground beef and sauté, breaking it up with a spoon or spatula as it cooks, for about 5 minutes, until no longer pink. Stir in the chili powder, oregano, and 1½ teaspoons salt and sauté for about 1 minute more. Pour in the water and stir to combine, using a wooden spoon to nudge loose any browned bits from the bottom of the pot. Add the tomatoes and their liquid and the kidney beans and stir to combine. Dollop the tomato paste on top. Do not stir.

2   Secure the lid and set the Pressure Release to **Sealing**. Press the **Cancel** button to reset the cooking program, then select the **Pressure Cook** or **Manual** program and set the cooking time for 10 minutes at high pressure. (The pot will take about 10 minutes to come up to pressure before the cooking program begins.)

3   When the cooking program ends, perform a quick pressure release by moving the Pressure Release to **Venting**. Open the pot, then select the **Sauté** setting and set the cooking time for 10 minutes. Let the chili simmer uncovered and without stirring, as stirring will cause spattering.

4   Wearing heat-resistant mitts, lift out the inner pot. Let the chili rest in the pot for 5 minutes, then use a wooden spoon to stir and nudge loose any browned bits from the bottom of the pot. Taste and adjust the seasoning with salt, if needed.

5   Ladle the chili into bowls and top with cheese and green onions. Serve piping hot.

Traditionally served over spaghetti, this chili resembles a thick meat sauce. It's a unique Midwestern specialty you've got to try if you haven't already. I've adapted this recipe from a stove-top version created by my friend and fellow classical singer Diana Pray of San Francisco. A Cincy native and an excellent cook, she's a true connoisseur of Cincinnati chili.

CINCINNATI CHILI

2 tablespoons sweet paprika

2 tablespoons ground cumin

1 tablespoon ground cinnamon

2 teaspoons ground coriander

2 teaspoons kosher salt

1½ teaspoons cocoa powder

1 teaspoon ground ginger

½ teaspoon ground cloves

¼ teaspoon cayenne pepper

2 tablespoons neutral vegetable oil

1 medium yellow onion, diced

2 garlic cloves, minced

2 pounds lean ground beef (93% lean)

2½ cups water

One 14½-ounce can diced tomatoes and their liquid

2 tablespoons yellow mustard, plus more for serving

2 tablespoons tomato paste

Kosher salt

Cooked spaghetti, cooked kidney beans (page 44), diced white onion, shredded Cheddar cheese, hot sauce (such as Tabasco), and/or oyster crackers for serving

PREP	5 MINUTES
COOK	1 HOUR, 15 MINUTES
PR	25 MINUTES NPR
REST	5 MINUTES
SERVES	6 TO 8

1   In a small bowl, stir together the paprika, cumin, cinnamon, coriander, salt, cocoa powder, ginger, cloves, and cayenne. Set aside.

2   Select the **Sauté** setting on the Instant Pot; add the vegetable oil, onion, and garlic; and sauté for about 5 minutes, until the onion is softened. Add the ground beef and sauté, breaking it up with a spoon or spatula as it cooks, for about 6 minutes, until it has cooked through and is no longer pink. Add the spice blend and sauté for about 1 minute more. Add the water, tomatoes and their liquid, and mustard, then stir to combine. Dollop the tomato paste on top. Do not stir.

3   Secure the lid and set the Pressure Release to **Sealing**. Press the **Cancel** button to reset the cooking program, then select the **Pressure Cook** or **Manual** setting and set the cooking time for 30 minutes at high pressure. (The pot will take about 20 minutes to come up to pressure before the cooking program begins.)

4   When the cooking program ends, let the pressure release naturally for 25 minutes, then move the Pressure Release to **Venting** to release any remaining steam. Open the pot and stir the chili. Select the **Sauté** setting and set the cooking time for 15 minutes. Let the chili simmer uncovered and without stirring, as stirring will cause spattering.

5   Wearing heat-resistant mitts, lift out the inner pot. Let the chili rest in the pot for 5 minutes, then use a wooden spoon to stir and nudge loose any browned bits from the bottom of the pot. Taste and adjust the seasoning with salt, if needed.

6   Serve the chili plain, or ladle it over cooked spaghetti and top with kidney beans, diced onion, and Cheddar. Pass hot sauce, mustard, and oyster crackers on the side.

Note: I think the seasonings in this chili are spot-on, but Diana's version used twice the amount of spices and salt. If you want a real flavor bomb of a chili, try it her way and double the spice blend!

This chili reminds me of enchiladas suizas, except in bowl form. The green chile base is enriched with sour cream, which adds a little tanginess. If you don't want to use dried beans, opt for two 15-ounce cans cannellini beans, rinsed and drained, and skip the soaking and initial 20-minute cooking steps—either works well, but dried beans add a little time to the preparation. Serve the chili with tortillas or Mexican-Style Rice (page 54).

WHITE CHICKEN CHILI

1 cup dried cannellini beans

4 cups water

Kosher salt

1 tablespoon olive oil

2 Anaheim or Hatch green chiles, seeded and diced

2 jalapeño chiles, seeded and diced

2 celery stalks, diced

1 medium yellow onion, diced

4 garlic cloves, minced

2 teaspoons ground cumin

2 teaspoons dried oregano

1 teaspoon ground coriander

¼ teaspoon cayenne pepper (optional)

1½ pounds boneless, skinless chicken breasts or tenders, cut into bite-size pieces

1 cup chicken broth (page 286)

1 cup sour cream

¼ cup chopped fresh cilantro

2 cups shredded Monterey Jack cheese for serving

2 green onions, tender green parts only, thinly sliced, for serving

PREP	8-HOUR SOAK
COOK	1 HOUR
PR	35 MINUTES NPR
SERVES	6

1   Combine the beans, water, and 1 teaspoon salt in the Instant Pot. Leave the pot turned off and let the beans soak for 8 to 10 hours.

2   Secure the lid and set the Pressure Release to **Sealing**. Select the **Bean/Chili**, **Manual**, or **Pressure Cook** setting and set the cooking time for 20 minutes at high pressure. (The pot will take about 15 minutes to come up to pressure before the cooking program begins.)

3   Let the pressure release naturally for 15 minutes, then move the Pressure Release to **Venting** to release any remaining steam. Open the pot and, wearing heat-resistant mitts, lift the inner pot out of the Instant Pot and drain the beans in a colander. Return the now-empty inner pot to the Instant Pot housing. Press the **Cancel** button to reset the cooking program.

4   Select the **Sauté** setting on the Instant Pot and heat the olive oil. Add all the chiles, the celery, onion, and garlic and sauté for about 5 minutes, until the vegetables are softened. Add the cumin, oregano, coriander, cayenne, and 1 teaspoon salt and sauté for about 1 minute more. Add the beans, chicken, and chicken broth and stir to combine.

5   Secure the lid and set the Pressure Release to **Sealing**. Press the **Cancel** button to reset the cooking program, then select the **Bean/Chili**, **Manual**, or **Pressure Cook** setting and set the cooking time for 10 minutes at high pressure. (The pot will take about 10 minutes to come up to pressure before the cooking program begins.)

6   Let the pressure release naturally for 20 minutes, then move the Pressure Release to **Venting** to release any remaining steam. Open the pot and stir in the sour cream and cilantro. Taste for seasoning and add more salt if needed.

7   Ladle the chili into bowls and sprinkle with the cheese and green onions. Serve piping hot.

This is my go-to football-game chili. The recipe makes a big pot, but it also works well as a half batch if you're serving a smaller group. On game day, you can leave the chili on the Keep Warm setting all afternoon, and people can ladle themselves a bowl whenever they please.

TURKEY AND PINTO BEAN CHILI

2 tablespoons olive oil

1 yellow onion, diced

4 garlic cloves, minced

2 jalapeño chiles, seeded and diced

2 pounds ground turkey (93% lean)

¼ cup chili powder

1 tablespoon ground cumin

2 teaspoons dried oregano

Kosher salt

1½ cups chicken broth (page 286)

One 14½-ounce can diced tomatoes and their liquid

6 cups cooked pinto beans (page 44), or two 28-ounce cans pinto beans, rinsed and drained

Diced white onion, chopped fresh cilantro, tortilla chips, and/or hot sauce (such as Cholula or Tapatío) for serving

1   Select the **Sauté** setting on the Instant Pot and heat the olive oil. Add the onion, garlic, and jalapeños and sauté for about 5 minutes, until the onion is softened. Add the ground turkey and sauté, breaking it up with a spoon or spatula as it cooks, for about 5 minutes more, until the turkey is cooked through. Add the chili powder, cumin, oregano, and ½ teaspoon salt and sauté for 1 minute more. Add the chicken broth, tomatoes and their liquid, and pinto beans and stir to combine.

2   Secure the lid and set the Pressure Release to **Sealing**. Press the **Cancel** button to reset the cooking program, then select the **Pressure Cook** or **Manual** setting and set the cooking time for 20 minutes at high pressure. (The pot will take about 20 minutes to come up to pressure before the cooking program begins.)

3   When the cooking program ends, let the pressure release naturally for 20 minutes, then move the Pressure Release to **Venting** to release any remaining steam. Open the pot, stir the chili, and taste and adjust the seasoning with salt if needed.

4   Ladle the chili into bowls and serve piping hot with diced onion, cilantro, tortilla chips, and hot sauce on the side.

PREP	0 MINUTES
COOK	50 MINUTES
PR	20 MINUTES NPR
SERVES	10 TO 12

Whole dried chiles make the best chile Colorado, giving the pork-based stew a deep flavor and a beautiful dark-red hue. You can find dried chiles in Mexican grocery stores and well-stocked supermarkets. Look for chiles that are plump and pliable, with a glossy shine to their skins.

CHILE COLORADO

3 cups vegetable broth (page 284) or chicken broth (page 286)

10 guajillo chiles, stemmed and seeded

5 pasilla chiles, stemmed and seeded

About 2½ pounds boneless pork shoulder or pork stew meat, trimmed and cut into ½-inch pieces

Kosher salt

1 teaspoon freshly ground black pepper

1 tablespoon avocado oil or other neutral oil with high smoke point

6 garlic cloves, minced

1 tablespoon ground cumin

1 teaspoon dried sage

1 teaspoon dried oregano

Warmed flour tortillas or Mexican-Style Rice (page 54) for serving

PREP	0 MINUTES
COOK	1 HOUR, 15 MINUTES
PR	20 MINUTES NPR
SERVES	4 TO 6

1 Add 2 cups of the vegetable broth to the Instant Pot and cover with the glass lid. Select the **Sauté** setting and set the cooking time for 10 minutes.

2 When the timer goes off, add all the chiles to the pot. Cover and let soak, for about 20 minutes, until softened.

3 Using tongs, transfer the soaked chiles to a blender. Wearing heat-resistant mitts, lift out the inner pot and pour the broth into the blender. Return the inner pot to the housing. Blend the chile mixture on high speed for about 1 minute, until smooth. Set aside.

4 Sprinkle the pork all over with 1½ teaspoons salt and the pepper.

5 Add the avocado oil to the Instant Pot, select the high **Sauté** setting, and heat for 2 minutes. Add half of the pork in a single layer to the pot and sear for about 4 minutes, until lightly browned on one side. Transfer the pork to a plate. Repeat with the remaining pork, returning the first batch of pork, including any accumulated juices, to the pot when the second batch is done. Add the garlic, cumin, sage, and oregano to the pot and sauté for about 1 minute, using a wooden spoon to nudge loose any browned bits from the bottom of the pot. Stir in the remaining 1 cup broth and the blended chiles.

6 Secure the lid and set the Pressure Release to **Sealing**. Press the **Cancel** button to reset the cooking program, then select the **Meat/Stew** program and set the cooking time for 25 minutes at high pressure. (The pot will take about 10 minutes to come up to pressure before the cooking program begins.)

7 When the cooking program ends, let the pressure release naturally for 20 minutes, then move the Pressure Release to **Venting** to release any remaining steam. Open the pot, then taste and adjust the seasoning with salt if needed.

8 Ladle the chile Colorado onto plates or into bowls. Serve piping hot with tortillas or rice.

This recipe makes twice as much of the chile verde base as you need for one meal. Freeze half for future use, and when you're ready, all you need to do is combine the pork and sauce in the pot! For a faster, weeknight-friendly meal, feel free to make just a half batch of the base, or substitute a 12-ounce jar of salsa verde for the pureed sauce.

PORK CHILE VERDE

2 tablespoons neutral vegetable oil

1 yellow onion, sliced

2 garlic cloves, peeled

2 serrano chiles, seeded and diced

1 jalapeño chile, seeded and diced

2 pounds tomatillos, husked and cut into quarters

1 cup water

Kosher salt

1 bunch cilantro, bottom 4 inches of stems trimmed and discarded

2 pounds boneless pork shoulder, trimmed of excess fat and cut into 1-inch pieces

Warmed tortillas or cooked long-grain rice (page 51) for serving

½ cup cilantro leaves for serving (optional)

½ cup pickled red onions (page 298) for serving (optional)

1 jalapeño chile, thinly sliced, for serving (optional)

1 lime, cut into wedges, for serving (optional)

PREP	0 MINUTES
COOK	1 HOUR
PR	25 MINUTES NPR
SERVES	8

1 Select the high **Sauté** setting on the Instant Pot and heat the vegetable oil. Add the onion, garlic, serranos, and jalapeño and sauté for about 10 minutes, until the onion is softened and browned. Add the tomatillos, water, and 1½ teaspoons salt.

2 Secure the lid and set the Pressure Release to **Sealing**. Press the **Cancel** button to reset the cooking program, then select the **Manual** or **Pressure Cook** setting and set the cooking time for 5 minutes at high pressure. (The pot will take about 10 minutes to come up to pressure before the cooking program begins.)

3 When the cooking program ends, let the pressure release naturally for 10 minutes, then move the Pressure Release to **Venting** to release any remaining steam. Open the pot and add the cilantro. Using an immersion blender, puree the mixture until smooth.

4 Ladle half the sauce into a silicone muffin or loaf pan and slip it into the freezer. When it's frozen solid, after about 4 hours, pop it out of the pan, transfer to a 1-gallon ziplock plastic freezer bag, and freeze for up to 6 months.

5 Add the pork to the remaining sauce in the Instant Pot, secure the lid, and set the Pressure Release to **Sealing**. Press the **Cancel** button to reset the cooking program, then select the **Meat/Stew** setting and set the cooking time for 25 minutes at high pressure. (The pot will take about 10 minutes to come up to pressure before the cooking program begins.)

6 When the cooking program ends, let the pressure release naturally for 15 minutes, then move the Pressure Release to **Venting** to release any remaining steam. Open the pot, then taste for seasoning and add more salt if needed.

7 Ladle the chili into bowls and sprinkle with cilantro, pickled onions, and jalapeño slices. Serve piping hot with lime wedges and tortillas or rice.

4

Vegetarian

Got some leftover mayonnaise or lemon aioli? Use it to make a simple dressing for this salad of arugula and romaine that's topped with soft-boiled eggs and crunchy toasted almonds. This is one of those salads that's much better than the sum of its ingredients, and I often make it for lunch.

ARUGULA AND ROMAINE SALAD WITH SOFT-BOILED EGGS

4 large eggs

¼ cup mayonnaise or lemon aioli (page 234)

¼ cup fresh lemon juice

¼ cup extra-virgin olive oil

2 green onions, white and tender green parts, finely chopped

½ teaspoon kosher salt

Freshly ground black pepper

1 head romaine lettuce, roughly chopped

One 6-ounce bag baby arugula

½ cup sliced almonds, toasted

PREP	0 MINUTES
COOK	20 MINUTES
PR	QPR
SERVES	4 AS A STARTER, 2 AS A MAIN DISH

1   Pour 1 cup water into the Instant Pot and place the wire metal steam rack in the pot. Place the eggs on the steam rack.

2   Secure the lid and set the Pressure Release to **Sealing**. Select the **Egg** or **Steam** setting and set the cooking time for 3 minutes at high pressure. (The pot will take about 10 minutes to come up to pressure before the cooking program begins.)

3   While the eggs are cooking, prepare an ice bath.

4   When the cooking program ends, perform a quick pressure release by moving the Pressure Release to **Venting**. Open the pot and transfer the eggs to the ice bath to cool.

5   In a large bowl, whisk together the mayonnaise, lemon juice, olive oil, green onions, salt, and ¼ teaspoon pepper until well combined. Add the romaine and arugula and toss to coat evenly with the dressing.

6   Transfer the greens to serving plates. Peel the eggs and halve them lengthwise, then place them on the salads. Sprinkle with the almonds and a few grinds of black pepper. Serve immediately.

This Instant Pot adaptation of a classic from Buvette in New York City brings together lentils and greens and is topped with a dollop of horseradish-spiked crème fraîche. The lacinato kale becomes silky and melds with the lentils, and the generous amount of olive oil makes everything taste rich and luxurious. It makes a big batch, and leftovers are great the next day.

LENTILS AND KALE WITH HORSERADISH CREAM

¼ cup extra-virgin olive oil, plus more for drizzling

2 shallots, diced

5 garlic cloves, minced

½ teaspoon red pepper flakes

½ teaspoon ground nutmeg

Kosher salt

About 16 ounces lacinato kale, stems discarded and leaves chopped into 1-inch pieces, or one 16-ounce bag washed and trimmed lacinato kale, cut into 1-inch pieces

2½ cups water

1 cup small green lentils, Puy lentils, or beluga lentils

½ cup crème fraîche

1½ tablespoons prepared horseradish

1 teaspoon red wine vinegar

PREP	0 MINUTES
COOK	50 MINUTES
PR	10 MINUTES NPR
SERVES	6

1   Select the **Sauté** setting on the Instant Pot and heat the olive oil. Add the shallots and garlic and sauté for about 4 minutes, until the shallots are softened. Add the red pepper flakes, nutmeg, and 1 teaspoon salt and sauté for 1 minute more. Stir in the kale and sauté for about 3 minutes, until fully wilted. Stir in the water and lentils, scraping down the sides of the pot to make sure the lentils are submerged.

2   Secure the lid and set the Pressure Release to **Sealing**. Press the **Cancel** button to reset the cooking program, then select the **Bean/Chili**, **Pressure Cook**, or **Manual** setting and set the cooking time for 30 minutes at high pressure. (The pot will take about 10 minutes to come up to pressure before the cooking program begins.)

3   While the lentils and kale are cooking, in a small bowl, stir together the crème fraîche, horseradish, vinegar, and ¼ teaspoon salt. Set aside.

4   When the cooking program ends, let the pressure release naturally for 10 minutes, then move the Pressure Release to **Venting** to release any remaining steam. Open the pot and give the mixture a stir. Taste and adjust the seasoning with salt if needed.

5   Ladle the lentils and kale into serving dishes, dollop with some of the horseradish cream, and drizzle with olive oil. Serve immediately.

Shakshouka, a Middle Eastern dish of eggs cooked in tomato sauce, is a great last-minute vegetarian main dish. It's fast and easy to make, and it's filling, too. In this version, the eggs are poached in a sauce made with canned tomatoes and jarred roasted peppers, so there's not a lot of prep involved. To complete the meal, I've also included couscous, prepared in the Instant Pot at the same time as the shakshouka.

SHAKSHOUKA WITH COUSCOUS

Couscous

1 cup fine couscous

1¼ cups water

½ teaspoon kosher salt

1 tablespoon unsalted butter or olive oil

Shakshouka

3 tablespoons extra-virgin olive oil, plus more for drizzling

3 garlic cloves, minced

1 yellow onion, thinly sliced

1 teaspoon ground cumin

1 teaspoon ground coriander

One 14½-ounce can diced tomatoes and their liquid

One 12-ounce jar roasted red bell peppers, drained and sliced into ¼-inch strips

½ cup water

4 eggs

PREP	5 MINUTES
COOK	20 MINUTES
PR	QPR
SERVES	4

1   To prepare the couscous: In a 1½-quart stainless-steel bowl, combine the couscous, water, and salt. Put the butter on top. Set aside.

2   To make the shakshouka: Select the **Sauté** setting on the Instant Pot and heat the olive oil and garlic for about 3 minutes, until the garlic is bubbling and just beginning to brown. Add the onion and sauté for about 4 minutes more, until softened. Add the cumin and coriander and sauté for about 1 minute more. Stir in the tomatoes and their liquid, roasted peppers, and water, using a wooden spoon to nudge loose any browned bits from the bottom of the pot.

3   Crack an egg into a small bowl, then pour it on top of the tomato mixture in the pot, taking care to place it closer to the center of the pot, so that the yolk is not touching the side of the pot. Repeat with the remaining eggs, spacing them as evenly apart as possible, in a single layer.

4   Place a tall steam rack in the pot, making sure its legs do not pierce the egg yolks and are resting firmly on the bottom of the pot. Place the bowl of couscous on the rack.

5   Secure the lid and set the Pressure Release to **Sealing**. Press the **Cancel** button to reset the cooking program, then select the **Pressure Cook** or **Manual** setting and set the cooking time for 0 (zero) minutes at low pressure. (The pot will take about 10 minutes to come up to pressure before the cooking program begins.)

6   When the cooking program ends, perform a quick pressure release by moving the Pressure Release to **Venting**. Open the pot and, wearing heat-resistant mitts, remove the bowl of couscous and the rack. Fluff the couscous with a fork.

7   Spoon the couscous into individual bowls, then spoon an egg and some of the sauce into each bowl and drizzle with olive oil. Serve immediately.

Salad bowls are a popular lunch in the Bay Area. At noontime, tech workers mob the fast-casual restaurants, dining on all-in-one bowls of whole grains, beans, and vegetables. This is my take. I use a mandoline or food processor to make quick work of shredding the vegetables while the chickpeas and rice cook in the Instant Pot. Tahini dressing ties everything together, its rich and tangy flavors contrasting with the warm spices in the chickpeas.

SPICED CHICKPEA RICE BOWLS WITH SHREDDED VEGGIES AND TAHINI DRESSING

1¼ cups dried chickpeas

4 cups water

1 teaspoon kosher salt

1½ cups long- or short-grain brown rice

1½ cups vegetable broth (page 284)

PREP	8-HOUR SOAK
COOK	50 MINUTES
PR	10 MINUTES NPR
SERVES	6

1 Combine the chickpeas, water, and salt in the Instant Pot. Leave the pot turned off and let the chickpeas soak for at least 8 hours or up to overnight.

2 Place a tall steam rack in the pot, making sure all of its legs are resting firmly on the bottom. In a 1½-quart stainless-steel bowl, stir together the rice and vegetable broth. Place the bowl on the rack. (The bowl should fit inside the pot and not touch the lid when the pot is closed.)

3 Secure the lid and set the Pressure Release to **Sealing**. Select the **Pressure Cook** or **Manual** setting and set the cooking time for 25 minutes at high pressure. (The pot will take about 20 minutes to come up to pressure before the cooking program begins.)

4 To make the tahini dressing: While the chickpeas and rice are cooking, in a widemouthed 1-pint jar, combine the tahini, water, lemon juice, garlic, salt, and cumin. Lower an immersion blender into the jar, so the head is fully submerged, then blend until smooth. (The dressing will thicken as it sits, so if you like a thinner dressing, blend in another 1 tablespoon water.)

5 Using a mandoline or a food processor fitted with a shredding disk, julienne or shred the carrots and broccoli. Set aside.

6 When the cooking program ends, let the pressure release naturally for 10 minutes, then move the Pressure Release to **Venting** to release any remaining steam. Open the pot and, wearing heat-resistant mitts, remove the bowl and rack from the pot. Fluff the rice with a fork. Lift out the inner pot and drain the chickpeas in a colander. Return the inner pot to the Instant Pot housing.

Tahini Dressing

½ cup tahini

⅓ cup water

3 tablespoons fresh lemon juice

1 garlic clove, peeled

½ teaspoon kosher salt

¼ teaspoon ground cumin

4 carrots, peeled

1 pound broccoli florets

2 tablespoons olive oil

2 teaspoons Middle Eastern spice blend (baharat or ras el hanout)

Kosher salt

1 tablespoon fresh lemon juice

½ cup chopped fresh flat-leaf parsley, plus fresh flat-leaf parsley leaves for sprinkling

½ cup chopped fresh mint, plus fresh mint leaves for sprinkling

7   Press the **Cancel** button to reset the cooking program, then select the **Sauté** setting and heat the olive oil. Add the drained chickpeas, the spice blend, and ½ teaspoon salt. Sauté for about 2 minutes, until the spices are fragrant, taking care not to mash the chickpeas. Press the **Cancel** button to turn off the pot, then remove the inner pot. Stir the lemon juice, chopped parsley, and chopped mint into the chickpeas.

8   Divide the rice, vegetables, and chickpeas evenly among six serving bowls. Drizzle 2 tablespoons of the dressing over each bowl, then sprinkle with parsley leaves and mint leaves. Serve warm.

Note: Individual servings freeze very well (without the dressing), stored in plastic freezer bags or other freezer-safe, tightly lidded containers. When you're ready to serve, transfer to a microwave-safe bowl, cover with a reusable silicone lid or plastic wrap, and heat in the microwave on high power for about 3 minutes. Uncover the bowl, taking care not to get burned by the steam, then drizzle with dressing. The vegetables will be tender and steamed rather than raw and crunchy.

Don't be afraid to venture beyond the green curry paste suggested here—any variety of Thai curry paste works well. The curry simmers under pressure, while the jasmine rice cooks in a bowl on top.

THAI GREEN CURRY TOFU WITH RICE

1½ cups water

1 cup jasmine rice, rinsed and drained

One 14-ounce block firm tofu, drained and cut into 1-inch thick slices

2 tablespoons coconut oil or neutral vegetable oil

3 shallots, quartered

¼ cup coconut cream

3 tablespoons Thai green curry paste

1 tablespoon coconut aminos or soy sauce (see Note)

½ cup coconut milk

6 ounces green beans, cut into 1-inch lengths

2 carrots, peeled and sliced ½-inch-thick rounds

PREP	5 MINUTES
COOK	40 MINUTES
PR	QPR
SERVES	4

Note: If you're not cooking for vegetarians or vegans, you can replace the coconut aminos with fish sauce.

1   In a 1½-quart stainless-steel bowl, combine 1 cup of the water and the rice. Set aside.

2   Place the sliced tofu between doubled layers of paper towels and press to remove excess moisture. Cut the tofu into 1-inch cubes.

3   In a nonstick skillet over medium-high heat, warm 1 tablespoon of the coconut oil. Add the tofu in a single layer, being careful not to get burned if the oil spatters. Sear for about 3 minutes, until lightly browned. Using a spatula, flip the pieces and sear for about 3 minutes more. Remove the skillet from the heat and set aside.

4   Select the **Sauté** setting on the Instant Pot and heat the remaining 1 tablespoon coconut oil. Add the shallots and sear for about 3 minutes, until beginning to brown. Stir in the coconut cream and curry paste and sauté for about 2 minutes, until bubbling and fragrant. Stir in the seared tofu, coconut aminos, and remaining ½ cup water, using a wooden spoon to nudge loose any browned bits from the bottom of the pot.

5   Place a tall steam rack in the pot, making sure all of its legs are resting firmly on the bottom. Place the bowl of rice on the rack.

6   Secure the lid and set the Pressure Release to **Sealing**. Press the **Cancel** button to reset the cooking program, then select the **Pressure Cook** or **Manual** setting and set the cooking time for 10 minutes at high pressure. (The pot will take about 10 minutes to come up to pressure before the cooking program begins.)

7   When the cooking program ends, perform a quick pressure release by moving the Pressure Release to **Venting**. Open the pot and, wearing heat-resistant mitts, remove the bowl of rice and the rack. Stir the coconut milk, green beans, and carrots into the pot.

8   **Cancel** the cooking program, then select the **Sauté** setting and set the cooking time for 10 minutes. Cook the curry uncovered, until the timer goes off. Wearing the heat-resistant mitts, lift out the inner pot. Fluff the rice with a fork, then stir the curry once more.

9   Spoon rice into bowls and ladle the curry over top.

This recipe is tailor-made for those times when the fridge is bare and the pantry is sparse. If you've got brown rice, dried black beans, and broth, you have the basis for these nutritious burrito bowls. The rice cooks in a bowl right on top of the beans, and the beans are ready at the same time. The recipe is vegan if you leave off the shredded cheese and sour cream. For extra vegan points, top with Chipotle Crema (see page 130).

BLACK BEAN BURRITO BOWLS

1½ cups long-grain brown rice

1½ cups water

1½ teaspoons kosher salt

2 tablespoons olive oil

2 garlic cloves, minced

1½ tablespoons chili powder

1 teaspoon dried oregano

½ teaspoon ground cumin

1 bay leaf

1¼ cups dried black beans

4 cups vegetable broth (page 284)

Shredded Mexican cheese blend, sour cream, shredded lettuce, sliced avocado, chopped white onion, chopped tomato, chopped fresh cilantro, and/or hot sauce (such as Cholula or Tapatío) for serving

PREP	5 MINUTES
COOK	50 MINUTES
PR	20 MINUTES NPR
SERVES	6

1   In a 1½-quart stainless-steel bowl, stir together the rice, water, and ½ teaspoon of the salt. Set aside.

2   Select the **Sauté** setting on the Instant Pot and heat the olive oil and garlic. Sauté for about 2 minutes, until the garlic is sizzling but not yet beginning to brown. Add the chili powder, oregano, cumin, bay leaf, and remaining 1 teaspoon salt and sauté for about 1 minute more. Add the black beans and vegetable broth and stir to combine.

3   Place a tall steam rack in the pot, making sure all of its legs are resting firmly on the bottom. Place the bowl of rice on the rack. (The bowl should fit inside the pot and not touch the lid when the pot is closed.)

4   Secure the lid and set the Pressure Release to **Sealing**. Press the **Cancel** button to reset the cooking program, then select the **Pressure Cook** or **Manual** setting and set the cooking time for 25 minutes at high pressure. (The pot will take about 20 minutes to come up to pressure before the cooking program begins.)

5   Let the pressure release naturally for 20 minutes, then move the Pressure Release to **Venting** to release any remaining steam. Open the pot and, wearing heat-resistant mitts, remove the bowl and rack from the pot. Fluff the rice with a fork.

6   Divide the rice among serving bowls. Using a slotted spoon, spoon the beans on top of the rice. Top with cheese, sour cream, lettuce, avocado, onion, tomato, and cilantro. Serve immediately, with hot sauce on the side.

This tofu scramble is packed with corn, tomatoes, and jalapeños, and it's seasoned with a Southwestern-inspired mixture of spices. The rice is cooked right on top of the tofu, making this a satisfying one-pot vegan meal.

SOUTHWESTERN SCRAMBLED TOFU WITH RICE

Rice

1½ cups long-grain white rice

1½ cups water

½ teaspoon kosher salt

Scrambled Tofu

2 tablespoons olive oil

3 garlic cloves, minced

1 yellow onion, diced

1 red, orange, or yellow bell pepper, seeded and diced

2 jalapeño chiles, seeded and diced

½ teaspoon kosher salt

1 tablespoon chili powder

1 teaspoon ground cumin

½ teaspoon freshly ground black pepper

½ teaspoon ground turmeric

½ teaspoon dried oregano

1 cup vegetable broth (page 284)

One 14-ounce block firm tofu, drained and crumbled

1 cup fresh, canned, or thawed frozen corn kernels

One 14½-ounce can diced tomatoes and their liquid

¼ cup nutritional yeast

Pitted, peeled, and sliced avocado; chopped fresh cilantro; and/or hot sauce (such as Cholula or Tapatío) for serving

PREP	5 MINUTES
COOK	40 MINUTES
PR	QPR
SERVES	4 TO 6

1   To make the rice: In a 1½-quart stainless-steel bowl, combine the rice, water, and salt. Set aside.

2   To make the scrambled tofu: Select the **Sauté** setting on the Instant Pot and heat the olive oil and garlic for about 2 minutes, until the garlic is bubbling. Add the onion, bell pepper, jalapeños, and salt. Sauté for about 4 minutes more, until the onion is softened. Add the chili powder, cumin, black pepper, turmeric, and oregano and sauté for 1 minute more. Stir in the vegetable broth, using a wooden spoon to nudge loose any browned bits from the bottom of the pot. Stir in the tofu and corn, then pour the tomatoes and their liquid on top. Do not stir.

3   Place a tall steam rack in the pot, making sure all of its legs are resting firmly on the bottom. Place the bowl of rice on the rack.

4   Secure the lid and set the Pressure Release to **Sealing**. Press the **Cancel** button to reset the cooking program, then select the **Pressure Cook** or **Manual** setting and set the cooking time for 10 minutes at high pressure. (The pot will take about 15 minutes to come up to pressure before the cooking program begins.)

5   When the cooking program ends, perform a quick pressure release by moving the Pressure Release to **Venting**. Open the pot and, wearing heat-resistant mitts, remove the bowl of rice and the rack. Fluff the rice with a fork. Add the nutritional yeast to the scrambled tofu and stir to combine. At this point, you can serve right away, or you can thicken the tofu.

6   To thicken, press the **Cancel** button to reset the cooking program, then select the **Sauté** setting. Bring the tofu mixture to a simmer and cook, stirring occasionally, for 8 to 10 minutes, until thickened. Press the **Cancel** button to turn off the pot.

7   Spoon the rice into serving bowls, then add the scrambled tofu and top with sliced avocado and cilantro. Serve immediately, with hot sauce on the side.

Browned bites of tender *paneer*, a mild Indian cheese, add texture and richness to a pot of braised spinach seasoned with garam masala. I buy my paneer at Costco, and it is also available in Indian grocery stores. (For a vegan version, or if you're not able to find paneer, substitute extra-firm tofu.) You'll brown the paneer (or tofu) in a nonstick skillet while the onions are cooking in the Instant Pot, which saves time and prevents a stuck-on mess in the pot. Make sure to use loosely packed, bagged frozen spinach rather than frozen spinach that comes boxed in a solid block; if boxed spinach is the only type available, thaw it before use.

PALAK PANEER

5 tablespoons avocado oil or other neutral oil with high smoke point

1 yellow onion, diced

1 pound paneer, pressed and dried between paper towels and cut into 1-inch cubes

1-inch knob fresh ginger, peeled and minced

3 garlic cloves, minced

½ teaspoon freshly ground black pepper

¼ teaspoon cayenne pepper

Kosher salt

One 16-ounce bag frozen chopped spinach

¼ cup water

One 14½-ounce can diced fire-roasted tomatoes and their liquid

¼ cup heavy cream or coconut milk

2 teaspoons garam masala

Cooked rice (page 51) for serving

Warmed naan for serving

PREP	0 MINUTES
COOK	30 MINUTES
PR	QPR
SERVES	4 TO 6

1   Select the high **Sauté** setting on the Instant Pot and heat 4 tablespoons of the avocado oil. Add the onion and sauté for about 10 minutes, until it begins to brown.

2   Meanwhile, warm the remaining 1 tablespoon oil in a nonstick skillet over medium-high heat. Add the paneer in an even layer, being careful not to get burned by the oil if it spatters. Sear for about 3 minutes, until golden brown, then use a thin, flexible spatula to turn the cubes. Sear for about 3 minutes more, until golden brown on the other side. Remove from the heat and set aside.

3   When the onions are ready, add the ginger and garlic and sauté for about 2 minutes, until the garlic is fragrant but not browned. Add the paneer, black pepper, cayenne, and 1 teaspoon salt and gently stir to combine, taking care not to break up the paneer. Gently stir in the frozen spinach. Pour the water and the tomatoes and their liquid over the top in an even layer but do not stir them in.

4   Secure the lid and set the Pressure Release to **Sealing**. Press the **Cancel** button to reset the cooking program, then select the **Pressure Cook** or **Manual** setting and set the cooking time for 5 minutes at high pressure. (The pot will take about 10 minutes to come up to pressure before the cooking program begins.)

5   When the cooking program ends, perform a quick pressure release by moving the Pressure Release to **Venting**. Open the pot and stir in the cream and garam masala. Taste for seasoning and add salt if needed.

6   Ladle the palak paneer onto serving plates or into bowls. Serve piping hot, with rice and naan.

Making tamales is a labor of love. There are many components to prepare, so they're perfect for entertaining kids in the kitchen on a leisurely afternoon. You'll soak dried corn husks and chiles, make salsa and masa dough from scratch, carefully fold up the tamales, then steam them in the Instant Pot. Unlike most large-batch tamale recipes, this one makes eight (enough to fill the Instant Pot), with enough sauce for a second batch.

MIXED VEGETABLE TAMALES

8 large dried corn husks (at least 6 inches across at the widest point)

6 cups boiling water

12 guajillo chiles, stemmed and seeded

Masa Dough

1½ cups masa for tamales

2 teaspoons baking powder

1 teaspoon kosher salt

1 cup warm water

½ cup vegetable shortening, melted

1 garlic clove, peeled

½ cup vegetable broth (page 284)

¾ teaspoon ground cumin

¾ teaspoon kosher salt

1 small Roma tomato, cored

1 medium zucchini, julienned

1 medium carrot, peeled and julienned

½ cup corn kernels (fresh or thawed frozen)

Lemon wedges or pico de gallo for serving

PREP	40 MINUTES
COOK	40 MINUTES
PR	20 MINUTES NPR
REST	15 MINUTES
MAKES	8 TAMALES

1   Place the corn husks in a large heatproof bowl, then pour in 4 cups of the boiling water. Cover with plastic wrap and set aside. Place the chiles in a second large heatproof bowl, pour in the remaining 2 cups boiling water, and let soak for about 20 minutes, until the chiles are softened.

2   To make the masa dough: While the chiles soak, in a medium bowl, combine the masa, baking powder, and salt and stir to mix. Add the warm water and melted shortening and stir until a smooth dough forms. Cover with plastic wrap and set aside.

3   Drain the chiles and add them to a blender, along with ¼ cup of the masa dough, the garlic, vegetable broth, cumin, salt, and tomato. Blend at high speed for about 30 seconds, until smooth.

4   In a bowl, combine the zucchini, carrot, and corn, then pour in half of the chile puree. Stir until the vegetables are evenly coated. (Freeze the remaining chile puree in an airtight container for up to 3 months.)

5   Drain the corn husks and stand them upright in their bowl so that the water continues to drain off of them.

6   Place a corn husk on your work surface with the rougher side facing up; the sides of the husk should curl inward. Scoop ¼ cup of the masa dough onto the wider end of the husk, then lay a plastic sandwich bag over the dough. Using a rolling pin or your hands, roll or pat the dough into a 5-inch square about ⅛ inch thick, rolling it all the way to the wide edge of the husk. Peel off the sandwich bag.

7   Spoon ¼ cup of the vegetables onto the middle of the masa square. Fold in one long side of the husk to cover the masa and filling, then fold in the other side of the husk. Fold up the bottom edge of the husk to form a tamale. Place the tamale, seam-side down, on a cutting board or plate. Repeat with the remaining corn husks, masa, and vegetables. Arrange the tamales, open ends up, in a wire-mesh steamer basket.

Note: Once the tamales are cooked, they can be cooled, transferred to freezer bags or freezer-safe containers, and then frozen for up to 3 months. To reheat them straight from the freezer, steam them in the Instant Pot for 15 minutes, using a natural pressure release.

Add 1½ cups water to the Instant Pot and place the steamer basket inside the pot.

8   Secure the lid and set the Pressure Release to **Sealing**. Select the **Steam** setting and set the cooking time for 25 minutes at high pressure. (The pot will take about 15 minutes to come up to pressure before the cooking program begins.)

9   Let the pressure release naturally for 20 minutes, then move the Pressure Release to **Venting** to release any remaining steam. Open the pot and, using tongs, transfer the cooked tamales to a serving platter. Wait about 15 minutes before unwrapping them; this prevents the dough from sticking to the husks.

10   Serve the tamales warm, with lemon wedges on the side.

This is one of my favorite dishes to prep on the weekend, because it sets me up with five lunches for the workweek. The secret star of this recipe is the vegan chipotle crema, which is good on just about anything. If you want to tone down the spiciness, substitute 1 tablespoon of sweet paprika for the chipotle.

SWEET POTATOES STUFFED WITH BLACK BEANS AND QUINOA

1 cup vegetable broth (page 284)

½ cup quinoa, rinsed and drained

½ teaspoon chili powder

¼ teaspoon dried oregano

¼ teaspoon kosher salt

1½ cups cooked black beans (page 44), or one 15-ounce can, rinsed and drained

5 sweet potatoes or yams, each about 2 inches diameter and 5 inches long (see Note)

Chipotle Crema

1 cup water

½ cup neutral vegetable oil

¼ cup apple cider vinegar

2 teaspoons soy sauce, tamari, or coconut aminos

½ cup raw slivered almonds or raw cashews

2 garlic cloves, peeled

1 chipotle chile in adobo sauce, or 1 tablespoon chipotle chile powder

3 tablespoons nutritional yeast

1½ teaspoons chili powder

½ teaspoon kosher salt

Chopped fresh cilantro for sprinkling

PREP	0 MINUTES
COOK	20 MINUTES
PR	10 MINUTES NPR
SERVES	5

1   Add the vegetable broth, quinoa, chili powder, oregano, and salt to the Instant Pot and stir to combine. Add the black beans in an even layer over the quinoa. Place a tall steam rack in the pot, making sure all of its legs are resting firmly on the bottom. Place the sweet potatoes in a single layer on the rack.

2   Secure the lid and set the Pressure Release to **Sealing**. Select the **Pressure Cook** or **Manual** setting and set the cooking time for 10 minutes at high pressure. (The pot will take about 10 minutes to come up to pressure before the cooking program begins.)

3   To make the chipotle crema: In a blender, combine the water, vegetable oil, vinegar, soy sauce, almonds, garlic, chipotle, nutritional yeast, chili powder, and salt. Blend on low speed for 1 minute, then increase to high speed and blend for about 1 minute more, until the mixture is smooth and creamy. Transfer to a 1-pint jar or other lidded container. (The chipotle crema will keep, refrigerated, for up to 5 days.)

4   When the cooking program ends, let the pressure release naturally for 10 minutes, then move the Pressure Release to **Venting** to release any remaining steam. Open the pot and, using tongs, transfer the sweet potatoes to serving plates. Wearing heat-resistant mitts, remove the rack. Stir the quinoa and beans to combine.

5   Using a fork, split each sweet potato down the middle. Evenly divide the quinoa–black bean mixture among each potato. Serve warm, topped with a dollop of the crema and sprinkled with chopped cilantro.

Note: The size of the sweet potatoes is important to the cooking time of this dish. If you use larger sweet potatoes, they will take longer to steam. Refer to page 302 for timing instructions, and steam larger sweet potatoes separately from the quinoa and black beans.

This comforting dish will please vegetarians and omnivores alike and can be served as a main dish or a side. Toasting the bread crumbs before sprinkling them onto the casserole adds a little extra crunch.

ZUCCHINI AND RICE CASSEROLE WITH CHEDDAR CHEESE AND BUTTERED BREAD CRUMBS

1 tablespoon olive oil

1 medium yellow onion, diced

2 garlic cloves, minced

1 teaspoon Italian seasoning

½ teaspoon kosher salt

½ teaspoon freshly ground black pepper

1 cup long-grain white rice

1 cup vegetable broth (page 284)

1 pound zucchini, halved lengthwise and cut crosswise into ¼-inch slices

1 cup tightly packed shredded sharp Cheddar cheese

Bread Crumb Topping

2 ounces crusty bread, cut into ½-inch cubes

1 tablespoon unsalted butter, melted

1 tablespoon fresh chopped flat-leaf parsley

PREP	0 MINUTES
COOK	20 MINUTES
PR	10 MINUTES NPR
SERVES	4 TO 6

1   Select the **Sauté** setting on the Instant Pot and heat the olive oil. Add the onion and garlic and sauté for about 3 minutes, until the onion begins to soften and the garlic is no longer raw. Add the Italian seasoning, salt, and pepper and sauté for 1 minute more. Add the rice and vegetable broth, then stir to combine. Scrape down any grains of rice stuck to the sides of the pot, making sure the rice is fully submerged in the cooking liquid. Scatter the zucchini slices in an even layer onto the rice.

2   Press the **Cancel** button to reset the cooking program, then select the **Pressure Cook** or **Manual** setting and set the cooking time for 3 minutes at high pressure. (The pot will take about 10 minutes to come up to pressure before the cooking program begins.)

3   To make the bread crumb topping: In a food processor or mini chopper, process the bread cubes for about 5 seconds, until they have formed rough bread crumbs; it's fine if a few bigger pieces still remain. Drizzle the butter evenly over the bread crumbs and then add the parsley. Process for five 1-second pulses, until the bread is coarsely ground. To toast, transfer to a medium skillet and cook over medium heat, stirring often, until golden brown, about 5 minutes. Transfer the toasted bread crumbs to a small bowl. Set aside.

4   When the cooking program ends, let the pressure release naturally for 10 minutes, then move the Pressure Release to **Venting** to release any remaining steam. Open the pot, then sprinkle the Cheddar evenly over the casserole and let the cheese melt for 2 minutes. Press the **Cancel** button to turn off the Instant Pot.

5   Scoop the casserole into bowls or onto plates, making sure to get all the way to the bottom so each serving gets a mixture of zucchini and rice. Sprinkle with the bread crumb topping and serve piping hot.

Note: The rice may brown a little bit on the bottom of the pot, which adds some nice flavor.

This delicious casserole can be served any time of day—for brunch, lunch, or dinner. It has all of the green chile and cheese flavors of traditional Mexican chiles rellenos but doesn't require any time-consuming stuffing and frying!

CHILE RELLENO CASSEROLE

¾ cup all-purpose flour

1½ teaspoons baking powder

3 eggs

¾ cup whole milk

Three 4-ounce cans diced fire-roasted green chiles, drained

3 ounces cotija cheese, coarsely grated

½ cup tightly packed shredded Mexican cheese blend or Monterey Jack

1 green onion, white and tender green parts, thinly sliced

Salsa Roja (page 289) or store-bought salsa for serving

PREP	10 MINUTES
COOK	40 MINUTES
PR	10 MINUTES NPR
REST	5 MINUTES
SERVES	4

1   Grease a 1½-quart soufflé dish or a 7-cup round heatproof glass container with butter or nonstick cooking spray, then set the dish on a long-handled silicone steam rack. Pour 1½ cups water into the Instant Pot.

2   In a medium bowl, whisk together the flour and baking powder. Add the eggs and milk and whisk until the dry ingredients are thoroughly incorporated. Stir in the chiles and cotija. Pour the batter mixture into the prepared dish and cover tightly with aluminum foil. Holding the handles of the steam rack, lower the dish into the Instant Pot.

3   Secure the lid and set the Pressure Release to **Sealing**. Select the **Pressure Cook** or **Manual** setting and set the cooking time for 30 minutes at high pressure. (The pot will take about 10 minutes to come up to pressure before the cooking program begins.)

4   When the cooking program ends, let the pressure release naturally for 10 minutes, then move the pressure release to **Venting** to release any remaining steam. Open the pot and, wearing heat-resistant mitts, grab the handles of the steam rack and lift the dish out of the pot. Uncover the dish, taking care not to get burned by the steam. Sprinkle the cheese on top, then let stand for about 5 minutes, until the cheese melts.

5   Cut the casserole into wedges and sprinkle with the green onion. Serve immediately with salsa roja on the side.

Lentils and mushrooms make this vegan Bolognese sauce as hearty and flavorful as the traditional meat-rich version. You can serve it over polenta instead of over pasta, or use it in Mini Lasagna Bolognese (page 218). This recipe makes about 7 cups of sauce.

VEGAN PASTA BOLOGNESE

4 tablespoons olive oil

3 garlic cloves, diced

1 yellow onion, diced

1 celery stalk, diced

1 carrot, peeled and diced

8 ounces button or cremini mushrooms, diced

Kosher salt

1 tablespoon Italian seasoning

½ teaspoon red pepper flakes

⅓ cup small green lentils, Puy lentils, or beluga lentils

1 cup vegetable broth (page 284)

1 bay leaf

One 28-ounce can fire-roasted whole tomatoes and their liquid

¼ cup chopped fresh flat-leaf parsley

Cooked pasta for serving

"Parmesan" (see page 136) for sprinkling

PREP	0 MINUTES
COOK	40 MINUTES
PR	15 MINUTES NPR
SERVES	6

1　Select the **Sauté** setting on the Instant Pot and heat 3 tablespoons of the olive oil and the garlic for about 2 minutes, until the garlic is bubbling. Add the onion, celery, carrot, mushrooms, and 1 teaspoon salt and sauté for about 5 minutes, until the onion is softened and the mushrooms begin to give up their liquid. Add the Italian seasoning and red pepper flakes and sauté for about 1 minute more. Stir in the lentils, vegetable broth, and bay leaf, then pour the tomatoes and their liquid on top. Do not stir.

2　Secure the lid and set the Pressure Release to **Sealing**. Press the **Cancel** button to reset the cooking program, then select the **Pressure Cook** or **Manual** setting and set the cooking time for 20 minutes at high pressure. (The pot will take about 10 minutes to come up to pressure before the cooking program begins.)

3　When the cooking program ends, let the pressure release naturally for 15 minutes, then move the Pressure Release to **Venting** to release any remaining steam. Open the pot and remove and discard the bay leaf. The sauce will look a bit watery when you open the pot, but it will thicken up as it cools over the next few minutes. Stir in the parsley and remaining 1 tablespoon oil. Using a wooden spoon, mash the tomatoes against the side of the pot until broken down into small pieces and incorporated into the sauce. Taste and adjust the seasoning with salt if needed.

4　Spoon the Bolognese over cooked pasta and sprinkle with "Parmesan." Serve immediately.

This is a hearty, flavorful rice dish with tender chunks of eggplant cooked in a bowl on top. Salting and rinsing the eggplant before cooking helps it cook up super-silky and tender, but you can skip those steps if you're short on time.

SMOKY VEGAN EGGPLANT JAMBALAYA

One 1- to 1¼-pound eggplant, peeled and cut into ¾-inch cubes

2 teaspoons kosher salt

3 tablespoons olive oil

2 garlic cloves, minced

1 yellow onion, diced

1 celery stalk, diced

1 red, orange, or yellow bell pepper, seeded and cut into ¼ by 1-inch strips

1½ teaspoons smoked paprika

½ teaspoon dried oregano

½ teaspoon freshly ground black pepper

¼ teaspoon cayenne pepper

2 cups vegetable broth (page 284)

1½ cups long-grain rice, rinsed and drained

Hot sauce (such as Crystal or Tabasco) for serving

PREP	0 MINUTES
COOK	35 MINUTES
PR	10 MINUTES NPR
SERVES	4

1   Put the eggplant in a bowl, sprinkle with 1½ teaspoons of the salt, and toss to coat. Let stand for about 30 minutes. Rinse the eggplant in a colander and pat it dry between paper towels, gently pressing the pieces to remove excess water. Transfer the eggplant to a 1½-quart stainless-steel bowl, drizzle with 1 tablespoon of the olive oil, and toss to coat.

2   Select the **Sauté** setting on the Instant Pot and heat the remaining 2 tablespoons oil and the garlic for about 3 minutes, until the garlic is bubbling and just beginning to brown. Add the onion, celery, and bell pepper and sauté for 4 minutes, until the onion begins to soften. Add the paprika, oregano, black pepper, cayenne, and remaining ½ teaspoon salt and sauté for about 1 minute more. Stir in the vegetable broth, using a wooden spoon to nudge loose any browned bits from the bottom of the pot. Add the rice and stir, making sure all the grains are submerged in the liquid.

3   Place a tall steam rack in the pot, making sure all of its legs are resting firmly on the bottom. Place the bowl of eggplant on the rack. (The bowl should fit inside the pot and not touch the lid when the pot is closed.)

4   Secure the lid and set the Pressure Release to **Sealing**. Select the **Pressure Cook** or **Manual** setting and set the cooking time for 15 minutes at low pressure. (The pot will take about 10 minutes to come up to pressure before the cooking program begins.)

5   When the cooking program ends, let the pressure release naturally for 10 minutes, then move the Pressure Release to **Venting** to release any remaining steam. Open the pot and, wearing heat-resistant mitts, remove the bowl of eggplant and the rack. Pour off the excess moisture from the eggplant. Add the eggplant to the pot, gently folding it into the rice mixture.

6   Spoon the jambalaya into bowls and serve immediately, with hot sauce.

Spaghetti squash is a healthful low-carb substitute for pasta, and it's the star ingredient in this casserole. The squash steams in less than half an hour in the Instant Pot—that's about twice as fast as cooking it in the oven. The tender pasta-like strands of squash are layered with garlic-sautéed vegetables, marinara sauce, and homemade vegan "cheese," then the lasagna is baked in the oven until hot and bubbling. It'll please vegans, vegetarians, and omnivores alike.

VEGAN SPAGHETTI SQUASH LASAGNA

One 3- to 3½-pound spaghetti squash

Vegetable Filling

2 tablespoons olive oil

2 garlic cloves, minced

8 ounces cremini or button mushrooms, sliced

½ teaspoon kosher salt

One 5- to 6-ounce bag baby spinach

"Parmesan"

1 cup raw cashews

¼ cup nutritional yeast

1 teaspoon garlic powder

1 teaspoon kosher salt

PREP	15 MINUTES
COOK	1 HOUR, 30 MINUTES
PR	QPR
SERVES	6 TO 8

1   Pour 1½ cups water into the Instant Pot and place the wire metal steam rack in the pot. Trim off the stem end of the squash, cut the squash lengthwise into quarters, and scoop out and discard the seeds. Place the squash quarters on the steam rack in the pot, arranging the pieces so they fit in a single layer.

2   Secure the lid and set the Pressure Release to **Sealing**. Select the **Steam** setting and set the cooking time for 7 minutes at high pressure. (The pot will take about 20 minutes to come up to pressure before the cooking program begins.)

3   When the cooking program ends, perform a quick pressure release by moving the Pressure Release to **Venting**. Open the pot and, wearing heat-resistant mitts, grab the handles of the steam rack and transfer the squash to a plate or cutting board. Still wearing the mitts, lift out the inner pot and discard the water. Return the inner pot to the housing. Let the squash cool enough to handle, about 10 minutes, then use a fork to separate the strands of spaghetti squash and loosen them from the skin of the squash.

4   To make the vegetable filling: Select the **Sauté** setting on the Instant Pot and heat the olive oil and garlic for about 2 minutes, until the garlic is bubbling. Add the mushrooms and salt and sauté for about 7 minutes, until the mushrooms are softened and just beginning to brown. Press the **Cancel** button to turn off the pot. Add the spinach and stir for about 1 minute, until the leaves are wilted.

5   To make the "Parmesan": In a food processor, combine the cashews, nutritional yeast, garlic powder, and salt. Process for about ten 1-second pulses, until the mixture resembles grated Parmesan cheese. Transfer to a bowl and set aside. Do not wash the food processor bowl and blade.

"Ricotta"

One 14-ounce block firm tofu, drained

¼ cup raw cashews

3 tablespoons nutritional yeast

3 tablespoons olive oil

1 teaspoon finely grated lemon zest, plus 2 tablespoons fresh lemon juice

1 teaspoon Italian seasoning

1 teaspoon dried basil

1 teaspoon garlic powder

1 teaspoon kosher salt

½ teaspoon freshly ground black pepper

2 cups Marinara Sauce (page 287) or your favorite jarred pasta sauce

6   To make the "ricotta": Cut the tofu into ½-inch-thick planks. Place the planks between doubled layers of paper towels and gently press to remove excess moisture. Add the tofu to the food processor along with the cashews, nutritional yeast, olive oil, lemon zest, lemon juice, Italian seasoning, basil, garlic powder, salt, and pepper and process for ten 1-second pulses, until no large cashew chunks remain, scraping down the sides of the bowl as needed. Transfer to a bowl and set aside.

7   Preheat the oven to 350°F.

8   Spread ½ cup of the marinara in an even layer in the bottom of a 9- by 13-inch baking dish. Scatter one-third of the spaghetti squash in an even layer on the sauce, then top with one-third of the vegetable filling. In small spoonfuls, dollop one-third of the "ricotta" evenly over the vegetables, then sprinkle on ¼ cup of the "Parmesan." Repeat these layers another two times using the remaining marinara, squash, vegetable filling, "ricotta," and "Parmesan." You will have some "Parmesan" left over; reserve it for serving.

9   Bake the lasagna, uncovered, until the sauce is bubbling and the "cheese" is lightly browned, about 30 minutes. Remove the lasagna from the oven and let cool for about 10 minutes.

10   Cut the lasagna into serving pieces and transfer to individual plates, leaving any excess liquid in the baking dish. Serve immediately, with the reserved "Parmesan" on the side.

5

Seafood

Seafood stew is often one of the pricier items on restaurant menus, but it's actually very easy and fairly economical to make at home. Served at Italian American restaurants up and down the wharf in San Francisco, cioppino is a hearty tomato-based soup filled with fish, shellfish, and calamari. To make my own, I buy bagged frozen seafood at Trader Joe's or Costco and thaw it overnight in the fridge before cooking, but you can use fresh, peeled, and deveined medium shrimp; calamari rings; bay scallops; and cod fillets, cut into 2-inch pieces, if you like.

CIOPPINO

2 tablespoons olive oil, plus more for drizzling

1 medium fennel bulb, quartered, cored, and thinly sliced

2 garlic cloves, chopped

2 shallots, chopped

½ teaspoon kosher salt

1 teaspoon dried oregano

½ teaspoon red pepper flakes

1 bay leaf

1 cup dry white wine

One 28-ounce can whole peeled tomatoes and their liquid

1 pound frozen seafood blend, thawed

1 pound frozen cod pieces, thawed

Chopped fresh flat-leaf parsley or fennel fronds for sprinkling

Warmed sourdough bread for serving

PREP	0 MINUTES
COOK	25 MINUTES
PR	QPR
SERVES	4 TO 6

1   Select the **Sauté** setting on the Instant Pot and heat the olive oil. Add the fennel, garlic, shallots, and salt and sauté for about 5 minutes, until the fennel begins to soften. Add the oregano, red pepper flakes, bay leaf, and wine. Bring to a simmer and cook for about 3 minutes, then stir in the tomatoes and their liquid, breaking them up a little with a spoon. Bring to a simmer, then stir in the seafood blend and cod.

2   Secure the lid and set the Pressure Release to **Sealing**. Press the **Cancel** button to reset the cooking program, then select the **Pressure Cook** or **Manual** program and set the cooking time for 0 (zero) minutes at low pressure. (The pot will take about 15 minutes to come up to pressure before the cooking program begins.)

3   When the cooking program ends, perform a quick pressure release by moving the Pressure Release to **Venting**. Open the pot and ladle the cioppino into bowls.

4   Drizzle the cioppino with olive oil and sprinkle with parsley. Serve piping hot, with slices of sourdough bread alongside.

You can steam potatoes, green beans, and eggs all at the same time in the Instant Pot! Make the vinaigrette as the ingredients cook, then compose the elements while the green beans and eggs chill in their ice bath. In no time, you've got a classic French salad that's a generous meal on its own. Store any leftover vinaigrette in the refrigerator in a sealed jar for up to 1 week; bring it to room temperature before using it as a dressing or marinade.

SALADE NIÇOISE WITH OIL-PACKED TUNA

8 ounces red potatoes, quartered

6 ounces green beans, trimmed

2 eggs

Vinaigrette

¼ cup extra-virgin olive oil

¼ cup neutral vegetable oil

¼ cup white wine vinegar

2 tablespoons water

2 teaspoons Dijon mustard

1½ teaspoons sugar

½ teaspoon dried tarragon or oregano

½ teaspoon kosher salt

½ small shallot, minced

1 head romaine or butter lettuce, torn into bite-sized pieces

¾ cup grape or cherry tomatoes, halved

¼ cup pitted Niçoise olives

One 7-ounce can oil-packed tuna, drained and flaked

Freshly ground black pepper

Chopped fresh flat-leaf parsley for sprinkling

PREP	0 MINUTES
COOK	25 MINUTES
PR	QPR
SERVES	2

1   Add 1 cup water to the Instant Pot and place a steamer basket in the pot. Add the potatoes, green beans, and eggs to the basket.

2   Secure the lid and set the Pressure Release to **Sealing**. Select the **Steam** setting and set the cooking time for 3 minutes at high pressure. (The pot will take about 15 minutes to come up to pressure before the cooking program begins.)

3   To make the vinaigrette: While the vegetables and eggs are steaming, in a widemouthed 1-pint jar, combine the olive oil, grapeseed oil, vinegar, water, mustard, sugar, tarragon, and salt. Lower an immersion blender into the jar, so the head is fully submerged. Blend until an emulsified vinaigrette forms, about 10 seconds. Stir in the shallot and set aside.

4   Prepare an ice bath.

5   When the cooking program ends, perform a quick release by moving the Pressure Release to **Venting**. Open the pot and, wearing heat-resistant mitts, lift out the steamer basket. Using tongs, transfer the eggs and green beans to the ice bath.

6   While the eggs and green beans are cooling, evenly divide the lettuce, tomatoes, olives, and tuna among two shallow serving bowls.

7   Drain the eggs and green beans. Peel and halve the eggs, then arrange them on the salads, along with the green beans and potatoes.

8   Spoon the vinaigrette over the salads, adding as much as you like, then sprinkle with pepper and parsley. Serve immediately.

Believe it or not, this recipe works best with shrimp straight from the freezer! For best results, use EZ-peel large shrimp (31 to 40 per pound). They cook up juicier and retain a firm yet tender texture, and, as the name implies, they're very easy to peel after cooking. Leave the tails on for a nice presentation, and serve the shrimp with a simple homemade cocktail sauce as an appetizer or first course. Both the shrimp and cocktail sauce can be refrigerated in separate airtight containers for up to 24 hours.

SHRIMP COCKTAIL

1 pound frozen large (31/40 size) EZ-peel shrimp

2 cups water

1½ teaspoons kosher salt

Cocktail Sauce

¼ cup ketchup

2 teaspoons prepared horseradish

½ teaspoon hot sauce such as Tabasco or Crystal

¼ teaspoon Worcestershire sauce

Lemon wedges for serving

PREP	0 MINUTES
COOK	20 MINUTES
PR	10 MINUTES NPR
SERVES	4

1   Add the shrimp to the Instant Pot, arranging them in as even a layer as possible. Pour in the water and sprinkle the salt evenly over the top.

2   Secure the lid and set the Pressure Release to **Sealing**. Select the **Steam** setting and set the cooking time for 0 (zero) minutes at low pressure. (The pot will take about 15 minutes to come up to pressure before the cooking program begins.)

3   To make the cocktail sauce: While the shrimp are cooking, in a small bowl, stir together the ketchup, horseradish, hot sauce, and Worcestershire. Set aside.

4   Prepare an ice bath and place a colander in the sink.

5   When the cooking program ends, let the pressure release naturally for 10 minutes, then move the Pressure Release to **Venting** to release any remaining steam. Open the pot and, wearing heat-resistant mitts, lift out the inner pot. Drain the shrimp in the colander, then transfer them to the ice bath. Let cool for 5 minutes and drain again. Peel the shrimp, leaving the tails on.

6   Arrange the shrimp on a serving plate, with the lemon wedges and cocktail sauce on the side.

With the Instant Pot, shrimp scampi with garlicky pasta doesn't take much time or effort—or even planning (the shrimp don't need to be thawed)—to put together. It's a kid-pleasing, one-pot, freezer-to-table meal.

SHRIMP SCAMPI WITH PENNE PASTA

1 pound frozen large (31/40 size) EZ-peel shrimp

4 cups water

Kosher salt

2 tablespoons unsalted butter

2 tablespoons olive oil

4 garlic cloves, minced

1 shallot, minced

½ teaspoon freshly ground black pepper

¼ cup dry white wine

8 ounces penne pasta

1 tablespoon fresh lemon juice

2 tablespoons chopped fresh flat-leaf parsley or basil

PREP	0 MINUTES
COOK	30 MINUTES
PR	15 MINUTES NPR
SERVES	4

1   Add the shrimp to the Instant Pot, arranging them in as even a layer as possible. Pour in 2 cups of the water and sprinkle 1 teaspoon salt evenly over the top.

2   Secure the lid and set the Pressure Release to **Sealing**. Select the **Steam** setting and set the cooking time for 0 (zero) minutes at low pressure. (The pot will take about 15 minutes to come up to pressure before the cooking program begins.)

3   Prepare an ice bath and place a colander in the sink.

4   When the cooking program ends, let the pressure release naturally for 10 minutes, then move the Pressure Release to **Venting** to release any remaining steam. Open the pot and, wearing heat-resistant mitts, lift out the inner pot. Drain the shrimp in the colander, then return the inner pot to the housing. Transfer the shrimp to the ice bath to cool.

5   Press the **Cancel** button on the Instant Pot to reset the cooking program, then select the **Sauté** setting. Add the butter, olive oil, garlic, shallot, pepper, and 1 teaspoon salt and sauté for about 2 minutes, until the butter is melted and the garlic loses its raw aroma. Add the wine and cook for about 3 minutes more. Stir in the pasta and remaining 2 cups water, nudging down any pasta that's sticking up way above the liquid; it's fine if a few pieces stick out a little bit.

6   Secure the lid and set the Pressure Release to **Sealing**. Press the **Cancel** button to reset the cooking program, then select the **Pressure Cook** or **Manual** setting and set the cooking time for 5 minutes at high pressure. (The pot will take about 5 minutes to come up to pressure before the cooking program begins.)

7   While the pasta is cooking, drain the shrimp, then peel them, removing the tails.

8   When the cooking program ends, let the pressure release naturally for 5 minutes, then move the Pressure Release to **Venting** to release any remaining steam. Open the pot and stir in the shrimp, lemon juice, and parsley. Taste and adjust the seasoning with salt if needed.

9   Spoon into bowls and serve immediately.

It's likely that most of the ingredients for this 30-minute pasta dinner are already in your pantry. I like to use canned whole baby clams, but the chopped kind work well, too. The pasta and sauce cook together in the Instant Pot, so there's no need to boil a pot of water.

LINGUINE WITH CLAM SAUCE

3 tablespoons extra-virgin olive oil

2 garlic cloves, minced

½ cup dry white wine

1½ teaspoons Italian seasoning

¼ teaspoon red pepper flakes

1 teaspoon kosher salt

½ teaspoon freshly ground black pepper

½ pound linguine, broken in half

1 cup water

One 10-ounce can baby clams with their juice

1 tablespoon chopped fresh flat-leaf parsley

PREP	0 MINUTES
COOK	20 MINUTES
PR	5 MINUTES NPR
SERVES	4 AS A STARTER, 2 AS A MAIN DISH

1   Select the **Sauté** setting on the Instant Pot and heat the olive oil and garlic. Sauté for about 3 minutes, until the garlic is sizzling and beginning to brown. Stir in the wine, Italian seasoning, red pepper flakes, salt, and pepper. Cook for about 3 minutes, until the aroma of the wine has cooked off. Then, add the linguine in an even layer, keeping the noodles pointing in the same direction so they don't poke up. Add the water and canned clams with their juice.

2   Secure the lid and set the Pressure Release to **Sealing**. Press the **Cancel** button to reset the cooking program, then select the **Pressure Cook** or **Manual** setting and set the cooking time for 5 minutes at high pressure. (The pot will take about 10 minutes to come up to pressure before the cooking program begins.)

3   When the program ends, let the pressure release naturally for 5 minutes, then move the Pressure Release to **Venting** to release any remaining steam. Open the pot and stir, breaking up any clumps of pasta. The sauce may appear too watery at first, but the pasta will absorb some of it within a minute or so.

4   Spoon the pasta into bowls and sprinkle with the parsley. Serve piping hot.

Steam a few lobster tails in the Instant Pot for the easiest lobster rolls ever. This Californian fully approves of using whatever type of hot dog rolls are available—West Coast supermarkets don't usually have the top-split kind used in New England. For maximum deliciousness, I make homemade mayo to toss with the cooked lobster meat.

LOBSTER ROLLS

Four 4- to 5-ounce lobster tails, fresh or thawed frozen

2 tablespoons mayonnaise

⅛ teaspoon kosher salt

⅛ teaspoon freshly ground black pepper

¼ cup minced celery

2 green onions, tender green parts only, thinly sliced

4 hot dog buns

2 tablespoons unsalted butter, at room temperature

PREP	5 MINUTES
COOK	25 MINUTES
PR	QPR
SERVES	4

1   Pour 1½ cups water into the Instant Pot and place the wire metal steam rack in the pot.

2   Using a pair of kitchen shears, cut open the top side of each lobster shell along its length. Gently pry apart the shell, then pull the meat up and out of the shell so that it can rest propped up on top of the shell. Place the lobster tails in a single layer on the steam rack.

3   Secure the lid and set the Pressure Release to **Sealing**. Select the **Steam** setting and set the cooking time for 3 minutes at low pressure. (The pot will take about 10 minutes to come up to pressure before the cooking program begins.)

4   While the lobster tails are cooking, prepare an ice bath.

5   When the cooking program ends, perform a quick pressure release by moving the Pressure Release to **Venting**. Open the pot and, using tongs, transfer the lobster tails to the ice bath. Let cool for 5 minutes.

6   Remove the lobster tails from the ice bath. Pull the meat out of the shells and discard the shells. Pat the meat dry with paper towels, then cut it into ½-inch pieces.

7   In a medium bowl, combine the lobster meat with the mayonnaise, salt, pepper, celery, and green onions and toss to mix.

8   Spread the inside of the hot dog buns with the butter and toast in a toaster oven on its light setting for about 2 minutes, until light golden brown.

9   Spoon the lobster mixture into the buns. Serve immediately.

Poaching fish is one of the trickiest things to do in a pressure cooker, because fish is so delicate and easily overcooks. In this recipe, much of the cooking takes place as the pot is coming up to pressure and also during the 10-minute pressure release after the cooking program ends. What results is a pair of flaky, tender, and flavorful salmon fillets. The garlicky aioli comes together in seconds with an immersion blender while the fish is cooking. Swap out the chopped tarragon for basil, if you like.

POACHED SALMON WITH TARRAGON AIOLI

Salmon

1 cup water

½ cup dry white wine

1 shallot, sliced

Four ½-inch-thick lemon slices

1 bay leaf

1 teaspoon kosher salt

Two 8-ounce salmon fillets

1½ teaspoons herbes de Provence

Tarragon Aioli

½ cup grapeseed oil or other light, neutral oil

1 egg yolk

1 small garlic clove, minced

2 tablespoons white wine vinegar

1 teaspoon Dijon mustard

1 teaspoon sugar

½ teaspoon kosher salt

¼ teaspoon freshly ground black pepper

1 tablespoon fresh chopped tarragon

Lemon wedges for serving

1   To prepare the salmon: Add the water, wine, shallot, lemon slices, bay leaf, and salt to the Instant Pot. Place the salmon fillets, skin-side down, in the pot and sprinkle the herbes de Provence over the fillets and the cooking liquid.

2   Secure the lid and set the Pressure Release to **Sealing**. Select the **Pressure Cook** or **Manual** setting and set the cooking time for 2 minutes at low pressure. (The pot will take about 10 minutes to come up to pressure before the cooking program begins.)

3   To make the tarragon aioli: While the fish is cooking, in a wide-mouthed 1-pint jar, combine the grapeseed oil, egg yolk, garlic, vinegar, mustard, sugar, salt, and pepper. Lower an immersion blender into the jar so the head is fully submerged. Using ½-second pulses, blend until an emulsified aioli forms, raising the blender head by ¼ inch or so after each pulse. By the time the blender head is at the top of the ingredients, the aioli should be fully emulsified, with all of the oil incorporated. Unplug the blender, then scrape any excess aioli off the blender into the jar. Stir in the tarragon and set aside. (The aioli will keep in an airtight container, refrigerated, for up to 1 week.)

4   When the cooking program ends, let the pressure release naturally for 10 minutes, then move the Pressure Release to **Venting** to release any remaining steam. Open the pot and use a fish spatula to transfer the salmon fillets to a plate. Remove and discard the lemon slices.

5   Serve the salmon with the aioli and lemon wedges on the side.

PREP	5 MINUTES
COOK	15 MINUTES
PR	10 MINUTES NPR
SERVES	2

In this Asian-inspired take on poached fish, ginger and green onions flavor the sake-spiked poaching liquid, and the sea bass comes out tender and moist. Serve the fillets with steamed rice and vegetables.

SAKE-POACHED SEA BASS WITH GINGER AND GREEN ONIONS

1 cup water

½ cup sake

2 tablespoons soy sauce

1 tablespoon sugar

1 teaspoon kosher salt

2 green onions, white and tender green parts, thinly sliced, plus 1 green onion, tender green part only, thinly sliced

1-inch knob fresh ginger, cut into 6 slices

Two 8-ounce sea bass fillets

Soy sauce for drizzling

Lemon wedges for serving

Steamed rice (page 51) for serving

PREP	5 MINUTES
COOK	15 MINUTES
PR	10 MINUTES NPR
SERVES	2

1   Add the water, sake, soy sauce, sugar, salt, 2 green onions, and ginger to the Instant Pot and stir to combine. Place the sea bass fillets, skin-side down, in the pot, spooning some of the poaching liquid over each fillet.

2   Secure the lid and set the Pressure Release to **Sealing**. Select the **Pressure Cook** or **Manual** setting and set the cooking time for 2 minutes at low pressure. (The pot will take about 10 minutes to come up to pressure before the cooking program begins.)

3   When the cooking program ends, let the pressure release naturally for 10 minutes, then move the Pressure Release to **Venting** to release any remaining steam. (The float valve may go down before the 10 minutes are up. If this happens, you should still wait the full 10 minutes before opening the pot.) Open the pot and use a fish spatula to transfer the fillets to serving plates.

4   Drizzle the fish with soy sauce and sprinkle with the remaining green onion. Serve right away with lemon wedges and steamed rice.

Fresh and frozen fish fillets poach equally well in the Instant Pot, so this recipe is a great option for those times when you've forgotten to defrost something else for dinner. This recipe includes a quick lemon-dill sauce made on the stove top while the fish poaches under pressure. For an even easier meal, you can skip the sauce and serve the fish with lemon wedges and store-bought tartar sauce instead. Complete the meal with some microwaved steamed vegetables and rice.

COD FILLETS WITH LEMON-DILL SAUCE

1 cup water

½ cup dry white wine

1 tablespoon white wine vinegar

1 shallot, thinly sliced

4 sprigs dill

1 teaspoon kosher salt

1 pound fresh or frozen cod fillets

Lemon-Dill Sauce

1 tablespoon fresh lemon juice

2 teaspoons Dijon mustard

½ teaspoon cornstarch

2 tablespoons unsalted butter

2 garlic cloves, minced

¼ cup white wine

¼ cup heavy cream

Kosher salt

¼ teaspoon freshly ground black pepper

1 tablespoon chopped fresh dill

PREP	5 MINUTES
COOK	15 MINUTES
PR	10 MINUTES NPR
SERVES	2 OR 3

1   Add the water, wine, vinegar, shallot, dill, and salt to the Instant Pot and stir to combine. Place the cod fillets in the pot in a single layer, then spoon some of the liquid over them.

2   Secure the lid and set the Pressure Release to **Sealing**. Select the **Pressure Cook** or **Manual** setting and set the cooking time for 2 minutes for fresh fillets or 5 minutes for frozen fillets. (The pot will take about 10 minutes to come up to pressure before the cooking program begins.)

3   To make the sauce: While the fish is cooking, in a small bowl, stir together the lemon juice, mustard, and cornstarch. Set aside. In a small saucepan over medium heat, melt the butter. Add the garlic and cook, stirring occasionally, for about 2 minutes, until the garlic begins to bubble and turn light blond. Add the wine, bring to a simmer, and cook for about 3 minutes, until it no longer smells like raw alcohol. Stir the lemon juice mixture to recombine, then add it to the saucepan, along with the cream, ½ teaspoon salt, and pepper. Bring to a simmer, whisking constantly, and cook until thickened, about 1 minute. Remove from the heat and stir in the dill. Taste and adjust the seasoning with salt if needed. Set aside.

4   When the cooking program ends, let the pressure release naturally for 10 minutes (don't open the pot before the 10 minutes are up, even if the float valve has gone down). Open the pot and use a fish spatula to gently transfer the fillets to serving plates.

5   Spoon the lemon-dill sauce over the fish and serve immediately.

Vegetables and fish fillets simmer in a Filipino-inspired, gingery, garlic-packed sweet-and-sour sauce. It's a lighter and simpler take on the traditional preparation of *escabeche*, in which a whole fish is fried in oil. Serve with cooked rice (page 51) or Crispy Smashed Potatoes (page 262).

TILAPIA IN ESCABECHE SAUCE

¼ cup water, plus 1 tablespoon (if thickening the sauce)

¼ cup cider vinegar

2 tablespoons soy sauce

2 tablespoons neutral vegetable oil

3 garlic cloves, minced

1-inch knob fresh ginger, peeled and minced

1 small yellow onion, thinly sliced

¼ cup firmly packed brown sugar

½ teaspoon kosher salt

½ teaspoon freshly ground black pepper

1 pound tilapia fillets

1 carrot, peeled and sliced ¼ inch thick on the diagonal

1 red, orange, or yellow bell pepper, seeded and cut into ¼-inch strips

1 tablespoon cornstarch (optional, for thickening the sauce)

PREP	5 MINUTES
COOK	20 MINUTES
PR	10 MINUTES NPR
SERVES	2 OR 3

1   In a small bowl, stir together the ¼ cup water, vinegar, and soy sauce. Set aside.

2   Select the **Sauté** setting on the Instant Pot and heat the vegetable oil, garlic, and ginger. Sauté for about 2 minutes, until bubbling. Add the onion and sauté for about 3 minutes more, until the onion is beginning to soften.

3   Add the vinegar mixture, brown sugar, salt, and pepper to the pot, using a wooden spoon to nudge loose any browned bits from the bottom of the pot. Using tongs, add the fish fillets to the pot in a single layer; it's fine if they overlap slightly. Spoon some of the liquid over the fillets, then sprinkle the carrot and bell pepper on top.

4   Secure the lid and set the Pressure Release to **Sealing**. Press the **Cancel** button to reset the cooking program, then select the **Pressure Cook** or **Manual** setting and set the cooking time for 2 minutes at low pressure. (The pot will take about 10 minutes to come up to pressure before the cooking program begins.)

5   When the cooking program ends, let the pressure release naturally for 10 minutes (don't open the pot before the 10 minutes are up, even if the float valve has gone down). Open the pot and use a fish spatula to transfer the fillets to serving plates. You can either ladle the sauce over the fish right away or thicken the sauce.

6   To thicken the sauce, in a small bowl, stir together the cornstarch and remaining 1 tablespoon water. Stir this mixture into the cooking liquid. Press the **Cancel** button to reset the cooking program, then select the **Sauté** setting and set the cooking time for 2 minutes. Cook, stirring constantly, until the sauce thickens. Press the **Cancel** button to turn off the pot.

7   Ladle the sauce and vegetables over the fish and serve right away.

6

Poultry

These chicken wings pressure-cook to tenderness in a tangy-sweet mustard sauce, which turns into a sticky-sweet glaze after a quick trip under the broiler. The wings take about half the time of most oven-baked versions, so they're great for a last-minute appetizer.

HONEY-MUSTARD CHICKEN WINGS

1 tablespoon neutral vegetable oil

2 garlic cloves, minced

¼ cup water

¼ cup prepared yellow mustard

3 tablespoons honey

2 tablespoons cider vinegar

½ teaspoon kosher salt

½ teaspoon freshly ground black pepper

About 2 pounds chicken wing drumettes and flats

1 green onion, thinly sliced

PREP	0 MINUTES
COOK	35 MINUTES
PR	QPR
SERVES	4

1   Select the **Sauté** setting on the Instant Pot and heat the vegetable oil and garlic for about 2 minutes, just until the garlic begins to bubble. Add the water, mustard, honey, vinegar, salt, and pepper and stir to combine. Add the chicken wings and stir to coat the wings in the sauce, then arrange them in a single layer in the pot.

2   Secure the lid and set the Pressure Release to **Sealing**. Press the **Cancel** button to reset the cooking program, then select the **Pressure Cook** or **Manual** program and set the cooking time for 10 minutes at high pressure. (The pot will take about 10 minutes to come up to pressure before the cooking program begins.)

3   While the chicken wings are cooking, preheat the broiler and line a rimmed baking sheet with aluminum foil.

4   When the cooking program ends, perform a quick pressure release by moving the Pressure Release to **Venting**. Open the pot and, using tongs, transfer the chicken wings to the prepared baking sheet, arranging them in a single layer.

5   Press the **Cancel** button on the Instant Pot to reset the cooking program, then select the **Sauté** setting and set the cooking time for 5 minutes. Simmer the cooking liquid, stirring occasionally, until it has thickened slightly and started to take on a glossy sheen. Wearing heat-resistant mitts, lift out the inner pot. Ladle half of the cooking liquid onto the wings.

6   Broil the wings for about 5 minutes, until browned and charred in spots. Remove the baking sheet from the oven, flip each wing, and ladle on the remaining cooking liquid. Broil the wings for 4 minutes more, until bubbling and charred on the second sides. Using tongs, transfer the wings to a serving plate.

7   Serve the wings warm with green onions sprinkled over top.

Variation: To make Sriracha chicken wings, substitute 2 tablespoons Sriracha for the mustard, and ¼ cup rice vinegar for the cider vinegar.

Adobo is one of my favorite weeknight dishes. You can just throw everything in the pot—no marinating or browning required! This is the Filipino version, which has soy sauce and vinegar as the base of its tangy sauce. The sauce is strong and flavorful, and pressure cooking helps the flavor penetrate the drumsticks through and through. Serve the adobo with some fluffy white rice for a simple dinner.

CHICKEN ADOBO DRUMSTICKS

About 3½ pounds chicken drumsticks

1 medium yellow onion, sliced

4 garlic cloves, minced

⅓ cup rice vinegar

⅓ cup soy sauce

1 tablespoon brown sugar

1 teaspoon black peppercorns

3 bay leaves

Steamed rice (page 51) for serving

PREP	5 MINUTES
COOK	30 MINUTES
PR	10 MINUTES NPR
SERVES	6

1   Add the chicken, onion, garlic, vinegar, soy sauce, brown sugar, peppercorns, and bay leaves to the Instant Pot. Use your hands to mix the ingredients and turn the drumsticks so that they're evenly coated with the mixture.

2   Secure the lid and set the Pressure Release to **Sealing**. Select the **Poultry**, **Pressure Cook**, or **Manual** setting and set the cooking time for 15 minutes at high pressure. (The pot will take about 15 minutes to come up to pressure before the cooking program begins.)

3   When the cooking program ends, let the pressure release naturally for 10 minutes, then move the Pressure Release to **Venting** to release any remaining steam. Open the pot, then remove and discard the bay leaves. Using tongs, transfer the chicken to a serving dish.

4   Ladle some of the sauce over the chicken and serve with rice.

Note: If you like, instead of drumsticks, you can use bone-in, skin-on chicken thighs or breasts. If using breasts, cut each one in half crosswise before adding to the pot.

Buffalo wings have nothing on this hot and spicy shredded chicken. It's great piled onto slider buns and offered as an appetizer, or on sandwich rolls and served as the main event. See Variation for a Buffalo chicken dip to serve with carrot and celery sticks.

SHREDDED BUFFALO CHICKEN

1 cup water, plus 1 tablespoon

Kosher salt

About 2½ pounds boneless, skinless chicken breasts

1 tablespoon cornstarch

½ cup hot sauce (preferably Frank's RedHot), plus more as needed

2 tablespoons honey

2 teaspoons Worcestershire sauce

4 tablespoons unsalted butter

4 garlic cloves, minced

Slider buns or sandwich rolls for serving

PREP	5 MINUTES
COOK	30 MINUTES
PR	QPR
SERVES	6

1   Add the 1 cup water, 1 teaspoon salt, and chicken breasts to the Instant Pot, placing the chicken in a single layer.

2   Secure the lid and set the Pressure Release to **Sealing**. Select the **Poultry**, **Pressure Cook**, or **Manual** setting and set the cooking time for 15 minutes at high pressure. (The pot will take about 10 minutes to come up to pressure before the cooking program begins.)

3   While the chicken is cooking, in a small bowl, stir together the remaining 1 tablespoon water and the cornstarch. Stir in the hot sauce, honey, and Worcestershire, then set aside.

4   When the cooking program ends, perform a quick pressure release by moving the Pressure Release to **Venting** to release any remaining steam. Open the pot and, using tongs, transfer the chicken to a cutting board. Wearing heat-resistant mitts, lift out the inner pot and pour out the cooking liquid, saving it for another use or discarding it. Return the inner pot to the housing. Using two forks, finely shred the chicken.

5   Press the **Cancel** button to reset the cooking program, then select the **Sauté** setting. Add 1 tablespoon of the butter and the garlic to the pot and sauté for about 2 minutes, until the garlic is no longer raw but has not begun to brown. Stir the hot sauce mixture to recombine, then pour it into the pot and cook for about 1 minute, stirring occasionally, until thickened. Press the **Cancel** button to turn off the pot. Add the remaining 3 tablespoons butter to the sauce and stir until melted and combined. Add the shredded chicken, tossing to coat it evenly. Taste and adjust the seasoning with more hot sauce and salt if needed.

6   Serve the chicken right away in slider buns.

Variation: To make Buffalo chicken dip, in a bowl, mix 2 cups shredded Buffalo chicken with 4 ounces room-temperature cream cheese until well combined. Transfer to a small baking dish and spread in an even layer, then sprinkle with ⅓ cup shredded Cheddar cheese. Bake at 375°F for about 15 minutes, until the dip is warmed through and the cheese is beginning to brown. Serve warm with carrot and celery sticks.

I've taken the sweet and spicy sauce of Chinese plum-chili chicken and used it for these meatballs. They have the flavor of chicken wonton filling, but there's no fussy folding or frying. Serve the meatballs with toothpicks as an appetizer, or over rice for dinner.

CHICKEN MEATBALLS IN PLUM SAUCE

Meatballs

1 pound ground chicken

1 small shallot, minced

2 tablespoons chopped fresh cilantro

1 tablespoon soy sauce

¼ teaspoon ground white pepper

⅛ teaspoon ground ginger

½ cup plum jam

½ cup water

2 tablespoons soy sauce

2 teaspoons sambal oelek (chile paste) or Sriracha sauce

¼ teaspoon ground ginger

1 garlic clove, minced

1 bunch green onions, white and tender green parts, thinly sliced; 2 tablespoons reserved for sprinkling

Steamed rice (page 51) for serving

PREP	10 MINUTES
COOK	25 MINUTES
PR	QPR
SERVES	4

1   To make the meatballs: In a medium bowl, combine the ground chicken, shallot, cilantro, soy sauce, white pepper, and ginger. Mix with your hands until all of the ingredients are evenly distributed. Shape the mixture into 1-inch meatballs, placing them on a plate as you go. Set aside.

2   Add the jam, water, soy sauce, sambal oelek, ginger, garlic, and green onions to the Instant Pot. Select the **Sauté** setting and cook for about 3 minutes, using a spoon to break up the jam and combine the ingredients.

3   Place the meatballs in a single layer in the pot. Don't worry if the meatballs are not completely covered.

4   Secure the lid and set the Pressure Release to **Sealing**. Press the **Cancel** button to reset the cooking program, then select the **Pressure Cook** or **Manual** setting and set the cooking time for 8 minutes at high pressure. (The pot will take about 5 minutes to come up to pressure before the cooking program begins.)

5   When the cooking program ends, perform a quick pressure release by moving the Pressure Release to **Venting**. Open the pot and use a slotted spoon to transfer the meatballs to a serving dish.

6   Press the **Cancel** button to reset the cooking program, then select the **Sauté** setting and set the cooking time for 7 minutes. Simmer, stirring often, until reduced to a glossy, pourable glaze. Wearing heat-resistant mitts, lift out the inner pot and pour the glaze over the meatballs. Sprinkle with the reserved green onion.

7   Serve the meatballs with steamed rice.

Note: If you like, you can brown the meatballs, which helps them hold their shape and adds depth of flavor, before simmering them in the Instant Pot, but because they tend to stick to the pot, which can cause a burn error, they're best browned in the oven. Place the meatballs on a parchment paper–lined baking sheet and bake at 375°F for about 15 minutes, until lightly browned.

A ziplock plastic bag makes mess-free work of dredging chicken thighs in seasoned flour, and you don't even have to sear the thighs before pressure-cooking. The flour coating thickens the Marsala-spiked mushroom sauce as the chicken cooks to tenderness.

CHICKEN MARSALA

1 ½ pounds boneless, skinless chicken thighs

¼ cup all-purpose flour

Kosher salt

½ teaspoon freshly ground black pepper

½ teaspoon sweet or smoked paprika

1 tablespoon olive oil

2 ounces prosciutto, cut into 1-inch squares

2 garlic cloves, minced

8 ounces cremini or button mushrooms, sliced

½ cup dry Marsala wine

½ teaspoon dried thyme

½ teaspoon dried oregano

½ cup chicken broth (page 286)

1 tablespoon tomato paste

1 tablespoon fresh lemon juice

1 tablespoon chopped fresh flat-leaf parsley

Steamed rice (page 51) or Creamy Mashed Potatoes (page 260) for serving

PREP	5 MINUTES
COOK	25 MINUTES
PR	QPR
SERVES	4

Note: You can make this recipe with bone-in, skin-on chicken thighs instead of boneless, skinless. Use 2 pounds, remove and discard the skin before coating with flour, and increase the cooking time to 15 minutes.

1   Line a large plate with paper towels. Pat the chicken dry with additional paper towels.

2   In a 1-gallon ziplock plastic bag, combine the flour, ¾ teaspoon salt, pepper, and parika. Seal the bag and shake to combine the flour and seasonings. Add the chicken, seal the bag, toss it around until the chicken is evenly coated with flour, then transfer the chicken to the prepared plate, shaking off the excess flour and placing in a single layer.

3   Select the **Sauté** setting on the Instant Pot and heat the olive oil. Add the prosciutto and garlic and sauté for about 2 minutes, until the garlic is no longer raw. Add the mushrooms and cook for about 3 minutes more, until they begin to soften. Add the Marsala, thyme, and oregano; bring to a simmer; and cook for about 5 minutes, until the raw alcohol smell of the Marsala has dissipated.

4   Stir the chicken broth, tomato paste, and lemon juice into the pot. Add the chicken, arranging the pieces in a single layer. Spoon some of the cooking liquid and mushrooms over each thigh.

5   Secure the lid and set the Pressure Release to **Sealing**. Press the **Cancel** button to reset the cooking program, then select the **Pressure Cook** or **Manual** setting and set the cooking time for 10 minutes at high pressure. (The pot will take about 5 minutes to come up to pressure before the cooking program begins.)

6   When the cooking program ends, perform a quick pressure release by moving the Pressure Release to **Venting**. Open the pot and, using a slotted spoon, transfer the chicken to a serving dish.

7   Press the **Cancel** button to reset the cooking program, then select the **Sauté** setting and set the cooking time for 3 minutes. Simmer the sauce, stirring occasionally, until lightly thickened. Taste the sauce and adjust the seasoning with salt if needed. Wearing heat-resistant mitts, lift out the inner pot and pour the sauce over the chicken.

8   Sprinkle the chicken with parsley and serve with rice or mashed potatoes.

With the Instant Pot, you can make a decadent, creamy pasta dish in just over half an hour and without having to boil a pot of water. Cooking dairy under pressure is a tricky proposition because it has a tendency to foam and curdle when boiled, and can clog up the mechanisms in the pot lid (see further explanation on page 301). Here the cheese and cream are stirred into the pasta and chicken at the very end. You'll never bother with jarred Alfredo sauces again once you try this version.

CHICKEN PENNE ALFREDO

2 tablespoons unsalted butter

1 garlic clove, chopped

1 pound boneless, skinless chicken breasts or tenders, cut into 1-inch pieces

1 teaspoon Italian seasoning

Kosher salt

½ teaspoon freshly ground black pepper

¼ teaspoon ground nutmeg

8 ounces penne pasta

2 cups chicken broth (page 286)

4 ounces cream cheese, at room temperature

½ cup grated Parmesan cheese

¼ cup heavy cream or whole milk

1 tablespoon chopped fresh flat-leaf parsley

PREP	0 MINUTES
COOK	25 MINUTES
PR	5 MINUTES NPR
REST	A FEW MINUTES
SERVES	4

1   Select the **Sauté** setting on the Instant Pot and melt the butter. Add the garlic and sauté for 1 minute. Add the chicken, Italian seasoning, ½ teaspoon salt, pepper, and nutmeg and sauté for about 5 minutes more, until the chicken is mostly cooked through. Add the penne in an even layer on top of the chicken, trying to get the pasta to lay as flat as possible. Pour the chicken broth over the penne, just covering it; use a spoon to nudge down any pasta that is sticking out above the liquid.

2   Secure the lid and set the Pressure Release to **Sealing**. Press the **Cancel** button to reset the cooking program, then select the **Pressure Cook** or **Manual** setting and set the cooking time for 5 minutes at high pressure. (The pot will take about 15 minutes to come up to pressure before the cooking program begins.)

3   When the cooking program ends, let the pressure release naturally for 5 minutes, then move the Pressure Release to **Venting** to release any remaining steam. Open the pot and stir in the cream cheese, Parmesan, and cream. Let stand for 2 minutes to allow the cheese to melt and for the sauce to thicken. Stir once more, then taste and adjust the seasoning with salt if needed.

4   Spoon the pasta into bowls and sprinkle with parsley. Serve immediately.

This is a dairy-free, gluten-free one-pot dinner made with brown rice and boneless, skinless chicken. The secret is cooking the rice on top of the mushrooms and chicken; this way, the rice won't scorch on the bottom of the pot. It's perfect for evenings when you want something tasty and nourishing with minimal effort.

ONE-POT CHICKEN, MUSHROOM, AND RICE CASSEROLE

2 tablespoons olive oil

1 medium yellow onion, diced

2 garlic cloves, minced

1 medium carrot, peeled and diced

1 celery stalk, diced

8 ounces cremini mushrooms, sliced

1 pound boneless, skinless chicken thighs or tenders, cut into 1-inch pieces

1 teaspoon dried thyme

1 teaspoon sweet paprika

Kosher salt

½ teaspoon freshly ground black pepper

1 cup long-grain brown rice or brown and wild rice blend

1 cup chicken broth (page 286)

¼ cup dry sherry

PREP	0 MINUTES
COOK	40 MINUTES
PR	10 MINUTES NPR
REST	A FEW MINUTES
SERVES	4

1   Select the **Sauté** setting on the Instant Pot and heat the olive oil. Add the onion, garlic, carrot, celery, and mushrooms and sauté for about 6 minutes, until the onion is softened and the mushrooms are beginning to wilt and soften. Add the chicken, thyme, paprika, 1 teaspoon salt, and pepper and stir to combine. Using a wooden spoon or spatula, nudge the mixture into a fairly even layer. Sprinkle the rice in an even layer in the pot, then pour in the chicken broth and sherry. Do not stir, so the rice stays on top of the chicken rather than ending up on the bottom of the pot.

2   Secure the lid and set the Pressure Release to **Sealing**. Press the **Cancel** button to reset the cooking program, then select the **Pressure Cook** or **Manual** program and set the cooking time for 25 minutes at high pressure. (The pot will take about 10 minutes to come up to pressure before the cooking program begins.)

3   When the cooking program ends, let the pressure release naturally for 10 minutes, then move the Pressure Release to **Venting** to release any remaining steam. Open the pot and stir to combine. Let stand for a few minutes, to allow the cooking liquid to be absorbed. Stir once more, then taste and adjust the seasoning with salt if needed.

4   Spoon the casserole into bowls and serve warm.

Salsa Chicken is popular for a reason—it's an easy, fast, and foolproof way to get dinner on the table. Steaming a bowl of cilantro rice right on top of the chicken makes this a complete Instant Pot dinner, but you can skip the rice and make just the chicken to use in tacos, burritos, or tostada salads.

SALSA CHICKEN WITH CILANTRO RICE

2 pounds boneless, skinless chicken breasts

1½ teaspoons chili powder

½ teaspoon dried oregano leaves

1 cup Salsa Roja (page 289) or jarred tomato salsa

1 cup long-grain white rice

1 cup water

Kosher salt

½ cup chopped fresh cilantro

2 green onions, thinly sliced

1 jalapeño chile, seeded and minced

1 tablespoon fresh lime juice

12 tostadas for serving (optional)

4 cups shredded iceberg lettuce for serving (optional)

2 green onions, thinly sliced, for serving (optional)

Shredded Mexican cheese blend for serving (optional)

PREP	5 MINUTES
COOK	40 MINUTES
PR	10 MINUTES NPR
SERVES	6

1 Add the chicken to the Instant Pot, sprinkle with the chili powder and oregano, then pour the salsa roja on top. Using tongs, turn the chicken breasts to coat with the salsa and spices, then arrange them in a single layer. Place a tall steam rack in the pot, making sure all of its legs are resting firmly on the bottom.

2 In a 1½-quart stainless-steel bowl, stir together the rice, water, and ½ teaspoon salt. Place the bowl on the rack. (The bowl should fit inside the pot and not touch the lid when the pot is closed.)

3 Secure the lid and set the Pressure Release to **Sealing**, then select the **Pressure Cook** or **Manual** program and set the cooking time for 15 minutes at high pressure. (The pot will take about 15 minutes to come up to pressure before the cooking program begins, or 10 minutes if you are cooking the chicken without the rice.)

4 When the cooking program ends, let the pressure release naturally for 10 minutes, then move the Pressure Release to **Venting** to release any remaining steam. (If you are cooking just chicken, you may perform a quick pressure release by moving the Pressure Release to **Venting** immediately after the cooking program ends.)

5 Open the pot and, wearing heat-resistant mitts, remove the bowl and rack from the pot. Using tongs, transfer the chicken breasts to a cutting board. Press the **Cancel** button to reset the cooking program, then select the **Sauté** setting. Let the salsa mixture cook for 6 to 8 minutes, until slightly thickened.

6 Meanwhile, add the ½ cup cilantro, green onions, jalapeño, and lime juice to the rice. Using a fork, gently incorporate the ingredients into the rice, fluffing the grains as you mix.

7 Press the **Cancel** button to turn off the pot. Using two forks, shred the chicken breasts into bite-size pieces. Return the chicken to the pot and stir to combine with the salsa mixture. Taste and adjust the seasoning with salt if needed.

8 Serve the chicken in a bowl over rice or on a tostada, topped with lettuce, shredded cheese, and green onions.

I know, I know, it's not a true paella unless there's a crunchy layer of rice on the bottom. But rice cooked on the bottom of a pressure cooker pot can scorch, especially when there's a heavy layer of meat weighing it down and preventing steam from building up in the pot. I prefer to go the safe route and make an upside-down paella, with the rice on top.

CHICKEN AND SAUSAGE PAELLA

1½ cups chicken broth (page 286)

1 pinch saffron threads

1 tablespoon olive oil

2 garlic cloves, minced

1 medium yellow onion, diced

1 red, yellow, or green bell pepper, seeded and cut into ¼-inch strips

1 tablespoon tomato paste

¾ teaspoon smoked paprika

½ teaspoon kosher salt

1 pound boneless, skinless chicken thighs, breasts, or tenders, cut into 1-inch pieces

8 ounces fully cooked, spicy chicken sausage, sliced into ¼-inch-thick rounds

1½ cups short-grain white rice

1 cup frozen peas

2 tablespoons chopped fresh flat-leaf parsley

PREP	0 MINUTES
COOK	35 MINUTES
PR	10 MINUTES NPR
SERVES	6

1   Combine the chicken broth and saffron in a microwave-safe liquid measuring cup, cover, and heat on high power for 3 minutes. Set aside.

2   Select the **Sauté** setting on the Instant Pot and heat the olive oil and garlic for about 2 minutes, until the garlic is sizzling but not browned. Add the onion and bell pepper and sauté for about 3 minutes more, until the onion is slightly softened.

3   Stir the tomato paste, paprika, salt, chicken, and sausage into the pot and sauté for about 3 minutes, until the chicken has begun to turn opaque (it does not need to be cooked all the way through). Using a spoon or spatula, arrange the chicken and vegetables in a fairly even layer. Sprinkle the rice on top of the chicken in as even a layer as possible. Pour the broth mixture over the rice. Scrape down any grains of rice on the sides of the pot, making sure that everything is submerged in the cooking liquid.

4   Secure the lid and set the Pressure Release to **Sealing**. Press the **Cancel** button to reset the cooking program, then select the **Pressure Cook** or **Manual** setting and set the cooking time for 15 minutes at high pressure. (The pot will take about 5 minutes to come up to pressure before the cooking program begins.)

5   When the cooking program ends, let the pressure release naturally for 10 minutes, then move the Pressure Release to **Venting** to release any remaining steam. Open the pot. Add the frozen peas and gently fold them in. Let the paella sit for about 2 minutes, until the peas are heated through.

6   Spoon the paella into bowls and sprinkle with parsley. Serve hot.

With the pot-in-pot method, you can cook Indian-style chicken and a bowl of steamed rice in the Instant Pot, all at the same time. Tender chunks of chicken are napped with a creamy, well-spiced (but not too spicy) sauce. You can also cook the chicken on its own, without the rice.

CHICKEN TIKKA MASALA WITH BASMATI RICE

Marinade

½ cup plain yogurt (page 32)

4 garlic cloves, minced

2 tablespoons garam masala

1 teaspoon sweet paprika

½ teaspoon ground turmeric

¼ teaspoon cayenne pepper (optional)

1½ teaspoons kosher salt

2 pounds boneless, skinless chicken breasts or tenders, cut into 1-inch pieces

1½ cups basmati rice

2 cups water

1 tablespoon ghee (page 291) or coconut oil

One 15-ounce can tomato sauce

½ cup heavy cream or coconut cream

¼ cup chopped fresh cilantro

Warmed naan for serving

PREP	20 MINUTES
COOK	30 MINUTES
PR	10 MINUTES NPR
SERVES	6

1   In a medium bowl, combine the marinade ingredients and stir to mix. Add the chicken and stir to evenly coat. Cover and let stand at room temperature for 15 to 20 minutes, or refrigerate for up to 6 hours.

2   While the chicken is marinating, in a 1½-quart stainless-steel bowl, combine the rice, 1½ cups of the water, and the remaining ½ teaspoon salt and stir to mix.

3   Select the **Sauté** setting on the Instant Pot and heat the ghee. Add the chicken in an even layer and pour the marinade over top. Cook for about 3 minutes, until the chicken is beginning to turn opaque, then stir and continue to cook for about 2 minutes more, until mostly opaque. It's fine if the chicken is not fully cooked through.

4   Pour in the tomato sauce and remaining ½ cup water and stir to combine. Place a tall steam rack in the pot, making sure all of its legs are resting firmly on the bottom. Place the bowl of rice on top of the rack. (The bowl should fit inside the pot and not touch the lid when the pot is closed.)

5   Secure the lid and set the Pressure Release to **Sealing**. Press the **Cancel** button to reset the cooking program, then select the **Pressure Cook** or **Manual** setting and set the cooking time for 10 minutes at high pressure. (The pot will take about 10 minutes to come up to pressure before the cooking program begins.)

6   Let the pressure release naturally for 10 minutes, then move the Pressure Release to **Venting** to release any remaining steam. Open the pot and, wearing heat-resistant mitts, remove the bowl and rack from the pot.

7   Press the **Cancel** button to reset the cooking program and select the **Sauté** setting. Stir the cream into the chicken mixture and cook for about 5 minutes, until the sauce is slightly thickened. Press the **Cancel** button to turn off the pot.

8   Transfer the chicken to a serving bowl and sprinkle with cilantro. Fluff the rice with a fork and serve alongside the chicken, with the naan.

Lots of fresh lemon juice, extra-virgin olive oil, and a Mediterranean blend of herbs and spices give a classic Greek flavor to boneless, skinless chicken. You can use thighs, breasts, or tenders, but thighs are my favorite. Serve the chicken and salad with cooked orzo or steamed rice for a complete, colorful dinner.

LEMON CHICKEN WITH GREEK SALAD

Chicken

2 teaspoons dried oregano

1½ teaspoons sweet paprika

1½ teaspoons kosher salt

1 teaspoon freshly ground black pepper

½ teaspoon red pepper flakes

½ teaspoon dried thyme

⅛ teaspoon ground cinnamon

1 tablespoon cornstarch

1 tablespoon water

2 tablespoons extra-virgin olive oil

2 garlic cloves, minced

2½ pounds boneless, skinless chicken thighs

½ cup chicken broth (page 286)

¼ cup fresh lemon juice

PREP	5 MINUTES
COOK	35 MINUTES
PR	QPR
SERVES	6

1   To prepare the chicken: In a small bowl, combine the oregano, paprika, salt, black pepper, red pepper flakes, thyme, and cinnamon and stir to mix. In a separate bowl, stir together the cornstarch and water.

2   Select the **Sauté** setting on the Instant Pot and heat the olive oil and garlic for about 3 minutes, until the garlic begins to brown. Add the herb-spice mixture and sauté for about 1 minute more. Add the chicken thighs, chicken broth, and lemon juice and stir to combine, then arrange the chicken in a single layer.

3   Secure the lid and set the Pressure Release to **Sealing**. Press the **Cancel** button to reset the cooking program, then select the **Pressure Cook** or **Manual** setting and set the cooking time for 15 minutes at high pressure. (The pot will take about 10 minutes to come up to pressure before the cooking program begins.)

4   To make the vinaigrette: While the chicken is cooking, in a jar with a tight-fitting lid or other leakproof container, combine the olive oil, lemon juice, vinegar, sugar, oregano, salt, black pepper, red pepper flakes, and garlic. Cover and shake vigorously to combine, then set aside.

5   When the cooking program ends, perform a quick pressure release by moving the Pressure Release to **Venting**. Open the pot and use a slotted spoon to transfer the chicken to a plate. Use two forks to shred the chicken into bite-size pieces.

6   Press the **Cancel** button to reset the cooking program and select the **Sauté** setting. Stir the cornstarch mixture to recombine, then stir the mixture into the cooking liquid and cook for 2 minutes, until slightly thickened. Press the **Cancel** button to turn off the pot. Return the chicken to the pot and stir to coat with the sauce.

7   To prepare the salad: In a large bowl, combine the lettuce, cucumbers, bell pepper, tomatoes, onion, olives, and feta and toss to mix.

Vinaigrette

¼ **cup extra-virgin olive oil**

2 **tablespoons fresh lemon juice**

1 **tablespoon red wine vinegar**

½ **teaspoon sugar**

½ **teaspoon dried oregano**

¼ **teaspoon kosher salt**

¼ **teaspoon freshly ground black pepper**

⅛ **teaspoon red pepper flakes**

1 **small garlic clove, minced**

Salad

½ **head iceberg lettuce or 1 head romaine lettuce, chopped, or 5 ounces baby spinach**

2 **Persian cucumbers or ½ English cucumber, halved lengthwise and sliced ¼ inch thick**

1 **red or yellow bell pepper, seeded and sliced into ¼-inch strips**

1 **cup grape or cherry tomatoes, halved**

½ **small red onion, thinly sliced**

½ **cup pitted Kalamata olives, halved lengthwise**

¾ **cup crumbled feta cheese**

Cooked orzo pasta or steamed rice (see page 51) for serving

8   Shake the vinaigrette to recombine, then pour it over the salad. Toss until evenly coated.

9   Serve the chicken over pasta or steamed rice, with the salad alongside.

Note: You can substitute 5 teaspoons store-bought Greek spice blend in place of the long list of spices in the chicken. I like the one from Spicely Organics. You can also substitute store-bought Greek vinaigrette instead of making your own (Primal Kitchen is a good brand), or even make the vinaigrette in advance and refrigerate it for up to 2 days; bring to room temperature before using.

Make a batch of caramelized onions over the weekend, then use half of them in this weeknight-friendly recipe for a whole chicken. The onions and cooking liquid come together to make a deeply flavorful gravy with a beautiful golden-brown hue. You can freeze the rest of the onions to have on hand for another chicken dinner or use them in Caramelized Onion Dip (page 238).

WHOLE CHICKEN WITH CARAMELIZED ONION GRAVY

One 3½- to 4-pound chicken

Kosher salt

¾ teaspoon freshly ground black pepper

1 teaspoon sweet paprika

2 tablespoons avocado oil or other neutral oil with high smoke point

½ cup dry red or white wine

1 teaspoon dried thyme

1 cup chicken broth (page 286)

1 tablespoon tomato paste

1½ tablespoons all-purpose flour

1¼ cups 30-Minute Caramelized Onions (page 290)

PREP	5 MINUTES
COOK	50 MINUTES
PR	QPR
SERVES	4

1   Pat the chicken dry with paper towels. Tuck the wing tips under the wings, so they sit flat against the chicken, tie the drumsticks together with kitchen string, then season the chicken all over with 1½ teaspoons salt, the pepper, and paprika.

2   Select the **Sauté** setting on the Instant Pot and heat the avocado oil for about 2 minutes, until shimmering. Swirl the oil around to make sure it coats the bottom of the pot. Using tongs, lower the chicken, back-side down, into the pot and sear for about 5 minutes, until browned. (Some of the chicken skin may stick to the pot bottom, and that's fine. This happens to me about half the time, which is why I sear it on the back side first. The sticking helps to form a protective layer on the pot so the skin on the breast side stays intact.) Flip the chicken onto its breast side and sear for about 5 minutes more, until browned. Transfer to a plate and set aside.

3   Add the wine and thyme to the pot and use a wooden spoon to nudge loose any browned bits from the bottom of the pot. Bring to a boil and cook for 3 minutes, then stir in the chicken broth and tomato paste. Place the wire metal steam rack in the pot. Using tongs, carefully lower the chicken, breast-side up, onto the rack.

4   Secure the lid and set the Pressure Release to **Sealing**. Press the **Cancel** button to reset the cooking program, then select the **Poultry**, **Pressure Cook**, or **Manual** setting and set the cooking time for 20 minutes at high pressure. (The pot will take about 10 minutes to come up to pressure before the cooking program begins.)

5   When the cooking program ends, perform a quick pressure release by moving the Pressure Release to **Venting**. Open the pot and, wearing heat-resistant mitts, grab the handles of the steam rack and lift the chicken out of the pot. Transfer the chicken to a cutting board to rest.

6   Wearing the mitts, lift out the inner pot and pour the cooking liquid into a fat separator or a bowl. Pour the liquid from the fat separator back into the inner pot, or, if using a bowl, skim off the fat with a ladle or spoon, then pour the liquid back into the inner pot. Discard the fat. Add the flour to the inner pot and, using an immersion blender, blend until no flour lumps remain. You may need to tilt the pot so the blender head is fully submerged in the liquid.

7   Return the inner pot to the housing, then stir the caramelized onions into the cooking liquid. Press the **Cancel** button to reset the cooking program, then select the **Sauté** setting. Bring the liquid to a boil and cook for about 2 minutes, until thickened. Immediately press the **Cancel** button to turn off the pot. Taste the gravy and adjust the seasoning with salt if needed.

8   Carve the chicken, arrange on a platter, and spoon the gravy over the top. Serve immediately.

Notes: If you are using a 6-quart Instant Pot, make sure your chicken weighs 4 pounds or less. If you are using an 8-quart Instant Pot, you can use a larger chicken, up to 6 pounds.

If you do not have caramelized onions, you can still make this recipe. After searing the chicken, add 1 large yellow onion, sliced thinly, and ½ teaspoon kosher salt to the pot. Sauté for about 10 minutes, until the onion is softened. Deglaze the pot with the wine and continue with the recipe as written. When it is time to separate the fat out from the cooking liquid, you'll strain the cooked onions over the fat separator, then add them back to the pot with the strained cooking liquid and flour.

If your chicken is frozen, make sure it is fully thawed before cooking. People regularly ask me if they can cook a whole frozen chicken in the Instant Pot, and I always tell them they should make something else for dinner that night. The best way to thaw a frozen bird is in the fridge for a day or two.

If you are using a brined chicken, you may want to use less salt (or none if you're sensitive to sodium) when seasoning the chicken.

The glaze for this kid-friendly Chinese-style chicken is sweet and tangy, and this recipe is fast and easy for last-minute weeknight cooking. I prefer to use chicken tenders, since they are, well, tender. Boneless, skinless breasts or thighs work, too.

ORANGE-GLAZED CHICKEN

½ cup fresh orange juice

½ cup tomato sauce

2 tablespoons soy sauce

1½ teaspoons Sriracha

¼ cup firmly packed brown sugar

1 teaspoon garlic powder

¼ teaspoon ground ginger

2 tablespoons avocado oil or other neutral oil with high smoke point

2 pounds chicken tenders, cut into 1-inch pieces

1 tablespoon cornstarch

1 tablespoon water

1 green onion, white and tender green parts, thinly sliced

Steamed rice (page 51) for serving

PREP	5 MINUTES
COOK	30 MINUTES
PR	10 MINUTES NPR
SERVES	6

1   In a liquid measuring cup, combine the orange juice, tomato sauce, soy sauce, Sriracha, brown sugar, garlic powder, and ginger. Stir until the sugar dissolves.

2   Select the **Sauté** setting on the Instant Pot and heat the avocado oil. Add the chicken in an even layer and sear for about 2 minutes, until just beginning to turn opaque. Stir the chicken and continue to cook for about 2 minutes more, until mostly opaque. It's fine if the chicken is not fully cooked at this point—you're just taking some of the chill off the meat. Stir in the orange juice mixture.

3   Secure the lid and set the Pressure Release to **Sealing**. Select the **Pressure Cook** or **Manual** setting and set the cooking time for 7 minutes at high pressure. (The pot will take about 10 minutes to come up to pressure before the cooking program begins.)

4   Let the pressure release naturally for 10 minutes, then move the Pressure Release to **Venting** to release any remaining steam. Open the pot and, using a slotted spoon, transfer the chicken to a shallow serving bowl. Press the **Cancel** button to reset the cooking program and select the **Sauté** setting. Let the sauce cook for about 5 minutes, until it has reduced by about ⅓ cup.

5   In a small bowl, stir together the cornstarch and water, then stir the mixture into the sauce. Cook for about 1 minute more, until thickened.

6   Wearing heat-resistant mitts, lift out the inner pot. Pour the sauce over the chicken and sprinkle the green onion on top. Serve immediately, with the rice alongside.

Pasta and turkey are smothered in a creamy mushroom sauce in this day-after-Thanksgiving classic. There's no need to parcook the noodles when you make tetrazzini in a pressure cooker, and you can use either diced cooked turkey or uncooked boneless, skinless turkey breasts or tenders.

TURKEY TETRAZZINI

1 tablespoon unsalted butter

8 ounces cremini or button mushrooms, sliced

1 garlic clove, minced

½ teaspoon dried thyme

Kosher salt

¼ teaspoon freshly ground black pepper

2 cups diced cooked turkey, or 1 pound boneless, skinless turkey breasts or tenders, cut into 1-inch pieces

8 ounces linguine, broken into 3-inch pieces

1½ cups chicken broth or turkey broth (page 286)

¼ cup dry sherry, vermouth, or white wine

1 cup frozen peas

¼ cup heavy cream or half-and-half

2 ounces cream cheese, at room temperature

½ cup grated Parmesan cheese

1 tablespoon fresh chopped parsley

1   Select the **Sauté** setting on the Instant Pot and melt the butter. Add the mushrooms, garlic, thyme, ½ teaspoon salt, and pepper and sauté for about 8 minutes, until the mushrooms have wilted and most of their liquid has evaporated. Add the turkey and stir to combine. If using raw turkey, sauté for about 3 minutes more, until beginning to turn opaque; it's fine if the turkey is not fully cooked at this point.

2   Add the linguine to the pot, scattering it in a layer on top of the other ingredients. Pour in the chicken broth and sherry and use a spoon to nudge the noodles into the liquid as much as possible. It's fine if some noodles are not completely submerged.

3   Secure the lid and set the Pressure Release to **Sealing**. Press the **Cancel** button to reset the cooking program, then select the **Pressure Cook** or **Manual** setting and set the cooking time for 5 minutes at high pressure. (The pot will take about 10 minutes to come up to pressure before the cooking program begins.)

4   When the cooking program ends, let the pressure release naturally for 5 minutes, then move the Pressure Release to **Venting** to release any remaining steam. Open the pot, then stir in the peas, cream, cream cheese, and Parmesan. Let stand for 2 minutes, then stir the mixture once more. Taste and adjust the seasoning with salt if needed.

5   Ladle the tetrazzini into bowls or onto plates, and sprinkle with parsley. Serve immediately.

PREP	0 MINUTES
COOK	25 MINUTES
PR	5 MINUTES NPR
SERVES	4

Barbecue sauce takes the place of ketchup to glaze this turkey meatloaf. The meat mixture cooks in a mini loaf pan, which fits perfectly in the Instant Pot. I like the traditional look of a meatloaf formed in a loaf pan, but you can also use a 7-inch round cake pan and shorten the cooking time to 25 minutes. Serve the meatloaf with steamed vegetables and Creamy Mashed Potatoes (page 260), then enjoy any leftovers sliced and layered in sandwich rolls.

BARBECUE TURKEY MEATLOAF

1 pound ground turkey (93% lean)

⅓ cup barbecue sauce (your favorite brand), plus 2 tablespoons

⅓ cup dried bread crumbs

1 egg

2 tablespoons mayonnaise

½ yellow onion, finely diced

1 garlic clove, minced

½ teaspoon kosher salt

½ teaspoon freshly ground black pepper

¼ cup pickled red onions (page 298) for serving (optional)

4 sandwich rolls or toasted bread for sandwiches (optional)

PREP	5 MINUTES
COOK	50 MINUTES
PR	QPR
SERVES	3 OR 4

1   Pour 1 cup water into the Instant Pot and place the wire metal steam rack in the pot. Lightly grease a 5½ by 3-inch loaf pan with olive oil or nonstick cooking spray.

2   In a medium bowl, combine the turkey, ⅓ cup barbecue sauce, bread crumbs, egg, mayonnaise, onion, garlic, salt, and pepper. Mix with your hands until all of the ingredients are evenly distributed. Transfer the meat mixture into the prepared pan, pressing it into an even layer. Cover the pan tightly with aluminum foil. Place the pan on a long-handled silicone steam rack. Holding the handles of the steam rack, lower it into the pot.

3   Secure the lid and set the Pressure Release to **Sealing**. Select the **Pressure Cook** or **Manual** setting and set the cooking time for 35 minutes at high pressure. (The pot will take about 10 minutes to come up to pressure before the cooking program begins.)

4   When the cooking program ends, perform a quick pressure release by moving the Pressure Release to **Venting**. Open the pot and, wearing heat-resistant mitts, grab the handles of the steam rack and lift the pan out of the pot. Uncover the pan, taking care to avoid getting burned by the steam. Brush the remaining 2 tablespoons barbecue sauce on top of the meatloaf.

5   Broil the meatloaf in a toaster oven (or a conventional oven) for a few minutes, just until the glaze becomes bubbly and browned. Cut into slices and serve hot, or enjoy leftovers as sandwiches in sandwich rolls or on toasted bread, topped with pickled onions.

7

Pork, Lamb, and Beef

Laab is a vibrantly flavored Thai dish of ground meat seasoned with lime juice and fish sauce. I tend to prepare a lot of dishes with ground meat because they're so economical and fast-cooking, and this one is in my rotation of easy weeknight meals. *Laab* can be made with any type of ground or minced meat, including pork, turkey, chicken, or beef.

LAAB

2 large shallots or ½ small red onion, thinly sliced

¼ cup fresh lime juice

2 tablespoons fish sauce

1 tablespoon plus 2½ teaspoons sweet or hot paprika

½ teaspoon cayenne pepper

1 pound ground pork

¼ cup water

1 tablespoon toasted rice powder (see Note)

1 cup fresh cilantro leaves

Steamed jasmine rice (page 51) for serving

Steamed green beans (see page 248) for serving

½ small head green cabbage, cut into 1-inch wedges

1 cup grape or cherry tomatoes, halved

PREP	5 MINUTES
COOK	25 MINUTES
PR	QPR
SERVES	4

1   In a small bowl, combine the shallots, lime juice, fish sauce, paprika, and cayenne and stir to mix. Set aside.

2   Add the pork and water to the Instant Pot and, using a spoon, break up the pork so that it forms an even layer. Secure the lid and set the Pressure Release to **Sealing**. Select the **Pressure Cook** or **Manual** setting and set the cooking time for 10 minutes at high pressure. (The pot will take about 10 minutes to come up to pressure before the cooking program begins.)

3   When the cooking program ends, perform a quick pressure release by moving the Pressure Release to **Venting**. Open the pot and, wearing heat-resistant mitts, lift out the inner pot. Use the spoon to break the pork into small crumbles. Stir in the rice powder, cilantro, and shallot mixture.

4   Transfer the laab to a shallow serving bowl. Serve warm or at room temperature, with steamed rice, green beans, cabbage wedges, and tomatoes on the side.

Note: Toasted rice powder is integral to this dish—it contributes a nutty flavor and helps absorb the cooking liquid. You can buy it at many Asian grocery stores, order it online, or make it at home. In a skillet over medium heat, toast ½ cup uncooked jasmine rice, shaking often, for about 20 minutes, until the grains are golden brown. Let the rice cool completely, then grind it in a spice grinder or with a mortar and pestle to a coarse powder. Store in a tightly sealed jar in the pantry for up to 3 months.

By cutting the pork into cubes before you cook it in the Instant Pot, you can make carnitas in just over an hour from start to finish. The blend of spices, onions, garlic, and orange juice infuses flavor into the pork as it cooks, and a touch of sugar helps it to brown. After pressure-cooking, I shred the pork and crisp it in a skillet or under the broiler.

CARNITAS

¾ cup fresh orange juice

2 tablespoons chili powder

1 teaspoon ground cumin

1 teaspoon red pepper flakes

1 teaspoon dried oregano

¼ teaspoon ground cinnamon

1 tablespoon brown sugar

1½ teaspoons kosher salt

1 yellow onion, cut into wedges

4 garlic cloves, smashed and peeled

1 bay leaf

One 3-pound boneless pork shoulder roast, cut into 2-inch cubes

Warmed corn tortillas, chopped white onion, chopped fresh cilantro, and/or hot sauce (such as Cholula or Tapatío) for serving

PREP	5 MINUTES
COOK	1 HOUR
PR	20 MINUTES NPR
SERVES	6 TO 8

1   Add the orange juice, chili powder, cumin, red pepper flakes, oregano, cinnamon, brown sugar, and salt to the Instant Pot and stir to combine. Add the onion, garlic, bay leaf, and cubed pork and stir to evenly coat the pork.

2   Secure the lid and set the Pressure Release to **Sealing**. Select the **Meat/Stew** setting and set the cooking time for 35 minutes at high pressure. (The pot will take about 15 minutes to come up to pressure before the cooking program begins.)

3   Let the pressure release naturally for 20 minutes, then move the Pressure Release to **Venting** to release any remaining steam. Open the pot and, using tongs, transfer the pork to a plate or carving board. Using two forks, shred the meat into bite-size pieces.

4   Wearing heat-resistant mitts, lift out the inner pot. Pour the cooking liquid into a fat separator, then pour the liquid back into the inner pot. Reserve 1 tablespoon of the fat for crisping the pork and discard the rest. Return the pork to the inner pot with the cooking liquid, then return to the Instant Pot housing.

5   Secure the lid, set the Pressure Release to **Venting**, and leave the pork in the Instant Pot on the **Keep Warm** setting for up to 10 hours, until you are ready to crisp it up and serve.

6   In a large, heavy skillet over medium-high heat, warm the reserved pork fat. Using a slotted spoon, transfer the pork to the skillet, spreading it in an even layer. Cook for 8 to 10 minutes, stirring occasionally, until the pork is crisp and browned. (Alternatively, use a slotted spoon to transfer the pork to a rimmed baking sheet, spreading it in an even layer, and broil until crisp, about 5 minutes.)

7   Serve the carnitas on warmed tortillas, sprinkled with onion and cilantro. Pass hot sauce alongside.

This classic Mexican pulled pork dish includes chorizo sausage for added richness and flavor. The sausage is removed from its casing before cooking, and it cooks down and combines with the shredded pork roast. A chipotle chile adds a kick of smoky spice. Serve the tinga spooned onto corn tortillas for an easy taco-night dinner.

PORK TINGA TACOS

One 2- to 2½-pound bone-in Boston butt pork roast

Kosher salt

1 teaspoon freshly ground black pepper

1 tablespoon avocado oil or other neutral oil with high smoke point

12 ounces Mexican-style fresh chorizo sausage, casing removed

1 yellow onion, diced

4 garlic cloves, minced

1½ teaspoons dried oregano

1 teaspoon dried thyme

½ cup vegetable broth (page 284) or chicken broth (page 286)

¼ cup water

One 14½-ounce can diced tomatoes and their liquid

1 chipotle chile in adobo sauce, minced

¼ cup chopped fresh cilantro

2 tablespoons fresh lime juice

Warmed corn tortillas; pitted, peeled, and sliced avocado; and/or thinly sliced white onion for serving

1   Pat the pork roast dry with paper towels. Season the roast on all sides with 1 teaspoon salt and the pepper.

2   Select the high **Sauté** setting on the Instant Pot and heat the avocado oil for about 2 minutes, until shimmering. Using tongs, lower the roast, fat-side down, into the pot. Sear for about 4 minutes, until browned on the first side. Flip the roast and sear for about 3 minutes more, until browned on the second side. Transfer the roast to a plate.

3   Add the chorizo, onion, and garlic to the pot and sauté for about 4 minutes, breaking up the chorizo with a wooden spatula as it cooks. Add the oregano and thyme and sauté for about 1 minute more. Stir in the vegetable broth and water, using the spatula to nudge loose any browned bits from the bottom of the pot. Stir in the tomatoes and their liquid and the chipotle chile. Return the pork, fat-side up, to the pot. Spoon some of the sauce mixture over the pork.

4   Secure the lid and set the Pressure Release to **Sealing**. Press the **Cancel** button to reset the cooking program, then select the **Meat/Stew** setting and set the cooking time for 1 hour at high pressure. (The pot will take about 10 minutes to come up to pressure before the cooking program begins.)

5   When the cooking program ends, let the pressure release for 20 minutes, then move the Pressure Release to **Venting** to release any remaining steam. Open the pot and, using tongs, carefully transfer the pork to a plate or cutting board.

PREP	5 MINUTES
COOK	1 HOUR, 35 MINUTES
PR	20 MINUTES NPR
SERVES	4 TO 6

6   Set a wire-mesh strainer over a fat separator or a bowl.

7   Wearing heat-resistant mitts, lift out the inner pot and pour the cooking liquid into the strainer. Return the inner pot to the housing, then add the solids in the strainer back to the pot. Pour the liquid from the fat separator into the pot, or, if using a bowl, skim off the fat with a ladle or spoon, then pour the liquid into the pot. Discard the fat.

8   Press the **Cancel** button to reset the cooking program, then select the medium **Sauté** setting and simmer the cooking liquid for about 10 minutes, until it has reduced and thickened slightly.

9   While the cooking liquid is simmering, use two forks to shred the pork. Discard the bone, along with any kitchen twine used to tie up the roast. Add the shredded pork to the pot, along with the cilantro and lime juice. Stir to combine, then taste and adjust the seasoning with salt if needed.

10   Serve the tinga on warmed tortillas, topped with avocado and onion.

Note: You can skip the straining step if you prefer your tinga rich with the rendered fat from the chorizo and pork.

Pork shoulder and tomatoes cook down into a rich wine- and fennel-infused pasta sauce that's a delicious alternative to the typical marinara or traditional Bolognese. The sauce freezes very well, too. I like to freeze 1-cup portions in silicone mini loaf pans, then pop them out into ziplock plastic freezer bags. Reheating a couple portions to serve over pasta makes for an easy dinner.

PORK RAGU WITH PAPPARDELLE

One 2½-pound bone-in pork shoulder roast

Kosher salt

Freshly ground black pepper

1 tablespoon avocado oil, ghee, or other neutral oil with high smoke point

1 yellow onion, sliced

3 garlic cloves, minced

1 cup dry white or red wine

½ cup chicken broth (page 286) or vegetable broth (page 284)

1 tablespoon Italian seasoning

1 teaspoon fennel seeds

½ teaspoon smoked paprika

½ teaspoon red pepper flakes

One 28-ounce can whole San Marzano tomatoes and their liquid

2 pounds pappardelle or pasta shape of choice, cooked and kept hot

Grated Parmesan cheese for sprinkling

PREP	5 MINUTES
COOK	1 HOUR, 30 MINUTES
PR	QPR OR NPR
SERVES	8

1   Pat the pork dry with paper towels. If needed, trim the fat layer on the top of the roast so that it is no more than ¼ inch thick. Season all over with 1 teaspoon salt and ½ teaspoon pepper.

2   Select the high **Sauté** setting on the Instant Pot and heat the avocado oil. Swirl the oil around to make sure it coats the center of the pot. Using tongs, lower the roast, fat-side down, into the pot and let it sear for about 5 minutes, until browned. Turn the roast over and sear for about 5 minutes more, until browned on the second side. Transfer the roast to a plate.

3   Add the onion and garlic to the pot and sauté for about 3 minutes, until the onion is slightly softened. Pour in the wine and, using a wooden spoon, nudge loose any browned bits from the bottom of the pot. Add the chicken broth, Italian seasoning, fennel seeds, paprika, and red pepper flakes and bring to a simmer. Add the tomatoes and their liquid, then use the spoon to nudge the tomatoes to the sides of the pot (there's no need to crush the tomatoes because they will break down with cooking). Return the pork to the pot, placing it in the center.

4   Secure the lid and set the Pressure Release to **Sealing**. Press the **Cancel** button to reset the cooking program, then select the **Meat/Stew** setting and set the cooking time for 60 minutes at high pressure. (The pot will take about 15 minutes to come up to pressure before the cooking program begins.)

5   When the cooking program ends, you can either perform a quick release by moving the Pressure Release to **Venting**, or you can let the pressure release naturally. Open the pot and, using tongs, transfer the roast to a plate. It may come apart as you lift it out of the pot.

6   Press the **Cancel** button to reset the cooking program, then select the medium **Sauté** setting and set the cooking time for 15 minutes. Let the sauce simmer uncovered and without stirring (stirring will cause spattering).

7   Meanwhile, use two forks to shred the pork into bite-size pieces; discard the bone.

8   When the timer goes off, the pot will turn off. Stir the shredded pork into the sauce and, using a spoon, break up any large pieces of tomato. Taste and adjust the seasoning with salt and pepper if needed.

9   Spoon the ragu over the pasta and sprinkle with Parmesan. Serve immediately.

Spareribs are pressure-steamed to tenderness over a mixture of apple juice and Chinese five-spice powder, then brushed with a simple hoisin and garlic glaze before being browned in the oven. For an easy dinner, serve the ribs with steamed rice and a vegetable slaw dressed with store-bought sesame vinaigrette.

HOISIN-GLAZED SPARERIBS

1 rack pork spareribs
(up to 3½ pounds)

¾ teaspoon kosher salt

¾ teaspoon freshly ground
black pepper

1½ cups apple juice

1 teaspoon Chinese five-spice
powder

⅓ cup hoisin sauce

2 teaspoons rice vinegar

1 garlic clove, minced

1 green onion, white and tender
green parts only, thinly sliced, for
serving (optional)

PREP	10 MINUTES
COOK	1 HOUR,
	5 MINUTES
PR	QPR
SERVES	3 TO 4

1   With the rack bone-side up, and starting at one end, slip a knife tip under the translucent membrane, loosening it from the bone. Once you have lifted enough to get a good grip, grasp the membrane with a paper towel and peel it off (or ask your butcher to do this). Cut the rack in half crosswise. Season the ribs all over with the salt and pepper.

2   Add the apple juice and five-spice powder to the Instant Pot and place the wire metal steam rack in the pot. Stack the ribs on top of the steam rack.

3   Secure the lid and set the Pressure Release to **Sealing**. Select the **Steam** setting and set the cooking time for 23 minutes at high pressure. (The pot will take about 15 minutes to come up to pressure before the cooking program begins.)

4   While the ribs are steaming, preheat the oven to 375°F and line a rimmed baking sheet with aluminum foil or a silicone baking mat.

5   In a small bowl, stir together the hoisin sauce, vinegar, and garlic.

6   When the cooking program ends, perform a quick pressure release by moving the Pressure Release to **Venting**. Open the pot and, using tongs, transfer the ribs to the prepared baking sheet. Discard the steaming liquid and press the **Cancel** button to turn off the pot.

7   Brush the ribs on both sides with the hoisin mixture. Bake for 25 minutes, bone-side down, until the glaze is caramelized and browned. Remove from the oven, then cut the ribs apart.

8   Serve hot sprinkled with green onion.

Note: You can double this recipe in the 8-quart Instant Pot. Use the same amount of apple juice and five-spice powder and pressure-steam two racks of ribs for the same amount of time, but double the quantity of hoisin glaze.

Country-style pork ribs aren't really ribs, but pork shoulder steak that's cut into thick strips. They become tender in only 30 minutes when cooked under pressure. In this recipe, the cooking liquid becomes a thick and sweet barbecue sauce, and there's plenty for ladling over Creamy Mashed Potatoes (page 260).

CIDER-BRAISED COUNTRY-STYLE RIBS

About 2½ pounds boneless country-style pork ribs

Kosher salt

Freshly ground black pepper

½ cup apple juice

2 tablespoons cider vinegar

¼ cup firmly packed brown sugar

¼ cup yellow mustard

1 tablespoon tomato paste

½ teaspoon smoked paprika

⅛ teaspoon ground cloves

1 tablespoon avocado oil or other neutral oil with high smoke point

1 yellow onion, sliced

2 garlic cloves, minced

PREP	5 MINUTES
COOK	55 MINUTES
PR	10 MINUTES NPR
SERVES	4 TO 6

1   Sprinkle the ribs with 1 teaspoon salt and 1 teaspoon pepper.

2   In a liquid measuring cup, whisk together the apple juice, vinegar, brown sugar, mustard, tomato paste, paprika, and cloves.

3   Select the high **Sauté** setting on the Instant Pot and heat the avocado oil for about 2 minutes, until shimmering. Using tongs, lower the ribs into the pot and sear for about 4 minutes, until browned on the first sides. Flip and sear for about 4 minutes more, until browned on the second sides. Transfer the ribs to a plate.

4   Add the onion and garlic to the pot and sauté for 3 minutes, until the onion begins to soften. Stir in the apple juice mixture, using a wooden spoon to nudge loose any browned bits from the bottom of the pot. Working quickly to minimize the amount of liquid that evaporates, return the ribs to the pot and coat with the cooking liquid.

5   Secure the lid and set the Pressure Release to **Sealing**. Press the **Cancel** button to reset the cooking program, then select the **Meat/ Stew** program and set the cooking time to 30 minutes at high pressure. (The pot will take about 10 minutes to come up to pressure before the cooking program begins.)

6   When the cooking program ends, let the pressure release naturally for 10 minutes, then move the Pressure Release to **Venting** to release any remaining steam. Open the pot and, using tongs, transfer the meat to a serving plate. Set a wire-mesh strainer over a fat separator or a bowl.

7   Wearing heat-resistant mitts, lift out the inner pot and pour the cooking liquid into the strainer. Return the inner pot to the housing, then add the onion in the strainer back to the pot. Pour the liquid from the fat separator into the pot, or, if using a bowl, skim off the fat with a ladle or spoon, then pour the liquid into the pot. Discard the fat.

8   You can serve the sauce as is or use an immersion blender to blend the onions into the liquid to make a thicker sauce. Taste and adjust the seasoning, adding more salt and/or pepper if needed.

9   Pour the sauce over the meat and serve.

In my version of the classic Southern dish, the pork chops are smothered in a buttermilk gravy that's a lot savory, a little tangy, and not too rich. Make sure to serve some Creamy Mashed Potatoes (page 260) on the side, so you can ladle some gravy over those, too.

SMOTHERED PORK CHOPS

Four 6- to 8-ounce bone-in center-cut pork loin chops, ¾ to 1 inch thick

¼ cup all-purpose flour

Kosher salt

1 teaspoon sweet paprika

½ teaspoon freshly ground black pepper

1 tablespoon avocado oil or other neutral oil with high smoke point

1 yellow onion, sliced

2 garlic cloves, minced

¾ teaspoon dried thyme

1 cup chicken broth (page 286) or vegetable broth (page 284)

½ cup buttermilk

1 teaspoon Dijon mustard

Chopped fresh flat-leaf parsley for sprinkling

PREP	5 MINUTES
COOK	40 MINUTES
PR	QPR OR NPR
SERVES	4

Note: If using double-cut pork chops—ones that are about 1½ inches thick—increase the cooking time to 20 minutes.

1   Pat the pork chops dry with paper towels.

2   Add the flour, 1½ teaspoons salt, paprika, and pepper to a large zip-lock plastic bag. Seal the bag and shake to combine. Add the pork chops to the bag, reseal, and shake to coat them with the flour. Transfer the chops to a plate, shaking off excess flour; the coating should be very light.

3   Select the **Sauté** setting on the Instant Pot and heat the avocado oil for about 2 minutes, until shimmering. Swirl the oil around to make sure it coats the center of the pot. Using tongs, add the pork chops in a single layer and sear for about 5 minutes, until browned on the first sides. Flip the chops and sear for about 5 minutes more, until browned on the second sides. Return the chops to the plate.

4   Add the onion and garlic to the pot and sauté for about 2 minutes, until the onion is slightly softened. Stir in the thyme and chicken broth, using a wooden spoon to nudge loose any browned bits from the bottom of the pot. Return the chops to the pot in a single layer.

5   Secure the lid and set the Pressure Release to **Sealing**. Press the **Cancel** button to reset the cooking program, then select the **Meat/Stew** setting and set the cooking time for 10 minutes at high pressure. (The pot will take about 5 minutes to come up to pressure before the cooking program begins.)

6   When the cooking program ends, perform a quick pressure release by moving the Pressure Release to **Venting**. Open the pot and, using tongs, transfer the pork chops to a serving dish.

7   **Cancel** the cooking program, then select the **Sauté** setting. Add the buttermilk and mustard to the pot and stir to combine. Simmer the sauce for about 8 minutes, stirring occasionally, until slightly reduced. Press the **Cancel** button to turn off the pot. Wearing heat-resistant mitts, lift out the inner pot. Using an immersion blender, blend the onion into the sauce, tilting the pot so that the blender head is fully submerged. Taste and adjust the seasoning, adding more salt if needed.

8   Ladle the sauce over the pork chops and sprinkle with parsley. Serve immediately.

Did you know you can quickly make a more healthful version of this Chinese American staple in the Instant Pot? The tangy sauce in this recipe packs a lot of flavor, so there's no need for frying. The onion, bell pepper, and pineapple take only 1 minute to cook under pressure, and they come out perfectly al dente in the finished dish. You can either use fresh or frozen pineapple chunks; if using frozen, defrost them for a couple minutes in the microwave or let them thaw overnight in the fridge before use.

SWEET AND SOUR PORK WITH PINEAPPLE AND BELL PEPPERS

½ cup pineapple juice, plus 1 ½ cups diced pineapple (fresh or thawed frozen)

½ cup tomato sauce

2 tablespoons apple cider

2 tablespoons soy sauce

¼ cup firmly packed brown sugar

1 teaspoon garlic powder

¼ teaspoon ground ginger

1 pound boneless pork sirloin cutlet chops, cut into 1-inch pieces

½ teaspoon kosher salt

½ teaspoon ground black pepper

2 tablespoons avocado oil, or other neutral oil with high smoke point

1 yellow onion, cut into 1-inch pieces

1 large green bell pepper, seeded and cut into 1-inch pieces

1 tablespoon cornstarch

1 tablespoon water

2 green onions, tender green parts only, thinly sliced

Steamed rice (page 51) for serving

PREP	5 MINUTES
COOK	25 MINUTES
PR	QPR
SERVES	4

1   In a medium bowl, combine the pineapple juice, tomato sauce, apple cider, soy sauce, brown sugar, garlic powder, and ginger. Stir until the sugar dissolves, then set aside.

2   Season the pork with the salt and pepper.

3   Select the high **Sauté** setting on the Instant Pot and heat the avocado oil. Add the pork in an even layer and let it sear for about 3 minutes, until it begins to turn opaque and brown just a bit. Give it a stir, then let cook for about 4 minutes more, until mostly opaque (it is fine if some traces of pink remain). Stir in the onion, bell pepper, diced pineapple, and pineapple juice mixture.

4   Secure the lid and set the Pressure Release to **Sealing**. Press the **Cancel** button to reset the cooking program, then select the **Pressure Cook** or **Manual** setting and set the cooking time for 1 minute at low pressure. (The pot will take about 10 minutes to come up to pressure before the cooking program begins.)

5   When the cooking program ends, perform a quick pressure release by moving the Pressure Release to **Venting**.

6   While the pressure is releasing, in a small bowl, stir together the cornstarch and water.

7   Open the pot and stir in the cornstarch mixture. Press the **Cancel** button to reset the cooking program, select the **Sauté** setting, and set the cooking time for 1 minute, to thicken the sauce.

8   Spoon the pork onto plates and sprinkle with the green onions. Serve the steamed rice alongside.

Apple juice, cider vinegar, and sliced apples make this pork roast a delicious fall treat. It's great for weeknights (you can start the roast in the morning and let it sit on the Keep Warm setting for up to 10 hours, then add the apples before serving), but it's also fancy enough for company.

PORK LOIN WITH APPLE CIDER AND ROSEMARY

One 2- to 2½-pound boneless pork loin roast

1 teaspoon kosher salt

¾ teaspoon freshly ground black pepper

1 tablespoon avocado oil or other neutral oil with high smoke point

1 medium yellow onion, thinly sliced

1 cup apple cider or juice

2 tablespoons cider vinegar

2 tablespoons honey

1 teaspoon Dijon mustard

1½ teaspoons chopped fresh rosemary

1 medium Fuji or Gala apple, cored and cut into ¼-inch-thick slices

2 teaspoons cornstarch or arrowroot powder

2 teaspoons water

Cooked rice (page 51) or Celery Root Puree (page 242) for serving

PREP	5 MINUTES
COOK	1 HOUR, 30 MINUTES
PR	QPR OR NPR
SERVES	4 TO 6

1   Season the pork roast on all sides with the salt and pepper.

2   Select the high **Sauté** setting on the Instant Pot and heat the avocado oil for about 2 minutes, until shimmering. Use tongs to lower the pork roast, fat-side down, into the pot and sear for about 6 minutes, until browned on the first side. Flip the roast and sear for about 6 minutes more, until browned on the second side. Transfer the roast to a plate.

3   Add the onion to the pot and sauté for about 5 minutes, until softened. Stir in the apple cider, vinegar, honey, mustard, and rosemary, using a wooden spoon to nudge loose any browned bits from the bottom of the pot. Return the roast, fat-side up, to the pot, then spoon some of the cooking liquid over the top.

4   Secure the lid and set the Pressure Release to **Sealing**. Press the **Cancel** button to reset the cooking program, then select the **Meat/Stew** setting and set the cooking time for 50 minutes at high pressure. (The pot will take about 15 minutes to come up to pressure before the cooking program begins.)

5   When the cooking program ends, perform a quick pressure release by moving the Pressure Release to **Venting,** or you can let the pressure release naturally. Open the pot and, using tongs, transfer the roast to a cutting board.

6   Press the **Cancel** button to reset the cooking program, then select the medium **Sauté** setting. Add the apple and cook for about 5 minutes, until almost tender.

7   In a small bowl, stir together the cornstarch and water. Stir the cornstarch mixture into the pot and simmer for about 1 minute, until the sauce has thickened slightly. Press the **Cancel** button to turn off the pot.

8   Carve the pork loin into ½-inch-thick slices. Serve with the sauce and apples poured over the top and with rice or celery root puree alongside.

Sauerkraut and a bouquet of fragrant spices give this Polish pork and sausage stew its distinct flavor. Recipes for bigos often yield enough to serve an army, but the Instant Pot makes a family-size batch that's perfect for a fall or winter evening.

BIGOS (PORK AND SAUSAGE STEW)

½ ounce mixed dried mushrooms

1 cup dry red wine

½ teaspoon allspice berries

½ teaspoon juniper berries

½ teaspoon black peppercorns

½ teaspoon caraway seeds

1 bay leaf

3 slices thick-cut bacon, diced

1½ pounds boneless pork shoulder, trimmed and cut into 1-inch cubes

1 yellow onion, diced

2 garlic cloves, minced

8 ounces cremini mushrooms, quartered if medium or small, cut into eighths if large

2 cups sauerkraut, drained

12 ounces kielbasa sausage, cut into ½-inch-thick slices

Steamed potatoes (page 258), sliced crusty bread, or cooked egg noodles for serving

PREP	5 MINUTES
COOK	1 HOUR, 5 MINUTES
PR	15 MINUTES NPR
SERVES	6

1   In a microwave-safe liquid measuring cup or bowl, combine the dried mushrooms and wine. Heat on high power for 1 minute, then leave in the microwave to let the mushrooms rehydrate.

2   Enclose the allspice berries, juniper berries, peppercorns, caraway seeds, and bay leaf in a piece of cheesecloth; gather the edges; and tie them with kitchen twine.

3   Select the **Sauté** setting on the Instant Pot and add the bacon. Sauté for about 6 minutes, until the bacon begins to brown and has rendered some fat. Using a slotted spoon, transfer the bacon to a plate.

4   Add the pork to the pot and sear for about 6 minutes, stirring once halfway through cooking. Use the slotted spoon to transfer the pork to the plate with the bacon.

5   Add onion and garlic to the pot and sauté for about 2 minutes, until the garlic is no longer raw. Add the cremini mushrooms and sauté for about 2 minutes more, until the onions are softened.

6   Pour the wine into the pot, leaving the mushrooms in the cup. Use a wooden spoon to nudge loose any browned bits from the bottom of the pot. Add the spice bundle to the pot.

7   Chop the rehydrated mushrooms and add them to the pot, along with the pork and bacon, sauerkraut, and sausage. Stir to combine.

8   Secure the lid and set the Pressure Release to **Sealing**. **Cancel** the cooking program, then select the **Meat/Stew** setting. Set the cooking time for 35 minutes at high pressure. (The pot will take about 15 minutes to come up to pressure before the cooking program begins.)

9   When the cooking program ends, let the pressure release naturally for 15 minutes, then move the Pressure Release to **Venting** to release any remaining steam. Open the pot, then remove and discard the spice bundle.

10   Ladle the stew into bowls and serve piping hot with potatoes, bread, or noodles.

Lamb is classic in shepherd's pie, but beef works equally well in this recipe. I buy my ground lamb from a local butcher who sources it from Superior Farms in Dixon, California. The meat has a mild flavor that's not at all gamy, so it pleases lamb lovers and skeptics alike. Of course, here it's cooked with plenty of thyme, black pepper, and a dash of Worcestershire sauce before being topped with mashed potatoes, so what's not to love? The potatoes steam on a tall steam rack above the filling, saving the time and trouble of simmering them separately on the stove. For a rustic mash, leave the skins on, but scrub the potatoes before cooking.

SHEPHERD'S PIE

1 tablespoon avocado oil or other neutral oil with high smoke point

1 pound ground lamb

1 yellow onion, diced

1 celery stalk, diced

1 large carrot, diced

1 garlic clove, minced

1 ¼ teaspoons kosher salt

1 teaspoon dried thyme

½ teaspoon freshly ground black pepper

1 tablespoon Worcestershire sauce

1 tablespoon tomato paste

1 cup vegetable broth (page 284)

1 cup frozen peas

4 medium russet potatoes, peeled

½ cup whole milk

PREP	0 MINUTES
COOK	55 MINUTES
PR	QPR
SERVES	4

1   Select the **Sauté** setting on the Instant Pot and heat the avocado oil. Add the lamb and sauté, breaking it up with a wooden spoon or spatula, for about 7 minutes, until cooked through and no traces of pink remain.

2   Set a colander in a bowl. Wearing heat-resistant mitts, lift out the inner pot and pour the lamb into the colander, letting it drain. Return the inner pot to the Instant Pot housing.

3   Add the onion, celery, carrot, garlic, and ½ teaspoon of the salt to the pot and sauté for about 4 minutes, until the onion is translucent. Stir in the thyme, pepper, Worcestershire, and tomato paste. Return the lamb to the pot, then add the vegetable broth and peas. Place a tall steam rack in the pot, making sure all of its legs are resting firmly on the bottom. Place the potatoes in a single layer on the rack.

4   Secure the lid and set the Pressure Release to **Sealing**. Press the **Cancel** button to reset the cooking program, then select the **Pressure Cook** or **Manual** program and set the cooking time for 15 minutes at high pressure. (The pot will take about 15 minutes to come up to pressure before the cooking program begins.)

5   When the cooking program ends, perform a quick pressure release by moving the Pressure Release to **Venting**.

6   Using tongs, transfer the potatoes to a bowl. Add the milk and remaining ¾ teaspoon salt, then use a potato masher to mash the potatoes until smooth.

7   Wearing heat-resistant mitts, remove the steam rack from the pot. Stir ½ cup of the mashed potatoes into the lamb mixture in the pot. Transfer the lamb mixture to a broiler-safe 8-inch square baking dish, dollop the mashed potatoes on top, and spread them out with a fork, creating a surface texture.

8   Broil the shepherd's pie in a toaster oven (or a conventional oven) for about 5 minutes, checking often, until the potatoes are lightly browned.

9   Spoon the shepherd's pie onto plates and serve immediately.

Note: If you like, instead of assembling and broiling the pie, you can simply serve the lamb mixture with the mashed potatoes on the side.

These well-spiced (but not spicy-hot) meatballs stay tender and moist with additions of crumbled feta cheese and grated zucchini. They're flavored with a Greek-inspired blend of oregano, mint, coriander, and cumin. Serve them in their tomato sauce with a dollop of the tangy yogurt sauce (or plain Greek yogurt) on top, and with pita bread on the side.

LAMB AND ZUCCHINI MEATBALLS WITH CUCUMBER-YOGURT SAUCE

Meatballs

1 pound ground lamb

1 egg

1 small zucchini, finely grated

1 garlic clove, chopped

½ cup crumbled feta cheese

¼ cup dried bread crumbs

1 teaspoon dried oregano

1 teaspoon dried mint

½ teaspoon ground coriander

½ teaspoon ground cumin

½ teaspoon kosher salt

½ teaspoon freshly ground black pepper

Tomato Sauce

2 tablespoons olive oil

1 medium yellow onion, diced

2 garlic cloves, minced

½ teaspoon kosher salt

½ teaspoon red pepper flakes

One 14½-ounce can diced tomatoes and their liquid

1 cup water

½ cup dry white wine

PREP	10 MINUTES
COOK	45 MINUTES
PR	10 MINUTES NPR
SERVES	4

1 To make the meatballs: In a medium bowl, combine the lamb, egg, zucchini, garlic, feta, bread crumbs, oregano, mint, coriander, cumin, salt, and pepper. Mix with your hands until the ingredients are evenly distributed. Shape the mixture into a dozen golf ball–size meatballs, then set aside.

2 To make the tomato sauce: Select the **Sauté** setting on the Instant Pot and add the olive oil, onion, garlic, salt, and red pepper flakes. Sauté for about 5 minutes, until the onion is softened. Add the tomatoes and their liquid, water, and wine and bring to a simmer.

3 Add the meatballs to the sauce in a single layer, spooning a little of the sauce over each meatball.

4 Secure the lid and set the Pressure Release to **Sealing**. Press the **Cancel** button to reset the cooking program, then select the **Pressure Cook** or **Manual** program and set the cooking time for 25 minutes at high pressure. (The pot will take about 10 minutes to come up to pressure before the cooking program begins.)

5 To make the yogurt sauce: While the meatballs are cooking, in a medium bowl, combine the yogurt, cucumber, olive oil, garlic, salt, pepper, and cumin and stir to mix. Set aside.

6 When the cooking program ends, let the pressure release naturally for 10 minutes, then move the Pressure Release to **Venting** to release any remaining steam.

7 Ladle the meatballs and tomato sauce onto plates and sprinkle with mint and parsley. Serve hot, with the yogurt sauce alongside.

Yogurt Sauce

1 cup Greek yogurt (see page 33)

1 Persian cucumber (or ⅓ regular cucumber, peeled and seeded), finely diced

1 tablespoon extra-virgin olive oil

1 garlic clove, minced

½ teaspoon kosher salt

¼ teaspoon freshly ground black pepper

¼ teaspoon ground cumin

Chopped fresh mint for serving

Chopped fresh flat-leaf parsley for serving

Note: Spicely Organics makes a gyro seasoning blend that can stand in for the herbs and spices that flavor the meatballs. Use 1 tablespoon gyro seasoning in place of the oregano, mint, coriander, and cumin.

The best way I can think of to describe this North African stew is "silky." The textures of the white beans, long-cooked carrots, and tender lamb meld so well, and they're all napped in a warmly spiced cooking liquid that thickens into a rich sauce. A final drizzle of olive oil and a sprinkle of chopped mint add fresh flavor to this comforting braise. Serve it with a bowl of couscous, or some naan or other flatbread for sopping up the sauce.

LAMB AND WHITE BEAN TAGINE

1 cup dried white beans

4 cups water

Kosher salt

1 tablespoon olive oil, plus more for drizzling

1½ to 2 pounds lamb stew meat, or boneless lamb shoulder, cut into 1-inch pieces

1 yellow onion, diced

3 garlic cloves, chopped

1½ tablespoons ras el hanout or 1½ teaspoons sweet paprika, ½ teaspoon ground coriander, ½ teaspoon ground cumin, ½ teaspoon ground allspice, ½ teaspoon ground cinnamon, and ¼ teaspoon cayenne pepper

1 cup vegetable broth (page 284)

2 large carrots, cut into 1-inch pieces

Chopped fresh mint for sprinkling

PREP	8-HOUR SOAK
COOK	1 HOUR, 5 MINUTES
PR	20 MINUTES NPR
SERVES	4 TO 6

1   Combine the beans, water, and 1½ teaspoons salt in the Instant Pot. Leave the pot turned off and let the beans soak for 8 to 10 hours.

2   Secure the lid and set the Pressure Release to **Sealing**. Select the **Bean/Chili** or **Manual** setting and set the cooking time for 15 minutes at high pressure. (The pot will take about 10 minutes to come up to pressure before the cooking program begins.)

3   Let the pressure release naturally for 10 minutes, then move the Pressure Release to **Venting** to release any remaining steam. Open the pot and, wearing heat-resistant mitts, lift out the inner pot and drain the beans in a colander. Return the inner pot to the Instant Pot housing and press the **Cancel** button to reset the cooking program.

4   Select the **Sauté** setting and heat the olive oil. Add the lamb in a single layer and sear for 3 minutes, until browned but not cooked through. Using a slotted spoon, transfer the lamb to a plate.

5   Add the onion and garlic to the pot and sauté for about 2 minutes, until the onion is beginning to soften. Add the ras el hanout and sauté for 1 minute more. Pour in the vegetable broth and, using a wooden spoon, nudge loose any browned bits from the bottom of the pot. Return the lamb to the pot, then stir in the beans and carrots.

6   Secure the lid and set the Pressure Release to **Sealing**. Press the **Cancel** button to reset the cooking program, then select the **Meat/Stew** setting and set the cooking time for 20 minutes at high pressure. (The pot will take about 15 minutes to come up to pressure before the cooking program begins.)

7   When the cooking program ends, let the pressure release naturally for 10 minutes, then move the Pressure Release to **Venting** to release any remaining steam. Open the pot and taste and adjust the seasoning with salt if needed.

8   Ladle the tagine into shallow bowls. Drizzle with olive oil and sprinkle with mint. Serve hot.

The strong flavor of lamb stands up to the assertive flavors of garlic, rosemary, and anchovies, and the shanks braise remarkably fast under pressure. Anchovies melt into the sauce and add a delicious savory note.

LAMB SHANKS WITH TOMATO SAUCE

1 tablespoon ground coriander

2 teaspoons dried oregano

1 teaspoon freshly ground black pepper

1 teaspoon kosher salt

4 small lamb shanks, about 3 pounds total

1 tablespoon avocado oil or other neutral oil with high smoke point

6 oil-packed anchovy fillets, rinsed and drained

3 garlic cloves, minced

1 yellow onion, thinly sliced

1 teaspoon chopped fresh rosemary

¾ cup dry red wine

1 tablespoon Dijon mustard

2 carrots, peeled, quartered lengthwise, and cut into 1-inch lengths

2 celery stalks, cut crosswise ½ inch thick

8 ounces Roma tomatoes, cored and diced

2 tablespoons chopped fresh flat-leaf parsley

Creamy Polenta with Parmesan (page 60) or Creamy Mashed Potatoes (page 260) for serving

PREP	5 MINUTES
COOK	1 HOUR, 15 MINUTES
PR	QPR
SERVES	4

1   In a small bowl, stir together the coriander, oregano, pepper, and salt. Pat the lamb shanks dry, then season them all over with the spice blend, rubbing it into the meat.

2   Select the high **Sauté** setting on the Instant Pot and heat the avocado oil for about 2 minutes, until shimmering. Working in batches if needed, use tongs to lower the lamb shanks into the pot, placing them in a single layer. Sear for 3 to 4 minutes, until browned on the first sides. Flip the shanks and sear for 3 to 4 minutes more, until browned on the second sides. Transfer the shanks to a plate.

3   Add the anchovies and garlic to the pot and sauté for about 1 minute, breaking up the anchovies with a spoon as they cook. Add the onion and rosemary and sauté for about 3 minutes more, until the onions are beginning to soften. Stir in the wine and mustard, using the wooden spoon to nudge loose any browned bits from the bottom of the pot. Add the carrots, celery, and tomatoes and stir to combine. Bring the mixture to a simmer, then return the shanks to the pot, arranging them in as even of a layer as possible.

4   Secure the lid and set the Pressure Release to **Sealing**. Press the **Cancel** button to reset the cooking program, then select the **Meat/Stew** program and set the cooking time for 50 minutes at high pressure. (The pot will take about 10 minutes to come up to pressure before the cooking program begins.)

5   When the cooking program ends, perform a quick pressure release by moving the Pressure Release to **Venting**. Open the pot and, using tongs, transfer the shanks to serving plates.

6   Set a wire-mesh strainer over a fat separator or a bowl.

7   Wearing heat-resistant mitts, lift out the inner pot and pour the cooking liquid into the strainer. Spoon the vegetables in the strainer around the shanks. Pour the liquid from the fat separator over the shanks and vegetables, or, if using a bowl, skim off the fat with a ladle or spoon, then pour over the liquid. Discard the fat.

8   Sprinkle the shanks and vegetables with the parsley and serve with polenta or mashed potatoes on the side.

These meatballs have a secret ingredient: Mexican-style chorizo. This is a totally different kind of sausage from the Spanish variety with the same name. Mexican-style chorizo is carried in the refrigerated meat case of most grocery stores, has a loose texture, and is meant to be squeezed out of its casing before cooking. It adds a ton of flavor and richness. The sauce is nice and spicy from chipotle chiles; cut back on the amount if you want a little less heat.

ALBONDIGAS IN CHIPOTLE TOMATO SAUCE

Meatballs

1 pound ground beef (93% lean)

½ pound Mexican-style fresh chorizo sausage

1 egg

¼ cup dried bread crumbs

1 teaspoon sweet paprika

½ teaspoon dried thyme

½ teaspoon ground cumin

½ teaspoon kosher salt

½ teaspoon ground black pepper

Sauce

1 tablespoon olive oil

1 medium yellow onion, chopped

1 garlic clove, chopped

½ teaspoon kosher salt

One 14½-ounce can diced fire-roasted tomatoes and their liquid

3 chipotle chiles in adobo sauce, chopped

1¼ cups water

Warmed flour or corn tortillas for serving

2 tablespoons chopped fresh cilantro for serving

¼ cup chopped white onion for serving

1   To make the meatballs: In a medium bowl, combine the ground beef, chorizo, egg, bread crumbs, paprika, thyme, cumin, salt, and pepper. Mix with your hands until all of the ingredients are evenly distributed; don't worry about overmixing. Shape the mixture into golf ball–size meatballs, placing them on a plate as you go. Set aside.

2   To make the sauce: Select the **Sauté** setting on the Instant Pot and heat the olive oil. Add the yellow onion, garlic, and salt and sauté for about 5 minutes, until the onion is softened. Stir in the tomatoes and their liquid, chipotles, and water and bring to a simmer.

3   Place the meatballs in a single layer in the pot and spoon a little sauce over each one.

4   Secure the lid and set the Pressure Release to **Sealing**. Press the **Cancel** button to reset the cooking program, then select the **Pressure Cook** or **Manual** setting and set the time for 25 minutes at high pressure. (The pot will take about 10 minutes to come up to pressure before the cooking program begins.)

5   When the cooking program ends, let the pressure release naturally for 10 minutes, then move the Pressure Release to **Venting** to release any remaining steam.

6   Serve the meatballs and the sauce on warmed tortillas, topped with cilantro and white onion.

PREP	10 MINUTES
COOK	45 MINUTES
PR	10 MINUTES NPR
SERVES	4

You can completely skip browning the meat and still end up with a rich, savory beef stew. The trick is to use umami-packed pantry staples such as tomato paste and beef broth to bump up the flavor. It takes only a little more than an hour from start to finish to make this simple yet satisfying stew.

CLASSIC BEEF STEW

1½ pounds beef stew meat, or boneless beef chuck, trimmed and cut into 1-inch cubes

Kosher salt

Freshly ground black pepper

2 tablespoons ghee (page 291) or neutral oil with high smoke point

1 medium yellow onion, diced

1 celery stalk, diced

3 garlic cloves, minced

8 ounces button or cremini mushrooms, quartered (see Note)

1 cup beef broth (page 285)

2 tablespoons Worcestershire sauce

1 tablespoon Dijon mustard

1 tablespoon tomato paste

1 teaspoon dried rosemary, crumbled, or 1 tablespoon chopped fresh rosemary

1 bay leaf

3 large carrots, sliced into 1-inch-thick rounds

2 medium russet or Yukon gold potatoes, peeled and cut into ¾-inch dice

1 tablespoon cornstarch

1 tablespoon water

Chopped fresh flat-leaf parsley for serving (optional)

PREP   5 MINUTES

COOK   1 HOUR,
         5 MINUTES

PR   QPR

SERVES   4

1   Sprinkle the beef all over with 1 teaspoon salt and 1 teaspoon pepper.

2   Select the **Sauté** setting on the Instant Pot and heat the ghee. Add the onion, celery, garlic, and mushrooms and sauté for about 5 minutes, until the onion has softened. Add the beef broth, Worcestershire, mustard, tomato paste, rosemary, and bay leaf and stir to combine. Stir in the beef.

3   Secure the lid and set the Pressure Release to **Sealing**. Press the **Cancel** button to reset the cooking program, then select the **Meat/Stew** setting and set the cooking time for 30 minutes at high pressure. (The pot will take about 10 minutes to come up to pressure before the cooking program begins.)

4   When the cooking program ends, perform a quick pressure release by moving the Pressure Release to **Venting**. Open the pot, remove and discard the bay leaf, and stir in the carrots and potatoes. Secure the lid once again and set the Pressure Release to **Sealing**. Press the **Cancel** button to reset the cooking program, then select the **Pressure Cook** or **Manual** setting and set the cooking time for 3 minutes at high pressure. (The pot will take about 15 minutes to come up to pressure before the cooking program begins.)

5   Perform a quick pressure release by moving the Pressure Release to **Venting**.

6   In a small bowl, stir together the cornstarch and water.

7   Open the pot and quickly stir the cornstarch mixture into the stew. Re-cover and let stand for about 5 minutes to thicken. Taste for seasoning and add more salt and pepper if needed.

8   Ladle the stew into bowls and sprinkle with parsley. Serve piping hot.

Note: If you don't want to include mushrooms, you may leave them out, but in that case add an extra ½ cup broth.

Use the winter squash of your choice here—kabocha can be cooked and eaten with the skin on, or you can peel and cube up a pumpkin or butternut squash. They all work well in this rich, coconutty curry. Its flavor greatly depends on the quality of your curry paste and fish sauce, so track down good ingredients. I like the massaman curry paste and coconut products from Mae Ploy and Aroy-D, and fish sauce made by Red Boat and Three Crabs. You can find them in most Asian grocery stores and online.

THAI MASSAMAN CURRY BEEF WITH WINTER SQUASH

1 tablespoon coconut oil or other neutral oil with high smoke point

1 yellow onion, cut into 1-inch pieces

½ cup coconut cream

¼ cup massaman curry paste

1½ pounds beef stew meat, or boneless beef chuck, trimmed and cut into 1-inch cubes

½ cup water

2 tablespoons fish sauce

One 1½-pound kabocha squash, seeded and cut into 1-inch cubes

1 cup coconut milk

1 cup loosely packed Thai basil leaves

Steamed rice (page 51) for serving

PREP	0 MINUTES
COOK	50 MINUTES
PR	QPR
SERVES	4

1   Select the high **Sauté** setting on the Instant Pot and heat the coconut oil. Add the onion and sauté for about 5 minutes, until it starts to brown. Add the coconut cream and curry paste and sauté for about 2 minutes more, until bubbling and fragrant. Stir in the beef, water, and fish sauce.

2   Secure the lid and set the Pressure Release to **Sealing**. Press the **Cancel** button to reset the cooking program, then select the **Meat/Stew** setting and set the cooking time for 20 minutes at high pressure. (The pot will take about 10 minutes to come up to pressure before the cooking program begins.)

3   When the cooking program ends, perform a quick pressure release by moving the Pressure Release to **Venting**. Open the pot and add the squash and coconut milk. Stir to combine, pushing down on the squash so all the pieces are submerged in the cooking liquid. Press the **Cancel** button to reset the cooking program, then select the medium **Sauté** setting. Let the stew cook, uncovered, for 10 minutes, or until the squash is fork tender. Press the **Cancel** button to turn off the pot. Stir in the basil.

4   Ladle the curry into bowls. Serve piping hot with the rice on the side.

Lots of paprika gives this goulash its vibrant color and authentic taste. Include potatoes for a heartier one-pot dish (see Note), or boil some egg noodles while the goulash is cooking.

BEEF GOULASH

1½ pounds beef stew meat or boneless beef chuck, trimmed of excess fat and cut into 1-inch cubes

Kosher salt

½ teaspoon freshly ground black pepper

1 tablespoon avocado oil or other neutral oil with high smoke point

1 large yellow onion, diced

1 garlic clove, minced

3 tablespoons sweet paprika

1½ cups beef broth (page 285)

2 tablespoons tomato paste

2 teaspoons cider vinegar

1 teaspoon finely grated lemon zest

4 medium carrots, peeled and sliced into ½-inch-thick rounds

1 bay leaf

Cooked egg noodles for serving (optional)

Sour cream for serving (optional)

2 tablespoons chopped fresh flat-leaf parsley

PREP	5 MINUTES
COOK	50 MINUTES
PR	10 MINUTES NPR
SERVES	4 TO 6

1   Sprinkle the beef all over with 1 teaspoon salt and the pepper.

2   Select the **Sauté** setting on the Instant Pot and heat the avocado oil for 1 minute. Add the onion and sauté for about 7 minutes, until beginning to brown. Add the garlic and paprika and sauté for 1 minute more. Stir in the beef, beef broth, tomato paste, vinegar, lemon zest, carrots, and bay leaf, using a wooden spoon to nudge loose any browned bits from the bottom of the pot.

3   Secure the lid and set the Pressure Release to **Sealing**. Press the **Cancel** button to reset the cooking program, then select the **Meat/ Stew** program and set the cooking time for 30 minutes at high pressure. (The pot will take about 10 minutes to come up to pressure before the cooking program begins.)

4   When the cooking program ends, let the pressure release naturally for 10 minutes, then move the Pressure Release to **Venting** to release any remaining steam. Open the pot, then remove and discard the bay leaf. Taste and adjust the seasoning with salt if needed.

5   Serve the goulash in bowls on its own or over egg noodles, topped with a dollop of sour cream and sprinkled with the parsley.

Note: If you'd like to add potatoes to your goulash, while the stew is cooking, peel 1 pound russet or Yukon gold potatoes and cut them into ¾-inch cubes. After opening the pot, add the potatoes in a layer on top of the stew; do not stir them in. Secure the lid and set the Pressure Release to **Sealing** once again. Press the **Cancel** button to reset the cooking program, then select the **Pressure Cook** or **Manual** setting and set the cooking time for 3 minutes at high pressure. (The pot will take about 10 minutes to come up to pressure before the cooking program begins.) When the cooking program ends, perform a quick pressure release by moving the Pressure Release to **Venting**. Open the pot, then remove and discard the bay leaf. Taste and adjust the seasoning with salt if needed. Serve as directed.

This is an ultra-easy, weeknight-friendly, one-pot dinner. I love the super-savory combination of mushrooms and beef, all covered in a lip-smacking Worcestershire-spiked gravy. Add the sour cream for a classic creamy stroganoff, or leave it out if you prefer yours dairy-free.

GROUND BEEF STROGANOFF

1 tablespoon olive oil

1 medium yellow onion, diced

2 garlic cloves, minced

8 ounces cremini mushrooms, sliced

Kosher salt

1 pound ground beef (93% lean)

1 tablespoon tomato paste

1 tablespoon Dijon mustard

1 tablespoon Worcestershire sauce

½ teaspoon dried thyme

½ teaspoon freshly ground black pepper

3 cups beef broth (page 285)

One 12-ounce package wide egg noodles

1 cup sour cream (optional)

2 tablespoons chopped fresh flat-leaf parsley

PREP	0 MINUTES
COOK	25 MINUTES
PR	5 MINUTES NPR
SERVES	4 TO 6

1   Select the high **Sauté** setting on the Instant Pot and heat the olive oil for 1 minute. Add the onion, garlic, mushrooms, and ½ teaspoon salt and sauté for about 5 minutes, until the onion is softened. Add the ground beef and sauté for about 4 minutes more, using a spoon or spatula to break up the meat as it cooks. It's fine if some pink remains; the beef does not have to be fully cooked at this point. Stir in the tomato paste, mustard, Worcestershire, thyme, pepper, beef broth, and noodles, using a wooden spoon to nudge most of the noodles into the liquid; it's fine if some noodles are not completely submerged.

2   Secure the lid and set the Pressure Release to **Sealing**. Press the **Cancel** button to reset the cooking program, then select the **Pressure Cook** or **Manual** setting and set the cooking time for 6 minutes at high pressure. (The pot will take about 10 minutes to come up to pressure before the cooking program begins.)

3   When the cooking program ends, let the pressure release naturally for 5 minutes, then move the Pressure Release to **Venting** to release any remaining steam. Open the pot, then stir in the sour cream. Taste and adjust the seasoning with salt if needed.

4   Ladle the stroganoff into bowls and sprinkle with the parsley. Serve piping hot.

Don't worry, no porcupines were harmed in the making of these meatballs! They just resemble roly-poly porcupines due to the grains of rice that poke out of their sides. This recipe is based on an oven-baked Betty Crocker classic, and in the Instant Pot, it cooks in about half the time as the original. I like to serve the meatballs with mixed steamed vegetables that I've prepared separately in the microwave or on the stove.

PORCUPINE MEATBALLS

1 medium yellow onion, chopped

2 garlic cloves, minced

1 pound lean ground beef (90% lean)

½ cup long-grain white rice

1 teaspoon kosher salt

½ teaspoon freshly ground black pepper

2 tablespoons olive oil

One 15-ounce can tomato sauce

½ cup water

1 tablespoon Worcestershire sauce

Chopped fresh flat-leaf parsely or small fresh basil leaves for serving (optional)

PREP	10 MINUTES
COOK	30 MINUTES
PR	QPR OR NPR
SERVES	4

1   In a medium bowl, combine half of the onion, half of the garlic, the ground beef, rice, salt, and pepper and mix with your hands until the rice is evenly distributed throughout the meat; don't worry about over-mixing. Shape the mixture into 12 evenly sized meatballs, each slightly larger than a golf ball.

2   Select the **Sauté** setting on the Instant Pot and heat the olive oil for 1 minute. Add the remaining onion and remaining garlic and sauté for about 5 minutes, until the onion is softened. Stir in the tomato sauce, water, and Worcestershire and bring to a simmer. Place the meatballs in a single layer in the pot and spoon a little sauce over each one.

3   Secure the lid and set the Pressure Release to **Sealing**. Press the **Cancel** button to reset the cooking program, then select the **Pressure Cook** or **Manual** setting and set the cooking time for 15 minutes at high pressure. (The pot will take about 10 minutes to come up to pressure before the cooking program begins.)

4   When the cooking program ends, you can either perform a quick pressure release by moving the Pressure Release to **Venting**, or you can let the pressure release naturally and leave the pot on the **Keep Warm** setting for up to 10 hours.

5   Serve the meatballs with the sauce spooned on top. Garnish with fresh herbs.

I love this recipe for busy weeknights. In about half an hour, you've got a well-seasoned beef filling for tucking into warm tortillas or piling into crispy taco shells. To be super-efficient, chop up your lettuce, onions, and any other fixin's you like while the meat is cooking.

GROUND BEEF TACOS

1 tablespoon avocado oil or other neutral oil with high smoke point

1 extra-large yellow onion, diced

2 garlic cloves, minced

2 pounds lean ground beef (90% lean)

3 tablespoons chili powder

2 teaspoons ground cumin

1 teaspoon dried oregano

½ cup beef broth (page 285) or water

Kosher salt

Tortillas or taco shells for serving

Chopped romaine lettuce for serving (optional)

1 cup shredded Cheddar cheese

2 Roma tomatoes, diced

½ cup chopped fresh cilantro

PREP	0 MINUTES
COOK	30 MINUTES
PR	QPR OR NPR
SERVES	4 TO 6

1   Select the high **Sauté** setting on the Instant Pot and heat the avocado oil. Add half of the onion and all of the garlic and sauté for about 3 minutes, until the onion is slightly softened. Add the ground beef and sauté for about 3 minutes more, using a spoon or spatula to break up the meat as it cooks. Stir in the chili powder, cumin, oregano, beef broth, and 1 teaspoon salt. It's fine if some pink remains; the beef does not have to be fully cooked at this point.

2   Secure the lid and set the Pressure Release to **Sealing**. Press the **Cancel** button to reset the cooking program, then select the **Pressure Cook** or **Manual** setting and set the cooking time for 10 minutes at high pressure. (The pot will take about 10 minutes to come up to pressure before the cooking program begins.)

3   When the cooking program ends, you can either perform a quick pressure release by moving the Pressure Release to **Venting**, or you can let the pressure release naturally and leave the pot on the **Keep Warm** setting for up to 10 hours.

4   Open the pot and give the meat a stir. Taste for seasoning and add more salt if needed.

5   Using a slotted spoon, spoon the meat onto tortillas or into taco shells. Top with lettuce, cheese, tomatoes, cilantro, and the remaining onion. Serve immediately.

This comfort-food classic gets a spicy update with the number-one condiment in my house: Sriracha. The kick of heat is subtle enough for most palates, but feel free to substitute a milder chili sauce, if you like. The recipe is easily doubled to serve a crowd, and Paleo-friendly substitutions are listed in the Notes.

SRIRACHA SLOPPY JOES

2 tablespoons neutral vegetable oil or ghee

1 pound lean ground beef (90% lean)

1 medium yellow onion, diced

2 large carrots, diced

1 large green bell pepper, seeded and diced

2 garlic cloves, chopped

1 cup tomato sauce

2 tablespoons Sriracha

2 tablespoons low-sodium soy sauce

2 tablespoons rice vinegar

¼ cup firmly packed brown sugar

4 hamburger buns, split and toasted

Thinly sliced red onion for serving

Sliced sandwich pickles for serving

PREP   0 MINUTES

COOK   45 MINUTES

PR   QPR OR NPR

SERVES   4

1   Select the **Sauté** setting on the Instant Pot and heat the vegetable oil. Add the ground beef and sauté until the meat is cooked through and no traces of pink remain, about 8 minutes, breaking up the meat with a spoon as it cooks. Add the onion, carrots, bell pepper, and garlic and sauté for about 5 minutes more, until the vegetables are softened. Stir in the tomato sauce, Sriracha, soy sauce, vinegar, and brown sugar.

2   Secure the lid and set the Pressure Release to **Sealing**. Press the **Cancel** button to reset the cooking program, then select the **Pressure Cook** or **Manual** setting and set the cooking time for 20 minutes at high pressure. (The pot will take about 10 minutes to come up to pressure before the cooking program begins.)

3   When the cooking program ends, you can either perform a quick pressure release by moving the Pressure Release to **Venting**, or let the pressure release naturally and leave the pot on the Keep Warm setting for up to 10 hours.

4   Stir the Sloppy Joe mixture, then ladle onto the hamburger buns and top with sliced red onion and pickles. Serve hot.

Notes: The Sloppy Joe mixture may look a little soupy when you open the pot, but in a minute or two after stirring, it sets up and thickens. Feel free to mix in a little tomato paste or a squeeze of ketchup if you like yours even thicker. Alternatively, cook the mixture on the **Sauté** setting for a few minutes, or until thickened to your liking.

For a Paleo diet, substitute equal amounts of coconut vinegar, coconut aminos, and coconut sugar for the rice vinegar, soy sauce, and brown sugar. Serve with cauliflower "rice" (page 233), in lettuce cups, or on top of roasted slices of sweet potato.

With a 7-inch cake pan, you can make a lasagna right in your Instant Pot. Start by making a batch of Bolognese sauce (or use store-bought), then layer it with no-boil noodles, baby spinach, and a cheesy filling. For a vegetarian version, substitute vegan Bolognese (page 134) or marinara (page 287) for the Bolognese sauce.

MINI LASAGNA BOLOGNESE

1 cup part-skim ricotta cheese

1 egg

1 ½ teaspoons Italian seasoning

½ cup grated Parmesan cheese

1 ½ cups tightly packed shredded mozzarella cheese

2 cups Bolognese sauce (page 288)

6 no-boil lasagna noodles

4 cups loosely packed baby spinach

PREP	10 MINUTES
COOK	30 MINUTES
PR	10 MINUTES NPR
SERVES	4

1   Pour 1½ cups water into the Instant Pot.

2   In a bowl, stir together the ricotta, egg, Italian seasoning, Parmesan, and 1 cup of the mozzarella until well mixed.

3   Ladle ½ cup of the Bolognese sauce into a 7-inch round cake pan and spread it in an even layer. Arrange 1½ lasagna noodles on the sauce, breaking the noodles as needed so you can fit a single layer into the pan. Spoon ½ cup of the ricotta cheese mixture onto the noodles and spread evenly, taking care not to move the noodles around underneath the cheese. Sprinkle 1 cup of the spinach leaves over the cheese. Repeat using the remaining ingredients, creating three more layers each of sauce, noodles, ricotta mixture, and spinach. Cover the pan tightly with aluminum foil. Place the pan on a long-handled silicone steam rack. Holding the handles of the steam rack, lower it into the pot.

4   Secure the lid and set the Pressure Release to **Sealing**. Select the **Steam** setting and set the cooking time for 20 minutes at high pressure. (The pot will take about 10 minutes to come up to pressure before the cooking program begins.)

5   When the cooking program ends, let the pressure release naturally for 10 minutes, then move the Pressure Release to **Venting** to release any remaining steam. Open the pot and, wearing heat-resistant mitts, grab the handles of the steam rack and lift the pan out of the pot. Uncover the pan, taking care to avoid getting burned by the steam.

6   Sprinkle the remaining ½ cup mozzarella evenly over the lasagna. Let the cheese melt for a couple minutes or broil the lasagna in a toaster oven (or a conventional oven) for about 3 minutes, until the cheese is bubbly and browned.

7   Slice the lasagna into wedges and serve hot.

After I sent my brother Dave and his family home with this brisket, he took one bite and texted me immediately, saying, "This brisket came out of the Instant Pot?!" He couldn't believe that such smoky flavor and tender texture were achievable without hours and hours on a smoker. Cook your brisket for an hour if you want to serve it in slices, or for 75 minutes for fall-apart, shred-able meat.

SMOKY BRISKET

2 teaspoons chili powder

2 teaspoons kosher salt

1 teaspoon freshly ground black pepper

1 teaspoon garlic powder

1 teaspoon smoked paprika

One 3- to 4-pound beef brisket

1 tablespoon avocado oil or other neutral oil with high smoke point

1 large yellow onion, sliced, plus sliced sweet onion for serving

1 cup beef broth (page 285)

Barbecue sauce for serving

Texas toast or sandwich bread for serving

Bread-and-butter pickle chips (page 296) for serving

PREP	1 HOUR REST
COOK	1 HOUR, 10 MINUTES
PR	30 MINUTES NPR
SERVES	6

1   In a small bowl, stir together the chili powder, salt, pepper, garlic powder, and paprika.

2   Pat the brisket dry with paper towels. If needed, trim the fat cap so that it is no more than ¼ inch thick. Cut the brisket in half crosswise, then sprinkle it all over with the seasoning mixture. Let the brisket stand at room temperature for 1 hour, or transfer to a covered dish or 1-gallon ziplock plastic bag and refrigerate for up to 24 hours.

3   Select the high **Sauté** setting on the Instant Pot and heat the avocado oil for 2 minutes, until shimmering. Using tongs, add one piece of the brisket fat-side down to the pot and sear for about 5 minutes, until browned. Transfer the brisket to a plate, then repeat with the second piece. (You do not have to sear both sides of the meat.)

4   Add the onion to the pot and sauté for about 3 minutes, until slightly softened. Pour in the beef broth and, using a wooden spoon, nudge loose any browned bits from the bottom of the pot. Return the brisket pieces to the pot, placing the larger half on the bottom.

5   Secure the lid and set the Pressure Release to **Sealing**. Press the **Cancel** button to reset the cooking program, then select the **Meat/Stew** setting and set the cooking time for 60 minutes if you plan to slice the brisket for serving, or 75 minutes if you plan to shred it. (The pot will take about 10 minutes to come up to pressure before the cooking program begins.)

6   When the cooking program ends, let the pressure release naturally for 30 minutes, then move the Pressure Release to **Venting** to release any remaining steam. Open the pot and, using tongs, carefully transfer the brisket to a carving board. If you have cooked it for the longer time, be careful—it may fall apart a bit as you remove it from the pot.

7   Wearing heat-resistant mitts, lift out the inner pot. Pour the cooking liquid into a fat separator, then pour the liquid back into the inner pot and discard the fat. Stir the onions back into the cooking liquid.

8   If slicing the brisket, cut it against the grain into ½-inch slices. If shredding the brisket, use two forks to pull the meat apart, then chop the longer shreds if needed.

9   Transfer the brisket to plates and spoon the cooking liquid and onions on top. Serve with barbecue sauce, Texas toast, bread-and-butter pickles, and sliced sweet onions alongside.

In the Instant Pot, corned beef cooks in about half the time it takes on the stove top. Serve it with steamed vegetables for dinner, use it in sandwiches for lunch, or make it into a hash with roasted bell peppers and potatoes for breakfast. Corned beef is easy to find during the week or two leading up to St. Patrick's Day, and it usually goes on sale immediately after. I like to cook one for the holiday and buy a couple on sale to freeze for later. Thaw frozen corned beef in the fridge for a day or two before cooking.

CORNED BEEF

One 4-pound corned beef, with spice packet

6 cups water

PREP	0 MINUTES
COOK	1 HOUR, 35 MINUTES
PR	30 MINUTES NPR
SERVES	8

1   Place the corned beef in the Instant Pot. Add the contents of the spice packet and the water.

2   Secure the lid and set the Pressure Release to **Sealing**. Select the **Meat/Stew** setting and set the cooking time for 55 minutes at high pressure. (The pot will take about 25 minutes to come up to pressure before the cooking program begins.)

3   When the cooking program ends, let the pressure release naturally; this will take about 30 minutes. Open the pot and, using tongs, transfer the corned beef to a cutting board. Let rest for 15 minutes, then carve against the grain into slices (for corned beef with vegetables or reuben sandwiches) or cut into ½-inch cubes (for hash). The corned beef may be served or used right away, or cooled to room temperature and then transferred to a tightly lidded container and stored in the refrigerator for up to 3 days.

Variations:

Corned Beef with Vegetables: After removing the corned beef from the Instant Pot, wear heat-resistant mitts to lift out the inner pot and discard all but 2 cups of the cooking liquid. Return the inner pot to the housing. Place a steamer basket in the pot and layer in 1 pound red or white potatoes, cut into 1-inch wedges; 1 pound carrots, peeled and cut into 1-inch pieces; and 1 small head green cabbage, cored and cut into 1½-inch wedges. Secure the lid and set the Pressure Release to **Sealing**. Select the **Steam** setting and set the cooking time for 5 minutes at high pressure. When the cooking program ends, perform a quick pressure release by moving the Pressure Release to **Venting**. Open the pot and, using a slotted spoon, transfer the vegetables to a platter, along with slices of the corned beef.

Reuben Sandwich: Spread Russian or Thousand Island dressing on a slice of rye bread, then pile on a few slices of corned beef, a thin layer of drained sauerkraut, and a slice of Swiss cheese. Top with another slice of rye bread. Toast the sandwich in a panini press or cook in a skillet over medium heat, until the bread is toasted on both sides and the cheese is melted.

This is my take on Mississippi pot roast, a Pinterest darling of a recipe. The pepperoncini season the meat, and their brine adds a little bit of vinegar tang. Serve the pot roast with mashed potatoes, or pile slices onto sandwich rolls for a twist on the classic French dip.

PEPPERONCINI POT ROAST

One 3-pound boneless beef chuck roast

1 teaspoon kosher salt

1 teaspoon freshly ground black pepper

2 tablespoons unsalted butter

1 yellow onion, diced

3 garlic cloves, minced

¼ cup pepperoncini brine, plus 10 pepperoncini

½ cup beef broth (page 285)

½ cup chopped fresh flat-leaf parsley

¼ cup chopped fresh dill

Creamy Mashed Potatoes (page 260) for serving

PREP	5 MINUTES
COOK	1 HOUR, 15 MINUTES
PR	30 MINUTES NPR
SERVES	4 TO 6

1   Pat the chuck roast dry with paper towels, then season on all sides with the salt and pepper.

2   Select the **Sauté** setting on the Instant Pot and heat the butter until bubbling. Using tongs, lower the roast into the pot and sear for 3 minutes, until browned on the first side. Flip the roast and sear it for about 2 minutes more, until browned on the second side. Transfer to a plate.

3   Add the onion and garlic to the pot and sauté for about 3 minutes, until the onion begins to soften. Stir in the pepperoncini brine and beef broth, using a wooden spoon to nudge loose any browned bits from the bottom of the pot. Return the roast to the pot. Sprinkle the pepperoncini around the meat. Add the parsley and dill, sprinkling them all over the roast and broth.

4   Secure the lid and set the Pressure Release to **Sealing**. **Cancel** the cooking program, then select the **Meat/Stew** setting and set the cooking time for 55 minutes at high pressure. (The pot will take about 10 minutes to come up to pressure before the cooking program begins.)

5   When the cooking program ends, let the pressure release naturally for 30 minutes, then move the Pressure Release to **Venting** to release any remaining steam. Open the pot, and, using tongs, carefully transfer the pot roast to a cutting board. Carve the pot roast against the grain into ½-inch-thick slices and transfer to a serving platter.

6   Set a wire-mesh strainer over a fat separator or a bowl.

7   Wearing heat-resistant mitts, lift out the inner pot and pour the cooking liquid into the strainer. Return the inner pot to the housing. Pour the liquid from the fat separator back into the pot, or, if using a bowl, skim off the fat with a ladle or spoon. Taste the cooking liquid, adjusting the seasoning with salt if needed. Discard the fat and solids, or, if you like, pick out the pepperoncini and use them for garnishing the pot roast.

8   Pour the cooking liquid over the pot roast and serve with mashed potatoes.

Traditional pot roast gets a sophisticated twist in this recipe. The braising liquid includes Dijon mustard, garlic, and fresh rosemary; the strong flavors really stand up to the beef, even after a long braise. Carrots and potatoes are added at the end of cooking, for a one-pot dinner.

ROSEMARY-DIJON POT ROAST

One 3-pound boneless beef chuck roast or bottom round roast

1 teaspoon kosher salt

1 teaspoon freshly ground black pepper

1 tablespoon avocado oil or other neutral oil with high smoke point

2 large shallots, sliced

4 garlic cloves, minced

1 cup beef broth (page 285)

3 tablespoons Dijon mustard

1 tablespoon chopped fresh rosemary

1¼ pounds Yukon Gold potatoes, cut into 1-inch pieces

1 pound carrots, peeled and cut into 1-inch pieces

PREP	5 MINUTES
COOK	1 HOUR, 30 MINUTES
PR	15 MINUTES NPR AND QPR
SERVES	4 TO 6

1   Place the beef on a plate, pat it dry with paper towels, and season on all sides with the salt and pepper.

2   Select the high **Sauté** setting on the Instant Pot and heat the avocado oil for 2 minutes. Using tongs, lower the roast into the pot and sear for about 4 minutes, until browned on the first side. Flip the roast and sear for about 4 minutes more, until browned on the second side. Return the roast to the plate.

3   Add the shallots to the pot and sauté for about 2 minutes, until slightly softened. Add the garlic and sauté for about 1 minute more. Stir in the beef broth, mustard, and rosemary, using a wooden spoon to nudge loose any browned bits from the bottom of the pot. Return the roast to the pot, then spoon some of the cooking liquid over the top.

4   Secure the lid and set the Pressure Release to **Sealing**. Press the **Cancel** button to reset the cooking program, then select the **Meat/Stew** setting and set the cooking time for 55 minutes at high pressure. (The pot will take about 5 minutes to come up to pressure before the cooking program begins.)

5   When the cooking program ends, let the pressure release naturally for 15 minutes, then move the Pressure Release to **Venting** to release any remaining steam. Open the pot and, using tongs, carefully transfer the pot roast to a cutting board. Tent with aluminum foil to keep warm.

6   Set a wire-mesh strainer over a fat separator or a bowl.

7   Wearing heat-resistant mitts, lift out the inner pot and pour the cooking liquid into the strainer. Return the inner pot to the housing, then add the shallots in the strainer back to the pot. Pour the liquid from the fat separator into the pot, or, if using a bowl, skim off the fat with a ladle or spoon, then pour the liquid into the pot. Discard the fat.

8   Add the potatoes and carrots to the pot. Once again secure the lid and set the Pressure Release to **Sealing**. Press the **Cancel** button to reset the cooking program, then select the **Pressure Cook** or **Manual** setting and set the cooking time for 5 minutes at high pressure. (The pot will take about 10 minutes to come up to pressure before the cooking program begins.)

9   When the cooking program ends, perform a quick pressure release by moving the Pressure Release to **Venting**. Open the pot and, using a slotted spoon, transfer the vegetables to a serving dish. Taste the cooking liquid, and adjust the seasoning with salt if needed. Wearing heat-resistant mitts, lift out the inner pot and pour the cooking liquid into a gravy boat or other serving vessel with a spout.

10   Carve the pot roast against the grain into ½-inch-thick slices and place on the dish with the vegetables. Pour some cooking liquid over the roast and serve, passing the remaining cooking liquid on the side.

Note: I prefer to use chuck roast for pot-roasting, but you can also use the leaner and more economical bottom round roast. If using bottom round, carve it a bit thinner for serving—about ¼ inch thick—and make sure to slice against the grain.

Short ribs are one of my favorite cuts of meat, but I never made them very often because they took so long to braise in the oven. Now that I cook them in the Instant Pot, I prepare them whenever they're on special at the butcher. This ingredient list is very similar to that of Classic Beef Stew (page 207), minus a few vegetables, and with an added glug of red wine. I do take the time to sear the short ribs, drain off any rendered fat, and reduce the cooking liquid into a rich sauce, as the ribs really benefit from these steps.

RED WINE SHORT RIBS

About 3 pounds bone-in beef short ribs

Kosher salt

Freshly ground black pepper

1 tablespoon avocado oil or other neutral oil with high smoke point

1 yellow onion, diced

2 garlic cloves, peeled and smashed

1 large carrot, diced

1 celery stalk, diced

½ cup dry, full-bodied red wine

½ cup beef broth (page 285)

1 tablespoon tomato paste

1 tablespoon Dijon mustard

1 sprig rosemary

Creamy Mashed Potatoes (page 260) for serving

PREP	5 MINUTES
COOK	1 HOUR, 5 MINUTES
PR	10 MINUTES NPR
SERVES	3 TO 4

1 Sprinkle the short ribs all over with 1 teaspoon salt and ½ teaspoon pepper.

2 Select the high **Sauté** setting on the Instant Pot and heat the avocado oil for 2 minutes, until shimmering. Using tongs, add the short ribs to the pot and sear them for about 4 minutes, until a bit browned. Flip the short ribs and sear for about 4 minutes more, until the second sides are browned. Transfer the ribs to a plate and set aside.

3 Add the onion, garlic, carrot, and celery to the pot and sauté for about 4 minutes, until the onion is softened. Stir in the wine, beef broth, tomato paste, mustard, and rosemary and, using a wooden spoon, nudge loose any browned bits from the bottom of the pot. Return the short ribs to the pot, nestling them in the cooking liquid, then pour in any accumulated juices from the ribs.

4 Secure the lid and set the Pressure Release to **Sealing**. Press the **Cancel** button to reset the cooking program, then select the **Meat/ Stew** setting and set the cooking time for 35 minutes at high pressure. (The pot will take about 5 minutes to come up to pressure before the cooking program begins.)

5 When the cooking program ends, let the pressure release naturally for 10 minutes, then move the Pressure Release to **Venting** to release any remaining steam. Open the pot and, using tongs, transfer the short ribs to a serving dish.

6 Set a wire-mesh strainer over a fat separator or a bowl.

7 Wearing heat-resistant mitts, lift out the inner pot. Pour the cooking liquid into the strainer, then return the inner pot to the Instant Pot housing. Pour the cooking liquid back into the inner pot, or, if using a bowl, skim off the fat with a ladle or a spoon. Discard the fat. (You may discard the vegetables, or save them to add back to the sauce to thicken.)

8   Press the **Cancel** button to reset the cooking program, then select the medium **Sauté** setting. Let the cooking liquid reduce for 8 minutes. Taste for seasoning and add more salt and pepper if needed. Ladle the liquid as is over the short ribs, or return the reserved vegetables to the pot, use an immersion blender to puree them into the liquid, then ladle the sauce over the short ribs.

9   Serve piping hot over mashed potatoes.

8

Vegetables
and Side Dishes

This recipe seems like it shouldn't work, but it does. There's hardly any liquid in the pot, but it's just enough to create a seal. The pot is set to zero minutes, which sounds kind of crazy. And yet, you end up with a pot of delicious, tender sprouts. Try 'em out!

SWEET CHILI BRUSSELS SPROUTS

3 tablespoons soy sauce

3 tablespoons rice vinegar

2 tablespoons honey, agave, or maple syrup

1 tablespoon sambal oelek or Sriracha

2 teaspoons toasted sesame oil

1 tablespoon neutral vegetable oil

2 shallots, minced

2 garlic cloves, minced

2 pounds brussels sprouts (halved if large), trimmed

1 teaspoon toasted sesame seeds

PREP	5 MINUTES
COOK	25 MINUTES
PR	QPR
SERVES	6 TO 8

1   In a small bowl or liquid measuring cup, stir together the soy sauce, vinegar, honey, sambal oelek, and sesame oil. Set aside.

2   Select the **Sauté** setting on the Instant Pot and add the vegetable oil, shallots, and garlic. Sauté for about 4 minutes, until the shallots begin to brown. Add the brussels sprouts and sauté for about 2 minutes, just to take off any chill. They will not be cooked through at this point.

3   Pour the soy sauce mixture over the brussels sprouts, quickly secure the lid on the pot, and set the Pressure Release to **Sealing**; work quickly so that moisture doesn't escape. Press the **Cancel** button to reset the cooking program, then select the **Steam** setting and set the cooking time for 0 (zero) minutes at low pressure. (The pot will take about 15 minutes to come up to pressure before the cooking program begins.)

4   When the cooking program ends, perform a quick pressure release by moving the Pressure Release to **Venting**. Open the pot and, using a slotted spoon, transfer the brussels sprouts to a serving bowl, leaving the liquid in the pot. If you like, press the **Cancel** button to reset the cooking program, then select the **Sauté** setting. Simmer the cooking liquid for 3 to 5 minutes, until it thickens into a glaze.

5   Pour the glaze over the sprouts and sprinkle with sesame seeds. Serve warm.

Browned bacon and sautéed shallot and garlic enhance tender steamed broccoli in this simple side dish. It's perfect for folks who take a little persuading to eat this green vegetable.

BROCCOLI WITH BACON

1½ pounds broccoli crowns, cut into 1-inch florets

3 slices bacon, diced

1 shallot, minced

2 garlic cloves, minced

Kosher salt

Freshly ground black pepper

PREP	0 MINUTES
COOK	15 MINUTES
PR	QPR
SERVES	4

1   Pour 1 cup water into the Instant Pot and place a steamer basket in the pot. Add the broccoli to the steamer basket.

2   Secure the lid and set the Pressure Release to **Sealing**. Select the **Steam** setting and set the cooking time for 0 (zero) minutes at low pressure. (The pot will take about 10 minutes to come up to pressure before the cooking program begins.)

3   While the broccoli is cooking, warm a medium skillet over medium heat. Add the bacon and sauté for about 5 minutes, until sizzling and beginning to brown. Add the shallot and garlic and sauté for about 3 minutes more, until the shallot is softened and the garlic is beginning to brown. Remove the skillet from the heat and set aside.

4   When the cooking program ends, perform a quick pressure release by moving the Pressure Release to **Venting**. Open the pot and, wearing heat-resistant mitts, lift out the steamer basket and pour the broccoli into the skillet with the bacon mixture. Add ¼ teaspoon salt and ¼ teaspoon pepper and toss to combine. Taste and adjust the seasoning with salt and pepper if needed.

5   Transfer the broccoli to a serving plate and serve warm.

This vegetable side dish is a great grain-free stand-in for plain steamed rice. Try it with main dishes, such as Beef, Bean, and Tomato Chili (page 108) or Sweet and Sour Pork (page 194).

CAULIFLOWER "RICE"

One 2-pound head cauliflower, cored and cut into 2-inch florets

1 tablespoon unsalted butter or olive oil

Kosher salt

PREP	0 MINUTES
COOK	20 MINUTES
PR	QPR
SERVES	6

1   Pour 1 cup water in the Instant Pot and place a steamer basket or wire metal steam rack in the pot. Place the cauliflower florets in the steamer basket or on the steam rack.

2   Secure the lid and set the Pressure Release to **Sealing**. Select the **Steam** setting and set the cooking time for 0 (zero) minutes at low pressure. (The pot will take about 15 minutes to come up to pressure before the cooking program begins.)

3   When the cooking program ends, perform a quick pressure release by moving the Pressure Release to **Venting**. Open the pot and, wearing heat-resistant mitts, remove the steamer basket; if you used the steam rack, transfer the cauliflower to a bowl, then, wearing heat-resistant mitts, grab the handles of the steam rack and lift the rack out of the pot. Lift out the inner pot and discard the water.

4   Return the cauliflower to the inner pot (there's no need to return the inner pot to the housing), along with the butter and ¼ teaspoon salt. Use a potato masher to roughly break up the cauliflower. The stems will not break down completely; if you like, remove and discard the stem pieces or remove them, chop them, and return them to the pot. Taste and adjust the seasoning with salt if needed.

5   Transfer the cauliflower "rice" to a serving bowl and serve hot.

Note: Alternatively, you can make cauliflower "rice" using the **Sauté** setting. Core the cauliflower, then very finely chop it or cut it into florets, then pulse the florets in a food processor until very finely chopped. Select the **Sauté** setting on the Instant Pot and melt the butter. Add the cauliflower and sauté for about 5 minutes, until translucent and tender. Taste and adjust the seasoning with salt if needed.

A few minutes in a grill pan gives steamed artichokes beautiful grill marks. Of course, you can also do them on a charcoal or gas grill if you happen to be cooking outdoors. Homemade lemony aioli is the perfect thing for dipping the leaves (and for spreading on hamburgers and sandwiches).

GRILLED ARTICHOKES WITH LEMON AIOLI

4 medium globe artichokes (see Note)

1 cup water

Lemon Aioli

½ cup grapeseed oil or other light, neutral oil

1 egg yolk

1 small garlic clove, minced

2 tablespoons fresh lemon juice, plus 1 teaspoon finely grated lemon zest

1 teaspoon Dijon mustard

1 teaspoon sugar

½ teaspoon kosher salt

¼ teaspoon freshly ground black pepper

1 tablespoon chopped fresh flat-leaf parsley

2 tablespoons olive oil

¼ teaspoon kosher salt

¼ teaspoon freshly ground black pepper

Chopped fresh flat-leaf parsley for sprinkling

PREP	10 MINUTES
COOK	20 MINUTES
PR	5 MINUTES NPR
SERVES	4

1   Holding one artichoke firmly on its side, use a serrated bread knife or a very sharp chef's knife to cut off the top one-third of the leaves. Next, cut off the stem even with the bottom of the artichoke. Using kitchen shears, trim off any thorny tips that remain on the leaves. Repeat with the remaining artichokes.

2   Pour the water into the Instant Pot and place a steamer basket inside. Place the artichokes in the basket. Secure the lid and set the **Pressure Release** to **Sealing**. Press the **Cancel** button to reset the cooking program, then select the **Steam** setting and set the cooking time for 10 minutes at high pressure. (The pot will take about 10 minutes to come up to pressure before the cooking program begins.)

3   To make the lemon aioli: While the artichokes are steaming, in a widemouthed 1-pint jar, combine the grapeseed oil, egg yolk, garlic, lemon juice, mustard, sugar, salt, and pepper. Lower an immersion blender into the jar, so the head is fully submerged. Using ½-second pulses, blend until an emulsified aioli forms, raising the blender head by ¼ inch or so after each pulse. By the time the blender head is at the top of the ingredients, the aioli should be fully emulsified, with all of the oil incorporated. Unplug the blender, then scrape any excess aioli off the blender into the jar. Stir in the lemon zest and parsley and set aside. (The aioli will keep in an airtight container, refrigerated, for up to 1 week.)

4   When the cooking program ends, let the pressure release naturally for 5 minutes, then move the Pressure Release to **Venting** to release any remaining steam. Open the pot and test an artichoke for doneness by trying to pull out an inner leaf. If it releases easily, the artichokes are ready. If it is difficult to free, the artichokes need to be cooked longer. In that case, secure the lid again and set the Pressure Release to **Sealing**. Press the **Cancel** button to reset the cooking program, then select the **Steam** setting and cook for 1 minute more.

Note: You can steam artichokes of any size in the Instant Pot. The 6-quart models will accommodate four medium (3-inch-diameter) or large (4-inch-diameter) artichokes or two jumbo artichokes (4½- to 5-inch-diameter). Set the cooking time for 10 minutes for medium artichokes, 12 minutes for large artichokes, or 15 minutes for jumbo artichokes.

5   Perform a quick pressure release by moving the Pressure Release to **Venting** and again test for doneness. If necessary, cook for 1 minute longer, using the same process until cooked. Using tongs, transfer the artichokes to a cutting board, allowing any excess liquid to drain back into the pot. Wearing heat-resistant mitts, slice each artichoke in half from top to bottom. Using a paring knife or teaspoon, scoop out the fuzzy chokes and small, flimsy inner leaves.

6   Warm a grill pan over medium heat for about 4 minutes, until hot. Brush the cut sides of the artichoke halves with the olive oil, then sprinkle all over with the salt and pepper. Place the artichoke halves, cut-sides down, in the pan and cook for about 4 minutes, until they have developed nice charred marks. Transfer the artichokes to a serving plate.

7   Sprinkle the artichokes with parsley and serve warm, with the aioli for dipping.

This is a creamy, cheesy, Italian-spiced dip loaded with artichokes and spinach. Serve it with baguette slices and crudités, then use leftovers for spreading on sandwiches or as a pasta sauce. Make sure to use loosely packed, bagged frozen spinach, rather than the kind that comes in a solid block. The dip freezes well, in 1- to 2-cup portions in tightly lidded containers, for up to 2 months. Defrost in the refrigerator for 24 hours before you plan to serve it, or in the microwave for when guests arrive unexpectedly.

ARTICHOKE-SPINACH DIP

2 tablespoons olive oil

6 garlic cloves, minced

1 yellow onion, diced

½ cup vegetable broth (page 284) or chicken broth (page 286)

One 1-pound bag frozen chopped spinach

Two 14-ounce cans artichoke hearts, drained and chopped

8 ounces cream cheese, at room temperature

1 cup tightly packed shredded mozzarella cheese

½ cup grated Parmesan cheese

½ cup mayonnaise

½ cup chopped fresh flat-leaf parsley

2 teaspoons Italian seasoning

1 teaspoon freshly ground black pepper

Kosher salt

1   Select the **Sauté** setting on the Instant Pot and heat the olive oil and garlic for about 3 minutes, until the garlic is bubbling and beginning to turn blond. Add the onion and sauté for about 5 minutes, until softened. Stir in the vegetable broth, using a wooden spoon to nudge loose any browned bits from the bottom of the pot. Stir in the spinach, breaking up any large chunks, then stir in the artichoke hearts.

2   Secure the lid and set the Pressure Release to **Sealing**. Press the **Cancel** button to reset the cooking program, then select the **Pressure Cook** or **Manual** setting and set the cooking time for 1 minute at high pressure. (The pot will take about 15 minutes to come up to pressure before the cooking program begins.)

3   When the cooking program ends, perform a quick pressure release by moving the Pressure Release to **Venting**. Open the pot, then stir in the cream cheese, mozzarella, Parmesan, mayonnaise, parsley, Italian seasoning, and pepper. Taste and adjust the seasoning with salt if needed.

4   Transfer the dip to a serving bowl and serve immediately, or leave it in the pot on the **Keep Warm** setting for up to 10 hours.

PREP	0 MINUTES
COOK	25 MINUTES
PR	QPR
MAKES	ABOUT 8 CUPS

A quick side dish of tender, lightly smoky collard greens is a welcome addition to the dinner table. For a shortcut, buy a 12-ounce bag of prewashed and chopped collards. Mustard greens or curly kale work well, too. For a vegan version, see Variation.

COLLARD GREENS WITH HAM

1 tablespoon olive oil

1 medium yellow onion, diced

1 medium carrot, peeled and diced

2 bunches collard greens, stems discarded and leaves sliced into 1-inch ribbons

8 ounces ham steak, diced

1 tablespoon tomato paste

¼ teaspoon freshly ground black pepper

½ cup water

Kosher salt

PREP	0 MINUTES
COOK	20 MINUTES
PR	QPR
SERVES	4 TO 6

1   Select the **Sauté** setting on the Instant Pot and heat the olive oil. Add the onion and carrots and sauté for about 4 minutes, until the onion begins to soften. Stir in the collards and sauté for about 2 minutes, until wilted. Stir in the ham, tomato paste, pepper, and water.

2   Secure the lid and set the Pressure Release to **Sealing**. Press the **Cancel** button to reset the cooking program, then select the **Pressure Cook** or **Manual** setting and set the cooking time for 5 minutes at high pressure. (The pot will take about 10 minutes to come up to pressure before the cooking program begins.)

3   When the cooking program ends, perform a quick pressure release by moving the Pressure Release to **Venting**. Open the pot and stir the mixture. Taste and adjust the seasoning with salt if needed.

4   Spoon the collards into a serving bowl or onto serving plates. Serve warm.

Variation: To make a vegan version, omit the ham, increase the carrots to a total of four, and add ½ teaspoon kosher salt and ½ teaspoon smoked paprika along with the tomato paste, pepper, and water.

The texture and flavor of the onions in this dip make it so tasty that you'll never want to go back to the store-bought variety again. Start by making some 30-Minute Caramelized Onions, then use half of them to whip up a batch of this creamy dip. It's a staple on any game-day coffee-table spread. Serve with chips and crudités for dipping.

CARAMELIZED ONION DIP

½ cup sour cream

½ cup mayonnaise

4 ounces cream cheese, at room temperature

1 teaspoon Worcestershire sauce

½ teaspoon kosher salt

½ teaspoon freshly ground black pepper

¼ teaspoon cayenne pepper

1¼ cups 30-Minute Caramelized Onions (page 290)

Tortilla or potato chips, carrot sticks, celery sticks, and/or sliced bell pepper for serving

1   Add the sour cream, mayonnaise, cream cheese, Worcestershire, salt, black pepper, and cayenne to the Instant Pot. Select the low **Sauté** setting. Whisk the mixture for 2 minutes, until no lumps remain and everything is warmed through.

2   Press the **Cancel** button to turn off the pot. Wearing heat-resistant mitts, lift out the inner pot. Gently stir in the caramelized onions, taking care not to break them up too much. Transfer the dip to a serving bowl.

3   Serve the dip right away, with chips and vegetables.

Note: The dip can be made ahead and kept in an airtight container, refrigerated, for up to 2 days. Remove it from the fridge about 1 hour before serving, to allow it to soften.

PREP	0 MINUTES
COOK	5 MINUTES
PR	N/A
MAKES	ABOUT 2 CUPS

Creamed spinach is one of my favorite vegetable side dishes, whether alongside a weeknight steak dinner or a Sunday roast. It has a mellow, kid-pleasing flavor, and this version is as easy and fast as they come. It's also gluten-free—the cream cheese adds just the right amount of richness and body so you don't have to make a flour-thickened sauce. Make sure to use bagged whole-leaf or chopped spinach for this recipe, not chopped spinach sold in solid blocks.

CREAMED SPINACH

2 tablespoons unsalted butter or olive oil

1 large yellow onion, diced

2 garlic cloves, chopped

Two 1-pound bags frozen spinach

1 cup vegetable broth (page 284) or chicken broth (page 286)

2 ounces cream cheese, at room temperature

¼ cup heavy cream

¼ teaspoon grated nutmeg

¼ teaspoon freshly ground black pepper

Kosher salt

PREP	0 MINUTES
COOK	25 MINUTES
PR	QPR
SERVES	8

1   Select the **Sauté** setting on the Instant Pot and melt the butter. Add the onion and garlic and sauté for about 5 minutes, until the onion is softened. Stir in the spinach and vegetable broth.

2   Secure the lid and set the Pressure Release to **Sealing**. Press the **Cancel** button to reset the cooking program, then select the **Pressure Cook** or **Manual** setting and set the cooking time for 1 minute at high pressure. (The pot will take about 15 minutes to come up to pressure before the cooking program begins.)

3   When the cooking program ends, perform a quick pressure release by moving the Pressure Release to **Venting**. Open the pot, then stir in the cream cheese, cream, nutmeg, pepper, and 1 teaspoon salt. Taste and adjust the seasoning with salt if needed.

4   Transfer the creamed spinach to a serving bowl and serve immediately, or leave it in the pot on the **Keep Warm** setting for up to 10 hours.

I like to think of creamed corn as a starch and vegetable side dish all in one. Creamy and mild, it goes well with just about any main dish you can think of, and it's total comfort food. I use frozen corn to make mine, since it's sweet all year round and requires zero kitchen prep. Bring this to a potluck and nobody will know how easy it was to put together.

CREAMED CORN

2 tablespoons unsalted butter or olive oil

1 large yellow onion, diced

2 pounds frozen corn kernels

1 cup vegetable broth (page 284) or chicken broth (page 286)

½ cup grated Parmesan cheese

2 ounces cream cheese, at room temperature

¼ cup heavy cream

Pinch of cayenne pepper

Kosher salt

PREP	0 MINUTES
COOK	25 MINUTES
PR	QPR
SERVES	8

1   Select the **Sauté** setting on the Instant Pot and melt the butter. Add the onion and sauté for about 5 minutes, until softened. Stir in the corn and vegetable broth.

2   Secure the lid and set the Pressure Release to **Sealing**. Press the **Cancel** button to reset the cooking program, then select the **Pressure Cook** or **Manual** setting and set the cooking time for 2 minutes at high pressure. (The pot will take about 15 minutes to come up to pressure before the cooking program begins.)

3   When the cooking program ends, perform a quick pressure release by moving the Pressure Release to **Venting**. Open the pot, then stir in the Parmesan, cream cheese, cream, cayenne, and ¼ teaspoon salt. Taste and adjust the seasoning with salt if needed.

4   Spoon the creamed corn into a serving bowl and serve immediately, or leave it in the pot on the **Keep Warm** setting for up to 10 hours.

There's no need to peel or chop a celery root to cook it in the Instant Pot. Once it's steamed, its skin is easily scraped off with a paring knife or the edge of a spoon. Mashed with butter and a little bit of lemon juice or wine vinegar to brighten things up, celery root makes a great side dish for hearty braises such as Red Wine Short Ribs (page 226) and Rosemary-Dijon Pot Roast (page 224).

CELERY ROOT PUREE

One 1½-pound celery root, scrubbed and trimmed of any stalks

2 tablespoons unsalted butter

1 teaspoon fresh lemon juice or white wine vinegar

Kosher salt

¼ teaspoon freshly ground black pepper

PREP	0 MINUTES
COOK	1 HOUR,
	5 MINUTES
PR	QPR
SERVES	3 OR 4

1   Pour 1½ cups water into the Instant Pot and place the wire metal steam rack in the pot. Place the celery root on top of the rack.

2   Secure the lid and set the Pressure Release to **Sealing**. Select the **Steam** setting and set the cooking time for 40 minutes at high pressure. (The pot will take about 10 minutes to come up to pressure before the cooking program begins.)

3   When the cooking program ends, perform a quick pressure release by moving the Pressure Release to **Venting**. Open the pot and insert a paring knife into the celery root to check for doneness. You should be able to easily pierce the root all the way to the middle. If the knife meets any resistance, the root is not quite cooked through. In this case, secure the lid once again and set the Pressure Release to **Sealing**. Select the **Steam** setting and set the cooking time for 5 minutes at high pressure.

4   When the cooking program ends, perform a quick pressure release by moving the Pressure Release to **Venting** and again test for doneness. If necessary, cook for 5 minutes longer, using the same process until cooked. If at any point most of the water has evaporated from the pot, pour in an additional ½ cup water to ensure that the pot will still be able to come up to pressure.

5   Once the celery root is cooked, wearing heat-resistant mitts, grab the handles of the steam rack, lift out the rack, and set it on a plate. Let stand until the celery root is cool enough to handle, about 10 minutes.

6   Meanwhile, wearing the heat-resistant mitts, lift out the inner pot and discard the water.

7   Using a paring knife, scrape the skin off the celery root and trim off any tough fibers. Return the celery root to the inner pot (there's no need to return the inner pot to the housing). Add the butter, lemon juice, ½ teaspoon salt, and pepper. Use a potato masher or an immersion blender to mash or puree the celery root until smooth. Taste and adjust the seasoning with salt if needed.

8   Transfer the puree to a serving bowl and serve warm.

For this dish, rather than cook fennel and shallots on a pressure setting, I use the Instant Pot's Sauté setting. It cooks in just 20 minutes, and leaving the pot uncovered for the last 10 minutes of cooking allows the orange juice to reduce into a shiny glaze. This is a lovely side dish for Whole Chicken with Caramelized Onion Gravy (page 174), especially in the winter, when fennel is plentiful and extra sweet.

ORANGE-BRAISED FENNEL AND SHALLOTS

1 tablespoon olive oil

1 tablespoon unsalted butter

12 ounces shallots, peeled and quartered

2 large fennel bulbs, trimmed, halved lengthwise, and sliced ¼ inch thick, plus 1 teaspoon chopped fennel fronds

½ teaspoon kosher salt

¾ cup fresh orange juice, plus 1 teaspoon finely grated orange zest

PREP	0 MINUTES
COOK	20 MINUTES
PR	N/A
SERVES	4 TO 6

1   Select the high **Sauté** setting on the Instant Pot and heat the oil and butter for 2 minutes, until the butter is melted and bubbling. Add the shallots and sear without stirring for about 3 minutes, until lightly browned on one side.

2   Add the fennel, salt, and orange juice to the pot and stir to combine. Cover with the glass lid and cook for about 5 minutes, until the fennel has begun to soften. Uncover and cook, stirring occasionally, for about 10 minutes more, until the orange juice reduces to a thick glaze. Press the **Cancel** button to turn off the pot. Transfer the vegetables to a serving dish.

3   Sprinkle the vegetable with the fennel fronds and orange zest. Serve warm.

When summer corn is at its sweetest, steam some up in the Instant Pot! These Mexican-inspired ears of corn are slathered with tangy homemade lime mayonnaise, then sprinkled with salty cotija cheese, chili powder, and fresh cilantro. They make a great side dish for Smoky Brisket (page 220) or Carnitas (page 185). Leave the ears whole (but trim them to fit into the pot, if needed) or break them in half before steaming for smaller portions.

CORN ON THE COB WITH COTIJA AND LIME MAYONNAISE

4 ears fresh corn, husks and silk removed, trimmed to fit into the pot if needed

Lime Mayonnaise

½ cup grapeseed oil or other light, neutral oil

1 egg yolk

2 tablespoons fresh lime juice, plus 1 teaspoon finely grated lime zest

½ teaspoon sugar

½ teaspoon kosher salt

¼ cup grated cotija cheese

½ teaspoon chili powder

1 tablespoon chopped fresh cilantro

PREP	0 MINUTES
COOK	20 MINUTES
PR	QPR
SERVES	4

1   Pour 1 cup water into the Instant Pot and place the wire metal steam rack in the pot. Lay the corn on the steam rack, stacking the ears on top of each other.

2   Secure the lid and set the Pressure Release to **Sealing**. Select the **Steam** setting and set the cooking time for 3 minutes at high pressure. (The pot will take about 15 minutes to come up to pressure before the cooking program begins.)

3   To make the lime mayonnaise: While the corn is cooking, in a wide-mouthed 1-pint jar, combine the grapeseed oil, egg yolk, lime juice, sugar, and salt. Lower an immersion blender into the jar, so the head is fully submerged. Using ½-second pulses, blend until an emulsified mayonnaise forms, raising the blender head by ¼ inch or so after each pulse. By the time the blender head is at the top of the ingredients, the mayonnaise should be fully emulsified, with all of the oil incorporated. Unplug the blender, then scrape any excess mayonnaise off the blender into the jar. Stir in the lime zest and set aside. (The mayonnaise will keep in an airtight container, refrigerated, for up to 1 week.)

4   When the cooking program ends, perform a quick pressure release by moving the Pressure Release to **Venting**. Open the pot and, using tongs, transfer the corn to a serving plate.

5   While the corn is still hot, spread 1 tablespoon lime mayonnaise all over each ear, then sprinkle with 1 tablespoon of the cheese, ⅛ teaspoon of the chili powder, and ¾ teaspoon of the chopped cilantro. Serve warm.

This is one of my favorite recipes in this book. I am a sucker for simple vegetable dishes that go from freezer to table in about 30 minutes. The combination of baby lima beans, corn, and tomatoes is pure summer, but you can make this colorful side to liven up your table any time of year. For anyone who hated lima beans growing up, I urge you to try the baby ones!

SUCCOTASH

1 tablespoon olive oil

1 tablespoon unsalted butter

1 medium yellow onion, diced

1 garlic clove, minced

One 16-ounce bag frozen baby lima beans

One 12-ounce bag frozen corn kernels

One 14½-ounce can diced tomatoes and their liquid

½ teaspoon dried thyme

½ teaspoon kosher salt

¼ teaspoon freshly ground black pepper

½ cup vegetable broth (page 284) or chicken broth (page 286)

1   Select the **Sauté** setting on the Instant Pot and heat the olive oil and butter. When the butter is melted, add the onion and garlic and sauté for about 5 minutes, until the onion is softened. Add the lima beans, corn, tomatoes and their liquid, thyme, salt, pepper, and vegetable broth. Stir to combine.

2   Secure the lid and set the Pressure Release to **Sealing**. Press the **Cancel** button to reset the cooking program, then select the **Pressure Cook** or **Manual** setting and set the cooking time for 3 minutes at high pressure. (The pot will take about 15 minutes to come up to pressure before the cooking program begins.)

3   When the cooking program ends, perform a quick pressure release by moving the Pressure Release to **Venting**. Open the pot and stir the succotash, then transfer to a serving bowl. Serve warm.

PREP	0 MINUTES
COOK	25 MINUTES
PR	QPR
SERVES	6 TO 8

Lightly steamed green beans with plenty of butter-toasted almonds sprinkled on top are a crowd-pleasing side. This is a fantastic and fresher-flavored alternative to the Thanksgiving-staple green bean casserole made with cream of mushroom soup. It'll please adults and kids alike at your next holiday (or weeknight) dinner.

GREEN BEANS AMANDINE

1 pound green beans, trimmed

2 tablespoons unsalted butter

½ cup sliced almonds

Kosher salt

Freshly ground black pepper

PREP	0 MINUTES
COOK	20 MINUTES
PR	QPR
SERVES	4

1   Pour 1 cup water into the Instant Pot and place a steamer basket in the pot. Add the green beans to the steamer basket.

2   Secure the lid and set the Pressure Release to **Sealing**. Select the **Steam** setting and set the cooking time for 3 minutes at low pressure. (The pot will take about 10 minutes to come up to pressure before the cooking program begins.)

3   When the cooking program ends, perform a quick pressure release by moving the Pressure Release to **Venting**. Open the pot and, wearing heat-resistant mitts, lift out the steamer basket. Lift out the inner pot, discard the water, and return the inner pot to the housing.

4   Press the **Cancel** button to reset the cooking program, then select the **Sauté** setting. Add the butter and almonds to the pot and sauté for about 4 minutes, until the almonds are toasted and the butter has browned. Add the green beans, ¼ teaspoon salt, and ¼ teaspoon pepper and stir to combine. Press the **Cancel** button to turn off the pot. Taste and adjust the seasoning with salt and pepper if needed. Wearing heat-resistant mitts, once again lift out the inner pot.

5   Transfer the green beans to a serving dish, scraping out all of the almonds from the pot. Serve warm.

When it comes to asparagus, I like to keep the preparation simple so the spears remain the star of the show. Topped with grated hard-boiled eggs and a lemony vinaigrette, they're a perfect side dish in the springtime. I almost always have hard-boiled eggs in the fridge, so I can make this dish in about 15 minutes flat. If you decide to cook the eggs just before cooking the asparagus, the Instant Pot will already be warm, so it will take only about 5 minutes to come up to pressure when cooking the asparagus. In this case, set the asparagus cooking time for 1 minute at low pressure.

ASPARAGUS WITH GRATED EGGS AND LEMON VINAIGRETTE

Lemon Vinaigrette

¼ cup extra-virgin olive oil

2 tablespoons fresh lemon juice

½ small shallot, minced

1 teaspoon Dijon mustard

½ teaspoon sugar

½ teaspoon herbes de Provence

¼ teaspoon kosher salt

¼ teaspoon freshly ground black pepper

1 pound asparagus spears, bottom inch trimmed off, remaining bottom 4 inches peeled

2 hard-boiled eggs (page 21)

Freshly ground black pepper

PREP	5 MINUTES
COOK	10 MINUTES
PR	QPR
SERVES	4

1   To make the vinaigrette: In a jar with a tight-fitting lid or other leak-proof container, combine the olive oil, lemon juice, shallot, mustard, sugar, herbes de Provence, salt, and pepper. Cover and shake vigorously. Set aside.

2   Pour 1½ cups water into the Instant Pot and place the wire metal steam rack in the pot. Place the asparagus on the rack.

3   Secure the lid and set the Pressure Release to **Sealing**. Select the **Steam** setting and set the cooking time for 0 minutes at low pressure. (The pot will take about 10 minutes to come up to pressure before the cooking program begins.)

4   When the cooking program ends, perform a quick pressure release by moving the Pressure Release to **Venting**. Open the pot and, wearing heat-resistant mitts, grab the handles of the steam rack and lift out the rack. Transfer the asparagus to a serving plate.

5   Shake the vinaigrette to recombine. Drizzle the asparagus with about 3 tablespoons of the vinaigrette. Peel the eggs, then grate them over the asparagus using a fine grater or a coarse Microplane. Drizzle on more vinaigrette and grind some pepper on top. Serve the asparagus warm or at room temperature.

Summer vegetables are the stars in this easy ratatouille. Serve it as a side dish to rotisserie chicken, tossed with pasta and sprinkled with cheese, or, my favorite way, as an appetizer with some crusty bread for sopping up the herby cooking liquid.

RATATOUILLE

1 medium globe eggplant, cut into 1-inch pieces

3 medium zucchini, cut into 1-inch pieces

1 teaspoon kosher salt

2 tablespoons olive oil, plus more for drizzling

1 large yellow onion, cut into 1-inch pieces

2 garlic cloves, minced

½ teaspoon freshly ground black pepper

1 teaspoon dried basil

½ teaspoon dried thyme

1 bay leaf

3 yellow, orange, or red bell peppers, stemmed and cut into 1-inch pieces

One 14½-ounce can diced tomatoes and their liquid

¼ cup dry white wine or vegetable broth (page 284)

Fresh basil or rosemary leaves for sprinkling

Warmed crusty bread for serving

1   In a large bowl, toss together the eggplant and zucchini with the salt. Let stand for 15 minutes.

2   Select the **Sauté** setting on the Instant Pot and heat the olive oil. Add the onion and garlic and sauté for about 4 minutes, until the onion is softened. Add the black pepper, basil, thyme, and bay leaf and sauté for about 1 minute. Add the eggplant-zucchini mixture and any liquid that has pooled in the bottom of the bowl, along with the bell peppers, tomatoes and their liquid, and wine. Stir to combine.

3   Secure the lid and set the Pressure Release to **Sealing**. Press the **Cancel** button to reset the cooking program, then select the **Pressure Cook** or **Manual** setting and set the cooking time for 2 minutes at low pressure. (The pot will take about 15 minutes to come up to pressure before the cooking program begins.)

4   When the cooking program ends, perform a quick pressure release by moving the Pressure Release to **Venting**. Open the pot and spoon the ratatouille into a serving bowl.

5   Drizzle the ratatouille with olive oil and sprinkle with fresh basil. Serve warm, with crusty bread.

PREP	15 MINUTES
COOK	25 MINUTES
PR	QPR
SERVES	6

Use cooked butternut squash in a simple mash with maple syrup (see opposite), puree it into soup (page 92), or use it in place of canned pumpkin in cheesecake. Use spaghetti squash for a vegan lasagna (page 136), or serve it as you would pasta, with meatballs (page 213) and marinara (page 287), for a low-carb meal. Minimal prep is required to cook winter squash in the Instant Pot—simply quarter the squash, remove the seeds, then steam the pieces under pressure. Once the squash is cooked and cooled, you can use a big spoon to scoop the flesh out of the skin of a butternut squash or a fork to separate the strands of a spaghetti squash.

STEAMED BUTTERNUT OR SPAGHETTI SQUASH

1 butternut squash or spaghetti squash, no larger than 3½ pounds

1   Pour 1½ cups water into the Instant Pot. Place the wire metal steam rack in the pot.

2   Trim off the stem end of the squash, cut the squash lengthwise into quarters, and scoop out and discard the seeds. Place the squash quarters on the steam rack in the pot, arranging the pieces in a single layer.

3   Secure the lid and set the Pressure Release to **Sealing**. Select the **Steam** setting and set the cooking time for 7 minutes at high pressure. (The pot will take about 10 minutes to come up to pressure before the cooking program begins.)

4   When the cooking program ends, perform a quick pressure release by moving the Pressure Release to **Venting**. Open the pot and, using tongs, transfer the squash to a plate or cutting board. Set aside until cool enough to handle, about 5 minutes. Use a spoon to scoop the flesh from the skin of the butternut squash, or a fork to separate the strands of the spaghetti squash. Discard the skin.

5   Use immediately, or let cool to room temperature, transfer to an airtight container, and refrigerate for up to 3 days.

Butternut squash becomes soft and scoopable in record time in the Instant Pot. It cooks in about half the time that it takes to roast in the oven. I like to mash the squash with butter, maple syrup, and spices for a sweet side dish.

MAPLE-BUTTERNUT PUREE

One 3- to 3½-pound butternut squash

4 tablespoons unsalted butter

2 tablespoons maple syrup

Kosher salt

¼ teaspoon ground cinnamon

¼ teaspoon grated nutmeg

PREP	5 MINUTES
COOK	25 MINUTES
PR	QPR
COOL	10 MINUTES
SERVES	6

1   Pour 1½ cups water into the Instant Pot and place the wire metal steam rack in the pot.

2   Trim off the stem end of the squash, cut the squash lengthwise into quarters, and scoop out the seeds. Place the squash quarters on the steam rack, arranging the pieces around each other so they all fit in the pot.

3   Secure the lid and set the Pressure Release to **Sealing**. Select the **Steam** setting and set the cooking time for 7 minutes at high pressure. (The pot will take about 20 minutes to come up to pressure before the cooking program begins.)

4   When the cooking program ends, perform a quick pressure release by moving the Pressure Release to **Venting**. Open the pot and, using tongs, transfer the squash, skin-side up, to a plate or cutting board. Set aside until cool enough to handle, about 10 minutes.

5   Wearing heat-resistant mitts, grab the handles of the steam rack and remove it from the pot. Still wearing the mitts, lift out the inner pot and discard the water. Return the inner pot to the housing.

6   Use a spoon to scoop the flesh from the skin of the squash; it should be very easy to remove. Return the squash to the pot and add the butter, maple syrup, 1 teaspoon salt, cinnamon, and nutmeg. For a rustic texture, mash the mixture with a potato masher; for a smooth consistency, puree with an immersion blender. Taste and adjust the seasoning with salt if needed.

7   Transfer the puree to a serving bowl and serve immediately.

This is an easy, kid-pleasing side dish to serve with a roasted or rotisserie chicken. The butter-honey glaze is an irresistible coating for steamed carrot coins, and the whole thing comes together in about 15 minutes.

CARROTS GLAZED WITH HONEY AND THYME

1 pound carrots, peeled and sliced into ¼-inch-thick rounds

1 tablespoon unsalted butter

1 tablespoon honey

1 teaspoon fresh thyme leaves

¼ teaspoon kosher salt

PREP	0 MINUTES
COOK	10 MINUTES
PR	QPR
SERVES	4

1   Pour 1 cup water into the Instant Pot and place a steamer basket in the pot. Add the carrots to the basket.

2   Secure the lid and set the Pressure Release to **Sealing**. Select the **Steam** setting and set the cooking time to 0 (zero) minutes at low pressure. (The pot will take about 10 minutes to come to pressure before the cooking program begins.)

3   When the cooking program ends, perform a quick pressure release by moving the Pressure Release to **Venting**. Open the pot and, wearing heat-resistant mitts, remove the steamer basket and set aside. Lift out the inner pot, discard the water, and return the inner pot to the Instant Pot housing.

4   Press the **Cancel** button to reset the cooking program, then select the **Sauté** setting. Add the butter, honey, thyme, and salt to the pot and stir until the butter has melted. Add the carrots and cook, stirring gently, for about 2 minutes, until the carrots are glazed.

5   Transfer the carrots to a serving bowl. Serve warm.

Steaming under pressure is my favorite way to cook beets—it's faster than any other method for getting the hardy root vegetables to a fork-tender state. I'll often steam a pound of them on the weekend for slicing into dinner salads all week long. This recipe showcases the beets as the main event, and they go so well with goat cheese, walnuts, cranberries, and arugula. A nice option for holiday dinners, the salad is easily doubled (the dressing already makes enough for two batches; store the rest in a tightly lidded container in the refrigerator for up to 1 week).

BEET SALAD WITH GOAT CHEESE AND ARUGULA

1 pound beets, each about 2½ inches in diameter

Balsamic Vinaigrette

¼ cup extra-virgin olive oil

¼ cup neutral vegetable oil

2 tablespoons red wine vinegar

2 tablespoons balsamic vinegar

1 tablespoon water

1 teaspoon Dijon mustard

1 teaspoon brown sugar

¼ teaspoon kosher salt

¼ teaspoon freshly ground black pepper

1 garlic clove, peeled

One 6-ounce bag baby arugula or arugula–baby spinach blend

½ cup crumbled fresh goat cheese (chèvre)

½ cup walnuts, roughly chopped, toasted

¼ cup dried cranberries

PREP	0 MINUTES
COOK	30 MINUTES
PR	QPR
SERVES	4 TO 6

1   Pour 1 cup water into the Instant Pot and place the wire metal steam rack in the pot. Arrange the beets in a single layer on the steam rack.

2   Secure the lid and set the Pressure Release to **Sealing**. Select the **Steam** setting and set the cooking time for 20 minutes at high pressure. (The pot will take about 10 minutes to come up to pressure before the cooking program begins.)

3   While the beets are cooking, prepare an ice bath.

4   To make the balsamic vinaigrette: In a widemouthed 1-pint jar, combine the olive oil, vegetable oil, red wine vinegar, balsamic vinegar, water, mustard, brown sugar, salt, pepper, and garlic. Lower an immersion blender into the jar, so the head is fully submerged. Blend until an emulsified vinaigrette forms. Set aside.

5   When the cooking program ends, perform a quick pressure release by moving the Pressure Release to **Venting**. Open the pot and, using tongs, transfer the beets to the ice bath and let cool for 10 minutes.

6   Using your fingers and a paring knife, remove the skins from the beets—they should peel off very easily. Trim and discard the ends of the beets, then slice them into ¼-inch-thick rounds.

7   In a large bowl, toss the arugula with ¼ cup of the vinaigrette. Arrange the arugula on a large serving plate or on individual salad plates, then top with the beets. Spoon another ¼ cup vinaigrette over the beets, then sprinkle with the cheese, walnuts, and cranberries. Serve immediately.

Potatoes vary in size, so these cooking times are given in ranges. If you are unsure of the weight of your potatoes, cook them for the minimum amount of time, then test for doneness. If they are not yet fork-tender, steam them for a few minutes more.

You can steam potatoes whole, quartered, sliced, or cubed. The 6-quart Instant Pot can hold a maximum of 4 pounds of potatoes, but I find that I get the most even and consistent results when I steam 3 pounds or less.

The following timetable applies to all kinds of potatoes, including starchy russets, waxy creamers, and sweet potatoes. Cook whole potatoes on the wire metal steam rack, and quartered, cubed, or sliced potatoes in a steamer basket.

STEAMED POTATOES (REGULAR AND SWEET)

Whole Potatoes	Cooking Time (in minutes, at high pressure)
Baby (1 to 2 ounces)	5
Small (3 to 4 ounces)	8 to 10
Medium (6 to 8 ounces)	10 to 12
Large (about 10 ounces)	12 to 15
Extra Large (12 to 14 ounces)	20 to 25
Jumbo (16 to 18 ounces)	28 to 30
Prepared Potatoes	Cooking Time (in minutes, at high pressure)
Quartered (medium)	5
Sliced (1⁄2 to 3⁄4 inch thick)	3 to 4
Cubed (1 inch)	3

1   Pour 1 cup water into the Instant Pot. If cooking whole potatoes, place the wire metal steam rack in the pot; if cooking prepared potatoes, place a steamer basket in the pot. Add the potatoes to the pot.

2   Secure the lid and set the Pressure Release to **Sealing**. Select the **Steam** setting, then refer to the time chart at left for setting the cooking time; use high pressure. (Depending on the quantity of potatoes, the pot will take 10 to 15 minutes to come up to pressure before the cooking program begins.)

3   When the cooking program ends, perform a quick pressure release by moving the Pressure Release to **Venting**. Open the pot and use tongs to remove whole potatoes or wear heat-resistant mitts to lift out the steamer basket or steam rack.

4   Serve immediately, or let cool to room temperature, transfer to an airtight container, and refrigerate for up to 3 days.

The mayonnaise-based dressing for this classic picnic side dish has a secret ingredient—a splash of tangy dill pickle brine. It seasons the potatoes as well as balances the richness of the mayonnaise. See the Note for suggestions for vegetable add-ins; you can make this salad as simple or as colorful as you like.

CLASSIC POTATO SALAD

2½ pounds russet potatoes, peeled and quartered

2 eggs

½ cup mayonnaise

1 tablespoon yellow mustard

½ teaspoon freshly ground black pepper

Kosher salt

¼ cup dill pickle brine (see page 295), plus 2 dill pickle spears, minced

½ small red onion, diced

2 celery stalks, diced

¼ cup chopped fresh flat-leaf parsley or chives

PREP	0 MINUTES
COOK	20 MINUTES
PR	QPR
SERVES	6 TO 8

1 Pour 1 cup water into the Instant Pot. Place a steamer basket in the pot and add the potatoes, then place the eggs on top of the potatoes.

2 Secure the lid and set the Pressure Release to **Sealing**. Select the **Steam** setting and set the cooking time for 5 minutes at high pressure. (The pot will take about 10 minutes to come up to pressure before the cooking program begins.)

3 While the potatoes and eggs are cooking, prepare an ice bath.

4 In a small bowl, stir together the mayonnaise, mustard, pepper, ½ teaspoon salt, and pickle brine to make a dressing.

5 When the cooking program ends, perform a quick pressure release by moving the Pressure Release to **Venting**. Open the pot and, using tongs, transfer the eggs to the ice bath. Wearing heat-resistant mitts, remove the steamer basket from the pot.

6 After the eggs have cooled for about 5 minutes, peel and roughly chop them, then put in a large bowl. The potatoes should now be cool enough to handle; cut them into 1-inch cubes and add them to the eggs. Add the onion, celery, parsley, minced pickles, and dressing, and toss until well combined. Taste and adjust the seasoning with salt if needed.

7 Transfer the salad to a serving bowl and serve immediately, or cover and refrigerate for up to 3 days.

Note: You can add as many other vegetables as you like to this salad to bump up the crunch and color. I often include diced carrot, sliced radish, and/or diced bell pepper, as well as sliced green onion.

In my house, we like our mashed potatoes with just enough dairy to make them creamy but not over-the-top rich. Peeled, sliced potatoes take about 15 minutes to steam (including the time it takes for the pot to come up to pressure), so the dish ends up taking about 20 minutes from start to finish. Serve the potatoes alongside Barbecue Turkey Meatloaf (page 179), Red Wine Short Ribs (page 226), Smothered Pork Chops (page 193), or Pork Loin with Apple Cider and Rosemary (page 196).

CREAMY MASHED POTATOES

1 ½ pounds russet potatoes, peeled and sliced into ¾-inch-thick rounds

½ cup half-and-half or whole milk

¼ cup sour cream

2 tablespoons unsalted butter

Kosher salt

Freshly ground black pepper

PREP	0 MINUTES
COOK	20 MINUTES
PR	QPR
SERVES	4

1   Pour 1 cup water into the Instant Pot and place a steamer basket in the pot. Add the potatoes to the basket.

2   Secure the lid and set the Pressure Release to **Sealing**. Select the **Steam** setting and set the cooking time for 4 minutes at high pressure. (The pot will take about 10 minutes to come up to pressure before the cooking program begins.)

3   When the cooking program ends, perform a quick pressure release by moving the Pressure Release to **Venting**. Open the pot and, wearing heat-resistant mitts, lift out the steamer basket. Lift out the inner pot and discard the water.

4   Return the potatoes to the still-warm inner pot. Add the half-and-half, sour cream, butter, ¾ teaspoon salt, and ¼ teaspoon pepper, then use a potato masher to mash the potatoes to your desired texture. Taste for seasoning and add more salt and pepper if needed.

5   Spoon the mashed potatoes into a serving bowl and serve warm.

Note: For a twist on this traditional mash, substitute 2 parsnips, peeled and sliced into ¾-inch rounds, for ½ pound of the potatoes.

These potatoes are soft in the middle and crispy on the outside, and they're the perfect side dish for Whole Chicken with Caramelized Onion Gravy (page 174) or Pork Loin with Apple Cider and Rosemary (page 196). You can steam the potatoes up to 3 days ahead of time, then smash and bake them while the rest of your meal is cooking.

CRISPY SMASHED POTATOES

2 pounds whole baby or small potatoes

2 tablespoons olive oil

½ teaspoon kosher salt

½ teaspoon freshly ground black pepper

PREP	0 MINUTES
COOK	40 MINUTES
PR	QPR
SERVES	4 TO 6

1   Preheat the oven to 425°F. Line a rimmed baking sheet with a silicone baking mat or aluminum foil.

2   Pour 1 cup water into the Instant Pot. Place the wire metal steam rack in the pot and add the potatoes.

3   Secure the lid and set the Pressure Release to **Sealing**. Select the **Steam** setting and set the cooking time for 5 minutes for baby potatoes, or 8 minutes for small potatoes, at high pressure. (The pot will take about 10 minutes to come up to pressure before the cooking program begins.)

4   When the cooking program ends, perform a quick pressure release by moving the Pressure Release to **Venting**. Open the pot and use tongs to remove the potatoes and arrange them in a single layer on the prepared baking sheet. Use a potato masher or the bottom of a drinking glass to flatten the potatoes to a ½-inch thickness; try not to break apart the potatoes. Drizzle the olive oil over the potatoes, then sprinkle them evenly with the salt and pepper.

5   Bake the potatoes for about 25 minutes, until golden brown and crispy. Transfer to a serving plate and serve warm.

The crispy, craggy texture of potatoes that have been steamed and then baked is incomparable. The contrast between the roughed-up outsides and creamy insides sets these spuds apart, and they're considerably less hands-on than skillet potatoes, since using a baking sheet means there's no need for constant stirring and flipping. Pair the home fries with a Basic 12-Egg Omelet (page 29) for an easy weekend brunch.

OVEN-BAKED HOME FRIES

2 pounds russet or waxy potatoes, peeled, cut into 1-inch cubes

2 tablespoons olive oil

½ teaspoon kosher salt

½ teaspoon freshly ground black pepper

½ teaspoon sweet paprika

¼ teaspoon garlic powder

PREP	0 MINUTES
COOK	40 MINUTES
PR	QPR
SERVES	4 TO 6

1   Preheat the oven to 425°F. Line a rimmed baking sheet with a silicone baking mat or aluminum foil.

2   Pour 1 cup water into the Instant Pot. Place a steamer basket in the pot and add the potatoes.

3   Secure the lid and set the Pressure Release to **Sealing**. Select the **Steam** setting and set the cooking time for 3 minutes at high pressure. (The pot will take about 10 minutes to come up to pressure before the cooking program begins.)

4   When the cooking program ends, perform a quick pressure release by moving the Pressure Release to **Venting**. Open the pot and, wearing heat-resistant mitts, lift out the steamer basket.

5   In a medium bowl, toss the potatoes with the olive oil, salt, pepper, paprika, and garlic powder. Spread the potatoes in a single layer on the prepared baking sheet.

6   Bake the potatoes for about 25 minutes, stirring once, until golden brown and crispy. Transfer to a serving bowl and serve warm.

9

Drinks and Desserts

I spent one summer working in a chocolate café, where we made dipped strawberries, fondue, and fantastic chocolate drinks, both hot and cold. The secret was starting with couverture chocolate disks rather than cocoa powder. This hot chocolate, which uses easier-to-find chocolate chips, is rich, comforting, and ready in 10 minutes, and you can leave it on the Keep Warm setting until you're ready to serve. If the hot chocolate forms a skin as it sits, stir it again before serving.

HOT COCOA

4 cups whole milk

¾ cup semisweet chocolate chips

2 tablespoons sugar

¾ teaspoon vanilla extract

¼ teaspoon kosher salt

Marshmallows for serving (optional)

PREP	0 MINUTES
COOK	10 MINUTES
PR	N/A
SERVES	4

1 Combine the milk, chocolate chips, sugar, vanilla, and salt in the Instant Pot and stir for 1 minute. Select the low **Sauté** setting and set the cooking time for 9 minutes. Cover the pot with the glass lid. After 4 minutes, open the pot, stir the mixture for 1 minute, then cover with the lid again. When the timer goes off, give the hot chocolate a final stir.

2 Ladle the hot chocolate into mugs and serve topped with marshmallows.

Variation: To make hot chocolate with cocoa powder, substitute ¼ cup cocoa powder for the chocolate chips and increase the sugar to 6 tablespoons.

Use the Sauté setting on the Instant Pot to heat up the cider, then leave it on the Keep Warm setting for your guests to enjoy all evening long. To make a small batch, halve all the ingredients and shorten the cooking time on the Sauté setting to 8 minutes. To make a quick version, substitute a 1-ounce packet or 3 tablespoons of mulling spice for the citrus zest, ginger, and spices. To make spiked spiced cider, add 1 cup aged rum or pear brandy. A dash of bitters on each serving is a nice addition.

SPICED CIDER

8 cups unfiltered apple cider

Zest of 1 orange, removed in strips with a vegetable peeler

Zest of 1 lemon, removed in strips with a vegetable peeler

2-inch knob fresh ginger, sliced into ¼-inch-thick rounds

1 cinnamon stick, broken into large pieces

2 teaspoons whole allspice berries

2 teaspoons whole cloves

PREP	5 MINUTES
COOK	45 MINUTES
PR	N/A
SERVES	6 TO 8

1   Pour the apple cider into the Instant Pot. Enclose all the zest strips, the ginger, cinnamon, allspice, and cloves in a piece of cheesecloth; gather the edges; and tie them in a bundle with kitchen twine. Add the spice bundle to the pot. (Alternatively, add these ingredients to a steamer basket and lower the basket into the pot, making sure everything is submerged in the cider.) Cover the pot with the glass lid. Select the **Sauté** setting and set the cooking time for 15 minutes.

2   When the cooking program ends, select the **Keep Warm** setting. Leave the spices in the cider for at least 30 minutes or up to 1 hour, depending on how strongly you want the cider to be spiced. Remove the spice bundle (or steamer basket) and discard the spices.

3   Stir the cider and ladle into mugs. Serve warm.

Here's a perfect winter warmer for holiday parties. My favorite wines to use for mulling are Malbec and Sangiovese. This recipe makes a big pot, but it works well to halve the ingredients and the cooking time for a smaller batch.

MULLED WINE

1 cup sugar

Two 750-ml bottles red wine

4 cups apple juice

¼ cup apple brandy (optional)

Juice and zest strips of 1 large orange, zest strips removed with a vegetable peeler, plus orange slices for serving

1 whole star anise

3 cinnamon sticks, broken into large pieces, plus more whole sticks for serving

1 tablespoon whole allspice berries

1½ teaspoons whole cloves

1   Add the sugar, wine, apple juice, brandy, and orange juice to the Instant Pot and stir to combine. Enclose the zest strips, star anise, cinnamon, allspice, and cloves in a piece of cheesecloth; gather the edges; and tie them into a bundle with kitchen twine. Add the spice bundle to the pot. (Alternatively, add these ingredients to a steamer basket and lower the basket into the pot, making sure everything is submerged in the liquid.) Cover the pot with the glass lid. Select the **Sauté** setting and set the cooking time for 16 minutes.

2   When the cooking program ends, select the **Keep Warm** setting. Leave the spices in the wine for 1 hour. Remove the spice bundle (or steamer basket) and discard the spices.

3   Stir the mulled wine and ladle into mugs. Serve warm, garnished with a slice of orange and a cinnamon stick.

PREP	5 MINUTES
COOK	1 HOUR, 15 MINUTES
PR	N/A
SERVES	12

Make a batch of homemade coconut yogurt, then use it to make some creamy, dairy-free frozen ice pops! Or, if you prefer, you can use store-bought coconut yogurt; I like COYO brand. The flavor of these ice pops reminds me of the slushy blended orange juice drinks my babysitter would make for me and my brother as an afternoon treat.

COCONUT YOGURT–ORANGE ICE POPS

1 cup plain coconut yogurt
(page 33)

¼ cup honey or agave nectar

1 teaspoon finely grated orange zest, plus 1 cup fresh orange juice

1 teaspoon vanilla extract

PREP	5 MINUTES
COOK	N/A
PR	N/A
FREEZE	4 HOURS
MAKES	ABOUT 6 ICE POPS

1   Combine the yogurt, honey, orange zest, orange juice, and vanilla in a blender. Blend at medium speed for about 30 seconds, until smooth. Lightly tap the blender jar on the counter a few times to encourage any bubbles to rise to the top. Let stand for 2 minutes.

2   Pour the mixture into ice-pop molds and freeze for at least 4 hours, or up to 6 months.

3   Unmold and serve.

Creamy, comforting rice pudding is delicious topped with a sprinkle of cinnamon. Make sure to let the pudding chill fully before serving. It will thicken up nicely in the fridge.

RICE PUDDING

⅔ cup long-grain, jasmine, or basmati rice

1½ cups water

2 cups whole milk

½ cup sugar

½ teaspoon kosher salt

½ teaspoon vanilla extract

2 eggs

⅔ cup raisins

Ground cinnamon for sprinkling

PREP	0 MINUTES
COOK	20 MINUTES
PR	10 MINUTES NPR
CHILL	3 HOURS
SERVES	6

1   Combine the rice and water in the Instant Pot.

2   Secure the lid and set the Pressure Release to **Sealing**. Select the **Pressure Cook** or **Manual** setting and set the cooking time for 3 minutes at high pressure. (The pot will take about 10 minutes to come up to pressure before the cooking program begins.)

3   While the rice is cooking, in a blender, combine the milk, sugar, salt, and vanilla. Begin to blend on low speed, then add the eggs one at a time, blending for about 5 seconds after each addition, just until the mixture is homogenous. Set aside.

4   When the cooking program ends, let the pressure release naturally for 10 minutes, then move the Pressure Release to **Venting** to release any remaining steam. Open the pot and use a whisk to break up the cooked rice. Whisking constantly, pour the milk mixture in a thin stream into the rice. Press the **Cancel** button to reset the cooking program, then select the **Sauté** setting. Cook the pudding for about 5 minutes, whisking constantly, until it just begins to bubble and the temperature reaches 175° to 180°F on an instant-read thermometer. The pudding will still be quite liquid at this point but will set as it cools. Press the **Cancel** button to turn off the pot. Stir in the raisins.

5   Wearing heat-resistant mitts, lift out the inner pot. Pour the pudding into a glass or ceramic dish or into individual serving bowls. Cover and refrigerate the pudding for at least 3 hours or up to overnight.

6   Just before serving, sprinkle the pudding with a light dusting of cinnamon.

The Instant Pot makes the most moist and tender bread pudding. This chocolate version is so good on its own that you don't need to make a special sauce for serving. Simply sprinkle the pudding with chocolate chips right after it comes out of the pot, then dust it with confectioners' sugar just before serving. The chips will melt from the pudding's heat, creating a sweet topping.

CHOCOLATE BREAD PUDDING

4 eggs

1 cup half-and-half

⅓ cup firmly packed dark brown sugar

3 tablespoons cocoa powder

½ teaspoon kosher salt

¼ teaspoon ground cinnamon

6 cups cubed brioche or challah bread

¼ cup semisweet chocolate chips

Confectioners' sugar for dusting

PREP	20 MINUTES
COOK	35 MINUTES
PR	10 MINUTES NPR
SERVES	6

1   Grease a 1½-quart soufflé dish or a 7-cup round heatproof glass container with butter or nonstick cooking spray.

2   In a blender, combine the eggs, half-and-half, brown sugar, cocoa powder, salt, and cinnamon. Blend on medium speed for about 30 seconds until combined, scraping down the sides if needed.

3   Put the cubed bread in a large bowl. Pour in the egg mixture and stir to combine, pressing the bread down to make sure all pieces are moistened. Transfer the mixture to the prepared dish, then cover tightly with aluminum foil. Let stand at room temperature for 10 minutes or refrigerate for up to 24 hours.

4   When you're ready to bake the bread pudding, pour 1½ cups water into the Instant Pot. Place the covered dish on a long-handled silicone steam rack. Holding the handles of the steam rack, lower it into the pot.

5   Secure the lid and set the Pressure Release to **Sealing**. Select the **Pressure Cook** or **Manual** setting and set the cooking time for 25 minutes at high pressure. (The pot will take about 10 minutes to come up to pressure from room temperature, or 15 from the fridge.)

6   When the cooking program ends, let the pressure release naturally for 10 minutes, then move the Pressure Release to **Venting** to release any remaining steam. Open the pot and, wearing heat-resistant mitts, grab the handles of the steam rack and lift the dish out of the pot. Uncover the dish, taking care to not get burned by the steam and to not drip condensation onto the pudding. The pudding will have puffed up, but it will settle down into the dish as it cools. Sprinkle with the chocolate chips and let stand for about 2 minutes to allow the chocolate to melt, then dust with confectioners' sugar.

7   Use a large spoon to scoop the bread pudding onto serving plates. Serve warm.

For this cobbler made with fluffy buttermilk biscuit dough, use fresh stone fruit when in season, and frozen fruit the rest of the year. Keep it unfussy, leaving the skins on if you're using fresh fruit. The dessert takes about an hour from start to finish, and it can cook in the Instant Pot while you're having dinner. Sprinkle cinnamon sugar on top and add scoops of ice cream just before serving.

PEACH COBBLER

Biscuit Dough

1 cup all-purpose flour

¼ cup sugar

1 teaspoon baking powder

½ teaspoon baking soda

¼ teaspoon kosher salt

6 tablespoons cold unsalted butter, cut into ½-inch cubes

½ cup buttermilk or whole milk

Filling

4 medium peaches, pitted and sliced, or two 10-ounce bags frozen sliced peaches, thawed

3 tablespoons sugar

2 tablespoons all-purpose flour

1½ teaspoons fresh lemon juice

Cinnamon Sugar

1 tablespoon sugar

¼ teaspoon ground cinnamon

Vanilla ice cream for serving (optional)

PREP	10 MINUTES
COOK	50 MINUTES
PR	10 MINUTES NPR
SERVES	6

1   To make the biscuit dough: In a medium bowl, whisk together the flour, sugar, baking powder, baking soda, and salt. Add the butter and use a pastry blender to cut the butter into the dry ingredients until the mixture resembles coarse sand and the butter pieces are no larger than pea-size. If you don't have a pastry blender, use your fingers to rub the butter into the dry ingredients. Add the buttermilk and stir with a silicone spoon or spatula just until all the dough is evenly moistened.

2   To make the filling: In a 1½-quart soufflé dish or a 7-cup round heat-proof glass container, toss the peaches with sugar, flour, and lemon juice.

3   Using two spoons or a small (1½-tablespoon) spring-loaded cookie scoop, dollop the biscuit dough onto the peaches. Cover the dish tightly with aluminum foil.

4   Pour 1½ cups water into the Instant Pot. Place the soufflé dish on a long-handled silicone steam rack. Holding the handles of the steam rack, lower it into the pot.

5   Secure the lid and set the Pressure Release to **Sealing**. Select the **Pressure Cook** or **Manual** setting and set the cooking time for 35 minutes at high pressure. (The pot will take about 15 minutes to come up to pressure before the cooking program begins.)

6   When the cooking program ends, let the pressure release naturally for 10 minutes, then move the Pressure Release to **Venting** to release any remaining steam. Open the pot and, wearing heat-resistant mitts, grab the handles of the steam rack and lift the dish out of the pot. Uncover the dish, taking care to not get burned by the steam. Let the cobbler cool for about 5 minutes.

7   To make the cinnamon sugar: In a small bowl, stir together the sugar and cinnamon.

8   Spoon the warm cobbler into bowls, sprinkle with the cinnamon sugar, and top with vanilla ice cream. Serve immediately.

Whether or not you're serving folks on a grain-free diet, this little cake is just the treat to welcome fall. It's sweet, dense, and moist with chopped apple, and it begs to be served warm, with a cup of tea alongside. Have it as an afternoon snack or for dessert.

GRAIN-FREE APPLE SPICE CAKE

½ cup coconut sugar

½ cup almond flour

½ cup tapioca flour

¼ cup coconut flour

2 tablespoons arrowroot powder

1 teaspoon pumpkin pie spice

1 teaspoon baking powder

½ teaspoon kosher salt

¾ cup coconut milk, at room temperature

1 egg, at room temperature

½ teaspoon vanilla extract

½ large apple, cored and chopped

Confectioners' sugar for dusting (optional)

PREP	10 MINUTES
COOK	45 MINUTES
PR	5 MINUTES NPR
COOL	20 MINUTES
SERVES	6 TO 8

1   Line the bottom of a 7 by 3-inch round cake pan with a circle of parchment paper. Grease the sides of the pan and the parchment with a neutral-flavored oil or nonstick cooking spray. Pour 1½ cups water into the Instant Pot.

2   In a medium bowl, whisk together the coconut sugar, almond flour, tapioca flour, coconut flour, arrowroot powder, pumpkin pie spice, baking powder, and salt. Make a well in the center of the dry ingredients and add the coconut milk, egg, and vanilla. Whisk just the wet ingredients until combined, then add the chopped apple. Using a silicone spoon or spatula, stir everything together just until the batter is evenly moistened.

3   Pour the batter into the prepared cake pan, then gently tap the pan on the counter a few times to make sure the batter is spread out in an even layer. Cover the pan tightly with aluminum foil and place it on a long-handled silicone steam rack. Holding the handles of the steam rack, lower the pan into the Instant Pot.

4   Secure the lid and set the Pressure Release to **Sealing**. Select the **Cake**, **Pressure Cook**, or **Manual** setting and set the cooking time for 33 minutes at low pressure. (The pot will take about 10 minutes to come up to pressure before the cooking program begins.)

5   When the cooking program ends, let the pressure release naturally for 5 minutes, then move the Pressure Release to **Venting** to release any remaining steam. Open the pot and, wearing heat-resistant mitts, grab the handles of the steam rack and lift the pan out of the pot. Uncover the pan, taking care to not get burned by the steam and to not drip any condensation onto the cake. Let the cake cool in the pan on a cooling rack for about 5 minutes.

6   Run a knife around the sides of the pan to make sure the cake isn't sticking to the pan. Invert the cake onto the rack, lift off the pan, and peel off the parchment paper. Let cool for 15 minutes, then invert the cake onto a serving plate. Dust the cake with confectioners' sugar, cut into wedges, and serve.

Smooth, creamy cheesecake is topped with a layer of tangy sour cream and a gorgeous garnet-red cherry compote. An Instagram-worthy dessert from your pressure cooker? Yes, I think so. Amazingly, the graham cracker crust stays firm even when steamed, and the cheesecake comes out perfectly silky every time.

CLASSIC NEW YORK CHEESECAKE WITH CHERRY COMPOTE

Crust

8 graham cracker sheets

1 tablespoon brown sugar

2 tablespoons unsalted butter, melted and cooled

Filling

Two 8-ounce packages cream cheese, at room temperature

½ cup granulated sugar

¼ cup heavy cream

1 tablespoon all-purpose flour

1 teaspoon vanilla extract

2 eggs, plus 1 egg yolk, at room temperature

½ cup sour cream

1 tablespoon confectioners' sugar

Compote

One 1-pound bag frozen pitted Bing cherries, thawed

⅓ cup granulated sugar

1 teaspoon vanilla extract

PREP	15 MINUTES
COOK	45 MINUTES
PR	20 MINUTES NPR
COOL	1 HOUR
CHILL	12 HOURS
SERVES	8

1   Line the base of a 7-inch round springform pan with an 8-inch round of parchment paper. Secure the collar on the springform pan, closing it onto the base so the parchment round is clamped in. Lightly grease the sides of the pan with butter or nonstick cooking spray.

2   To make the crust: In a food processor, process the graham crackers to fine crumbs. Add the brown sugar and melted butter. Using 1-second pulses, process until the mixture resembles damp sand.

3   Transfer the crumb mixture to the prepared pan and press firmly into an even layer on the bottom and about ½ inch up the sides of the pan. Place the pan in the freezer to allow the crust to firm up a bit while you make the filling. Wipe out the food processor.

4   To make the filling: In the food processor, combine the cream cheese, granulated sugar, cream, flour, and vanilla. Process in about five 1-second pulses, just until smooth, stopping to scrape down the sides of the bowl as needed. One at a time, add the eggs and egg yolk, processing for two 1-second pulses after each addition. Do not overprocess the filling, or the batter may overflow the pan and you will end up with an overly fluffy cheesecake. Using a rubber spatula, gently stir in any large streaks of egg yolk, but it's fine if a few small streaks remain.

5   Pour the filling into the prepared crust. Tap the pan firmly against the countertop a few times to remove any air bubbles in the filling. Place the pan on a long-handled silicone steam rack.

6   Pour 1½ cups water into the Instant Pot. Holding the handles of the steam rack, lower it into the pot.

7   Secure the lid and set the Pressure Release to **Sealing**. Select the **Cake**, **Pressure Cook**, or **Manual** setting and set the cooking time for 32 minutes at high pressure. (The pot will take about 10 minutes to come up to pressure before the cooking program begins.)

CONTINUED

CLASSIC NEW YORK CHEESECAKE WITH CHERRY COMPOTE
CONTINUED

8   While the cheesecake is cooking, in a small bowl, whisk together the sour cream and confectioners' sugar.

9   When the cooking program ends, let the pressure release naturally for 20 minutes, then move the Pressure Release to **Venting** to release any remaining steam. Open the pot, taking care to not drip condensation from the lid onto the cheesecake. Wearing heat-resistant mitts, grab the handles of the steam rack, lift the pan out of the pot, and set the pan on a cooling rack. Use a paper towel to dab up any moisture that may have settled on the surface. The cake will be puffed up and jiggle a bit in the center when it comes out of the pot, but it will settle and set up as it cools.

10   When the cheesecake has deflated about ½ inch, spread the sour cream mixture on top in a smooth, even layer. Let the cheesecake cool on the rack for about 1 hour, then cover and refrigerate for at least 12 hours or up to 24 hours.

11   To make the cherry compote: While the cheesecake is cooling, wearing heat-resistant mitts, lift the inner pot from the Instant Pot. Discard the water, and return the inner pot to the housing.

12   Press the **Cancel** button to reset the cooking program, then select the **Sauté** setting. Add the cherries, granulated sugar, and vanilla to the pot. Cook for 10 to 12 minutes, stirring often, until the mixture thickens enough to coat the back of a spoon. Wearing heat-resistant mitts, lift out the inner pot. Press the **Cancel** button to turn off the pot. Transfer the compote to an airtight container and refrigerate for up to 5 days.

13   Unclasp the collar on the pan and lift it off, then use the parchment border to tug the cheesecake off the base of the pan and onto a plate.

14   Top the cheesecake with the cherry compote, then slice and serve.

Every layer of this cheesecake is infused with deep, dark chocolate flavor, from the chocolate cookie crust to the silky chocolate filling to the decadent ganache topping. The whipped cream and fresh strawberry garnishes make this dessert as beautiful as it is delicious, but it's equally good served without the extra toppings.

TRIPLE CHOCOLATE CHEESECAKE

Crust

8 chocolate graham cracker sheets, or 4½ ounces Nabisco Famous Chocolate Wafers

1 tablespoon dark brown sugar

2 tablespoons unsalted butter, melted and cooled

Filling

Two 8-ounce packages cream cheese, at room temperature

⅔ cup semisweet chocolate chips, melted (see Note)

¼ cup heavy cream, at room temperature

¼ cup granulated sugar

1 tablespoon all-purpose flour

1 teaspoon vanilla extract

2 eggs, plus 1 egg yolk, at room temperature

Ganache

¼ cup semisweet chocolate chips

¼ cup heavy cream

1 cup whipped cream

1 cup sliced strawberries

PREP	15 MINUTES
COOK	45 MINUTES
PR	20 MINUTES NPR
COOL	1 HOUR
CHILL	12 HOURS
SERVES	8

1   Line the base of a 7-inch round springform pan with an 8-inch round of parchment paper. Secure the collar on the springform pan, closing it onto the base so the parchment round is clamped in. Lightly grease the sides of the pan with butter or nonstick cooking spray.

2   To make the crust: In a food processor, process the graham crackers to fine crumbs. Add the brown sugar and melted butter. Using 1-second pulses, process until the mixture resembles damp sand.

3   Transfer the crumb mixture to the prepared pan and press firmly into an even layer on the bottom and about ½ inch up the sides of the pan. Place the pan in the freezer to allow the crust to firm up a bit while you make the filling. Wipe out the food processor.

4   To make the filling: In the food processor, combine the cream cheese, melted chocolate chips, cream, granulated sugar, flour, and vanilla. Process in about five 1-second pulses, just until smooth, stopping to scrape down the sides of the bowl as needed. One at a time, add the eggs and egg yolk, processing for two 1-second pulses after each addition. Do not overprocess the filling, or the batter may overflow the pan and you will end up with an overly fluffy cheesecake. Using a rubber spatula, gently stir in any large streaks of egg yolk, but it's fine if a few small streaks remain.

5   Pour the filling into the prepared crust. Tap the pan firmly against the countertop a few times to remove any air bubbles in the filling. Place the pan on a long-handled silicone steam rack.

6   Pour 1½ cups water into the Instant Pot. Holding the handles of the steam rack, lift the pan and lower it into the pot.

7   Secure the lid and set the Pressure Release to **Sealing**. Select the **Cake**, **Pressure Cook**, or **Manual** setting and set the cooking time for 33 minutes at high pressure. (The pot will take about 10 minutes to come up to pressure before the cooking program begins.)

8   When the cooking program ends, let the pressure release naturally for 20 minutes, then move the Pressure Release to **Venting** to release any remaining steam.

9   To make the ganache: When 10 minutes remain on the **Keep Warm** setting, in a small saucepan, combine the chocolate chips and heavy cream. Set the pan over low heat and warm the mixture, stirring constantly, for a few minutes, just until the ganache is smooth and shiny. Remove from the heat and set aside.

10   Open the Instant Pot, taking care to not drip condensation from the lid onto the cheesecake. Wearing heat-resistant mitts, grab the handles of the steam rack, lift the pan out of the pot, and set the pan on a cooling rack. Use a paper towel to dab up any moisture that may have settled on the surface. The cake will be puffed up and jiggle a bit in the center when it comes out of the pot, but it will settle and set up as it cools.

11   When the cheesecake has deflated about ½ inch, pour the ganache on top. Let the cheesecake cool on the rack for about 1 hour, then cover and refrigerate for at least 12 hours or up to 24 hours.

12   Unclasp the collar on the pan and lift it off, then use the parchment border to tug the cheesecake off the base of the pan and onto a plate. Cut into wedges and serve, topping each piece with a dollop of the whipped cream and a spoonful of the sliced strawberries.

Note: To melt the chocolate chips for the filling, place them in a microwave-safe bowl and microwave on high power in 20-second intervals, stirring after each interval, until fully melted.

This isn't so much a cake as it is a round, impressively tall pan of fudge brownie. I think it's pretty glorious, especially when it's still a little warm. Serve it in wedges, with vanilla ice cream and caramel sauce.

FUDGE BROWNIE CAKE WITH TOASTED WALNUTS

¾ cup unsalted butter, melted and cooled

3 eggs

1 cup firmly packed brown sugar

1½ teaspoons instant coffee crystals

1½ teaspoons vanilla extract

¼ teaspoon kosher salt

¾ cup all-purpose flour

¾ cup cocoa powder

¾ cup semisweet chocolate chips

¾ cup walnuts, coarsely chopped and toasted

PREP	10 MINUTES
COOK	45 MINUTES
PR	10 MINUTES NPR
COOL	20 MINUTES
SERVES	8 TO 10

1   Line the base of a 7-inch round springform pan with an 8-inch round of parchment paper. Secure the collar on the springform pan, closing it onto the base so the parchment round is clamped in. Lightly grease the sides of the pan with butter or nonstick cooking spray.

2   Put the melted butter in a large bowl. One at a time, whisk in the eggs, then the brown sugar, coffee, vanilla, and salt until combined. Add the flour and cocoa powder and whisk just until the dry ingredients are fully incorporated. Fold in the chocolate chips and walnuts.

3   Pour the batter into the prepared pan. Tap the pan firmly against the countertop a few times to remove any air bubbles in the batter. Cover the pan tightly with aluminum foil. Place the pan on a long-handled silicone steam rack.

4   Pour 1½ cups water into the Instant Pot. Holding the handles of the steam rack, lift the pan and lower it into the pot.

5   Secure the lid and set the Pressure Release to **Sealing**. Select the **Cake**, **Pressure Cook**, or **Manual** setting and set the cooking time for 35 minutes at high pressure. (The pot will take about 10 minutes to come up to pressure before the cooking program begins.)

6   When the cooking program ends, let the pressure release naturally for 10 minutes, then move the Pressure Release to **Venting** to release any remaining steam. Open the pot and, wearing heat-resistant mitts, grab the handles of the steam rack, lift the pan out of the pot, and set the pan on a cooling rack.

7   Remove the foil from the pan, being careful not to get burned by the steam. Let the cake cool for about 20 minutes, until warm, or cool to room temperature.

8   Unclasp the collar on the pan and lift it off, then use the parchment border to tug the cake off the base of the pan and onto a plate. Slice the cake into wedges and serve.

This cake gets an impressive rise in the Instant Pot, doming up as it bakes. If you're fussy about presentation, you might want to slice off some of the dome before glazing the cake. I don't mind, though. It comes out dense as a pound cake should be, but not waterlogged, like some pressure cooker cakes. The not-too-sweet cake is offset by a sugary, zesty glaze.

GLAZED ORANGE POUND CAKE

Cake

2 cups all-purpose flour

⅔ cup granulated sugar

2 teaspoons baking powder

½ teaspoon kosher salt

2 eggs

6 tablespoons unsalted butter, melted and cooled

1 teaspoon finely grated orange zest, plus ½ cup fresh orange juice

Orange Glaze

½ cup confectioners' sugar

1 teaspoon finely grated orange zest, plus 2 teaspoons fresh orange juice (or orange liqueur)

PREP	10 MINUTES
COOK	55 MINUTES
PR	10 MINUTES NPR
COOL	10 MINUTES
SERVES	8

1   To make the cake: Grease a 1-quart Bundt pan with butter or non-stick cooking spray and dust with flour, shaking and rotating the pan to coat it evenly. Tap out the excess.

2   In a medium bowl, whisk together the flour, granulated sugar, baking powder, and salt. Make a well in the center. Add the eggs to the well and whisk to break up the yolks a bit. Add the butter, orange zest, and orange juice and whisk just until the dry ingredients are fully incorporated.

3   Pour the batter into the prepared pan and spread it in an even layer. Tap the pan firmly against the countertop a few times to remove any air bubbles in the batter. Cover the pan tightly with aluminum foil. Place the pan on a long-handled silicone steam rack.

4   Pour 1½ cups water into Instant Pot. Holding the handles of the steam rack, lift the pan and lower it into the pot.

5   Secure the lid and set the Pressure release to **Sealing**. Select the **Cake**, **Pressure Cook**, or **Manual** setting and set the cooking time for 45 minutes at high pressure. (The pot will take about 10 minutes to come up to pressure before the cooking program begins.)

6   To make the orange glaze: While the cake is cooking, in a small bowl, combine the confectioners' sugar, orange zest, and orange juice and whisk until smooth. Transfer to a ziplock plastic bag, seal the bag, and set aside.

7   When the cooking program ends, let the pressure release naturally for 10 minutes, then move the Pressure Release to **Venting** to release any remaining steam. Open the pot and, wearing heat-resistant mitts, grab the handles of the steam rack, lift the pan out of the pot, and set the pan on a cooling rack. Remove the foil from the pan, taking care not to get burned by the steam. Let the cake cool in the pan for 5 minutes, then invert the pan onto the cooling rack, lift off the pan, and let the cake cool for 5 minutes more.

8   Set the rack with the cake over a large plate to catch drips when you glaze the cake. Cut off a small corner of the ziplock bag and squeeze the glaze all over the cake. Let cool to room temperature, then transfer to a serving plate.

9   Cut the cake into wedges and serve.

VEGETABLE BROTH

PREP	0 MINUTES
COOK	40 MINUTES
PR	30 MINUTES NPR
MAKES	ABOUT 2 QUARTS

1 tablespoon olive oil

1 large yellow onion, diced

4 garlic cloves, smashed and peeled

2 large carrots, diced

4 celery stalks, preferably the dark green outer stalks, diced

2 teaspoons kosher salt

2 tablespoons tomato paste

2 tablespoons nutritional yeast

8 cups water

1 teaspoon black peppercorns

2 bay leaves

1 bunch flat-leaf parsley

1   Select the **Sauté** setting on the Instant Pot and heat the olive oil. Add the onion, garlic, carrots, celery, and salt. Sauté for about 10 minutes, until the vegetables have given up some of their liquid and begun to brown just a bit. Stir in the tomato paste and nutritional yeast, then add 1 cup of the water and use a wooden spoon to nudge loose any browned bits from the bottom of the pot. Add the peppercorns, bay leaves, parsley, and remaining 7 cups water, making sure not to fill the pot more than two-thirds full.

2   Secure the lid and set the Pressure Release to **Sealing**. Press the **Cancel** button to reset the cooking program, then select the **Soup/Broth** setting and set the cooking time for 10 minutes at high pressure. (The pot will take about 20 minutes to come up to pressure before the cooking program begins.)

3   Place a wire-mesh strainer over a large stainless steel bowl. For a clearer broth, line the strainer with a doubled layer of cheesecloth.

4   When the cooking program ends, let the pressure release naturally for 30 minutes, then move the Pressure Release to **Venting** to release any remaining steam. Open the pot and, wearing heat-resistant mitts, lift out the inner pot and pour the broth

through the prepared strainer into the bowl. Discard the vegetables. Let the broth cool to room temperature. (To speed the cooling process, set the bowl in a larger bowl containing an ice bath.)

5   The broth can be used right away, stored in an airtight container in the refrigerator for up to 3 days, or frozen for up to 6 months.

MUSHROOM BROTH

PREP	0 MINUTES
COOK	35 MINUTES
PR	45 MINUTES NPR
MAKES	ABOUT 10 CUPS

1 ounce dried shiitake mushrooms

1 ounce mixed dried mushrooms

2 teaspoons kosher salt

1 teaspoon black peppercorns

1 bay leaf

10 cups water

1   Combine all the mushrooms, the salt, peppercorns, bay leaf, and water in the Instant Pot.

2   Secure the lid and set the Pressure Release to **Sealing**. Select the **Soup/Broth** setting and set the cooking time for 10 minutes at high pressure. (The pot will take about 25 minutes to come up to pressure before the cooking program begins.)

3   When the cooking program ends, let the pressure release naturally for 45 minutes, then move the Pressure Release to **Venting** to release any remaining steam. Open the pot and, using a slotted spoon, remove the mushrooms; if you like, save them for another use.

4   Set a wire-mesh strainer over a large stainless steel bowl and line the strainer with a doubled layer of cheesecloth.

5   Wearing heat-resistant mitts, lift out the inner pot and pour the broth through the prepared strainer into the bowl. Discard the solids in the strainer. Let the broth cool to room temperature. (To speed the cooling process, set the bowl in a larger bowl containing an ice bath.)

6   The broth can be used right away, stored in an airtight container in the refrigerator for up to 3 days, or frozen for up to 6 months.

BEEF BONE BROTH

PREP	0 MINUTES
COOK	2 HOURS
PR	45 MINUTES NPR
MAKES	ABOUT 8 CUPS

2 pounds beef soup bones (such as knucklebones), shanks, or oxtails (see Notes)

3 celery stalks, cut into 3-inch lengths

2 large carrots, halved lengthwise, then cut crosswise into 3-inch lengths

1 large yellow onion, cut into wedges

1 teaspoon kosher salt

½ teaspoon black peppercorns

1 bay leaf

8 cups water

1   Combine the beef bones, celery, carrots, onion, salt, peppercorns, and bay leaf in the Instant Pot. Pour in the water, making sure the pot is no more than two-thirds full.

2   Secure the lid and set the Pressure Release to **Sealing**. Select the **Soup/Broth** setting and set the cooking time for 120 minutes at high pressure. (The pot will take about 30 minutes to come up to pressure before the cooking program begins.)

3   When the cooking program ends, let the pressure release naturally; this will take about 45 minutes.

4   Place a wire-mesh strainer over a large heat-safe bowl or pitcher.

5   Open the pot and, wearing heat-resistant mitts, lift out the inner pot and pour the broth into the strainer. Discard the bones and vegetables. You can pick the meat off the bones if you like, but it will have given up most of its flavor to the broth. Pour the broth into a fat separator to remove the fat, or chill the broth in the refrigerator until the fat solidifies on top, then scoop off the fat from the surface with a large spoon. Let the broth cool to room temperature. (To speed the cooling process, set the bowl in a larger bowl containing an ice bath.)

6   The broth can be used right away, stored in an airtight container in the refrigerator for up to 5 days, or frozen for up to 6 months.

Notes: For deeper flavor and color, roast the bones before you make the broth. Spread the bones on a rimmed baking sheet and roast in a 400°F oven for about 45 minutes.

I find the best broth is made with oxtails, but they are expensive and it can be a wasteful way to use them unless you harvest the meat from the bones. I pick off the meat after cooking, then freeze it for later use, or add it to Beef and Cabbage Soup (page 94).

CHICKEN BROTH

PREP	0 MINUTES
COOK	1 HOUR, 15 MINUTES
PR	30 MINUTES NPR
MAKES	ABOUT 8 CUPS

1 teaspoon avocado oil or other neutral oil with high smoke point

About 2½ pounds bony chicken parts (such as drumsticks, wings, necks, and backs)

3 celery stalks, cut into 3-inch lengths

2 medium carrots, halved lengthwise, then cut crosswise into 3-inch lengths

1 medium yellow onion, cut into wedges

3 garlic cloves, smashed and peeled

1 teaspoon kosher salt

½ teaspoon black peppercorns

1 bay leaf

8 cups water

1   Select the **Sauté** setting on the Instant Pot and heat the avocado oil. Using tongs, place the chicken pieces in a single layer in the pot and cook, flipping once, for about 5 minutes on each side, until browned. Don't worry if some skin sticks to the pot. Add the celery, carrots, onion, garlic, salt, peppercorns, and bay leaf to the pot and then the water, pouring slowly to prevent splashing. Make sure the pot is no more than two-thirds full.

2   Secure the lid and set the Pressure Release to **Sealing**. Press the **Cancel** button to reset the cooking program, then select the **Soup/Broth** setting and set the cooking time for 50 minutes at high pressure.

3   When the cooking program ends, let the pressure release naturally for 30 minutes, then move the Pressure Release to **Venting** to release any remaining steam. If you like, you can also leave the pot on the **Keep Warm** setting for up to 10 hours.

4   Place a wire-mesh strainer over a large heatproof bowl or pitcher.

5   Open the pot and, wearing heat-resistant mitts, lift out the inner pot and pour the broth into the strainer. Discard the bones and vegetables—they will have given up their flavor to the broth. Pour the broth into a fat separator to remove the fat, or chill the broth in the refrigerator until the fat solidifies on top, then scoop off the fat from the surface with a large spoon; if you like, reserve the fat for another use. Let the broth cool to room temperature. (To speed the cooling process, set the bowl in a larger bowl containing an ice bath.)

6   The broth can be used right away, stored in an airtight container in the refrigerator for up to 5 days, or frozen for up to 6 months.

ROASTED TURKEY BROTH

PREP	15 MINUTES
COOK	1 HOUR, 50 MINUTES
PR	1 HOUR, 15 MINUTES NPR
MAKES	ABOUT 10 CUPS

3½ pounds bony turkey parts (such as necks, backs, and wings)

1 teaspoon kosher salt

½ teaspoon dried rosemary

1 medium yellow onion, cut into wedges

2 medium carrots, halved lengthwise, then cut crosswise into 3-inch lengths

2 bay leaves

1 teaspoon black peppercorns

10 cups water

1   Preheat the oven to 425°F.

2   Pat the turkey parts dry with paper towels, place in a roasting pan, and sprinkle all over with the salt and rosemary. Arrange the onion and carrot pieces around the turkey parts. Roast for about 45 minutes, until the turkey parts are golden brown and the onion is beginning to brown on the edges. Using tongs, transfer the turkey parts and vegetables to the Instant Pot. Add the bay leaves, peppercorns, and water, pouring slowly to prevent splashing. Make sure the pot is no more than two-thirds full.

3 Secure the lid and set the Pressure Release to **Sealing**. Select the **Soup/Broth** setting and set the cooking time for 40 minutes at high pressure. (The pot will take about 25 minutes to come up to pressure before the cooking program begins.)

4 When the cooking program ends, let the pressure release naturally; this will take about 1¼ hours. Alternatively, let the pressure release for 1 hour, then move the Pressure Release to Venting to release any remaining steam. If you like, you can also leave the pot on the **Keep Warm** setting for up to 10 hours.

5 Place a wire-mesh strainer over a large heatproof bowl or pitcher.

6 Open the pot and, wearing heat-resistant mitts, lift out the inner pot and pour the broth into the strainer. Discard the bones and vegetables—they will have given up most of their flavor to the broth. Pour the broth into a fat separator to remove the fat, or chill the broth in the refrigerator until the fat solidifies on top, then scoop off the fat from the surface with a large spoon; if you like, reserve the fat for another use. Let the broth cool to room temperature. (To speed the cooling process, set the bowl in a larger bowl containing an ice bath.)

7 The broth can be used right away, stored in an airtight container in the refrigerator for up to 5 days, or frozen for up to 6 months.

Note: To make turkey gravy with roasted turkey broth, select the **Sauté** setting on the Instant Pot and heat 2 tablespoons of the reserved turkey fat (or substitute neutral vegetable oil or unsalted butter). Add 2 tablespoons all-purpose flour and whisk for about 3 minutes, until bubbling and blond in color. Whisking constantly, slowly pour in 2 cups turkey broth. Bring to a boil and cook for about 3 minutes more, whisking occasionally, until thickened. Taste and adjust the seasoning with salt and pepper if needed. Press the **Cancel** button to turn off the pot. Transfer the gravy to a serving vessel.

MARINARA SAUCE

PREP	0 MINUTES
COOK	15 MINUTES
PR	N/A
MAKES	ABOUT 3½ CUPS

¼ cup olive oil

3 garlic cloves, minced

One 28-ounce can whole San Marzano tomatoes and their liquid

2 teaspoons Italian seasoning

Kosher salt

½ teaspoon red pepper flakes (optional)

1 Select the **Sauté** setting on the Instant Pot and heat the olive oil and garlic for about 3 minutes, until the garlic turns light blond but is not browned. Add the tomatoes and their liquid and use a wooden spoon or spatula to crush the tomatoes against the side of the pot. Stir in the Italian seasoning, 1½ teaspoons salt, and red pepper flakes. Cook for about 10 minutes more, stirring occasionally, until the sauce has thickened a bit. Press the **Cancel** button to turn off the pot. Taste the sauce and adjust the seasoning with salt if needed.

2 The sauce can be used right away, stored in an airtight container in the refrigerator for up to 3 days, or frozen for up to 4 months.

Note: If you wish to process for longer storage, follow your preferred canning method. The sauce will keep, in a cool, dark place, for up to 1 year.

BOLOGNESE SAUCE

PREP	0 MINUTES
COOK	55 MINUTES
PR	15 MINUTES NPR
MAKES	ABOUT 10 CUPS

2 tablespoons olive oil

1 medium yellow onion, finely diced

2 garlic cloves, minced

2 celery stalks, finely diced

1 medium carrot, peeled and grated

1½ teaspoons kosher salt

1 pound ground beef (90% lean)

1 pound ground pork

½ cup dry red or white wine

2 bay leaves

½ teaspoon freshly ground black pepper

One 28-ounce can whole San Marzano tomatoes and their liquid

¼ cup tomato paste

1   Select the **Sauté** setting on the Instant Pot and add the olive oil, onion, garlic, celery, carrot, and salt. Sauté for about 5 minutes, until the onion is softened and translucent. Add the beef and pork and sauté for about 10 minutes, breaking them up with a wooden spoon or spatula as they cook, until no traces of pink remain. Stir in the wine, bay leaves, and pepper, using the spoon to nudge loose any browned bits from the bottom of pot. Add the tomatoes and their liquid, leaving the tomatoes whole. Dollop the tomato paste on top of the whole tomatoes. Do not stir.

2   Secure the lid and set the Pressure Release to **Sealing**. Press the **Cancel** button to reset the cooking program, then select the **Meat/Stew** setting and set the cooking time for 20 minutes at high pressure.

3   When the cooking program ends, let the pressure release naturally for 15 minutes, then move the Pressure Release to **Venting** to release any remaining steam. Open the pot and, using the spoon, crush the tomatoes against the side of the pot and stir in the tomato paste. Taste the sauce and adjust the seasoning with salt and pepper if needed.

4   The sauce can be used right away, stored in an airtight container in the refrigerator for up to 4 days, or frozen for up to 6 months.

BRUSCHETTA SAUCE

PREP	0 MINUTES
COOK	15 MINUTES
PR	N/A
MAKES	2 CUPS

1½ pounds ripe Roma or San Marzano tomatoes

¼ cup plus 3 tablespoons water

¼ cup white wine vinegar (5% acidity)

3 tablespoons good-quality aged balsamic vinegar (6% acidity)

2 tablespoons Italian seasoning

1 tablespoon sugar

1½ teaspoons kosher salt

1 garlic clove, minced

1   Cut the tomatoes lengthwise into quarters, then cut out the cores and remove the seeds. Cut the tomato flesh into ½-inch dice, discarding the cores and seeds.

2   Add the diced tomatoes, water, wine vinegar, balsamic vinegar, Italian seasoning, sugar, salt, and garlic to the Instant Pot and stir to combine, then cover with the glass lid.

3   Select the low **Sauté** setting and cook for about 6 minutes, until the mixture begins to simmer. Uncover the pot, stir once more, and cook, uncovered, for about 5 minutes more, until the cooking liquid has reduced and thickened slightly. Press the **Cancel** button to turn off the pot. Wearing heat-resistant mitts, lift out the inner pot. Transfer the tomato mixture to an airtight container. Let cool to room temperature, then cover the container.

4   The sauce will keep, refrigerated, for up to 1 week.

Notes: This recipe is easily doubled; just increase the covered cooking time from 6 minutes to 10 minutes.

If you wish to process for longer storage, follow your preferred canning method. The sauce will keep, in a cool, dark place, for up to 1 year.

SALSA ROJA

PREP	0 MINUTES
COOK	35 MINUTES
PR	N/A
MAKES	5 CUPS

8 medium pasilla chiles, stemmed and seeded

3 cups water

1 ½ pounds Roma tomatoes, cored and halved lengthwise

4 jalapeño chiles, stemmed

2 bunches green onions, trimmed

5 garlic cloves, smashed and peeled

6 tablespoons fresh lime juice

½ bunch cilantro, bottom 4 inches of stems discarded, cut into 1-inch lengths

2 teaspoons kosher salt

1   Preheat the broiler and line a baking sheet with aluminum foil.

2   Place the chiles and water in the Instant Pot and cover with the glass lid. Select the **Sauté** setting and set the cooking time for 8 minutes. When the timer goes off, let the chiles soak for 10 minutes.

3   While the chiles soak, arrange the tomatoes, jalapeños, green onions, and garlic in a single layer on the prepared baking sheet. Broil for about 5 minutes, until lightly charred. Using tongs, flip all the vegetables, then broil for about 5 minutes more, until charred on the second sides. The green onions and garlic will brown the most. Remove from the oven and set aside.

4   Using tongs, transfer the soaked chiles to a blender, then pour in ½ cup of the soaking liquid. Wearing heat-resistant mitts, lift out the inner pot and discard the remaining soaking liquid. Return the inner pot to the housing.

5   Using the tongs, transfer the charred vegetables to the blender with the chiles. Add the lime juice, cilantro, and salt, then blend for about 15 seconds, until no large chunks of vegetables remain but you can still see charred bits throughout the salsa. Pour the mixture into the Instant Pot and cover with the glass lid.

6   Select the **Sauté** setting and set the cooking time for 3 minutes. When the timer goes off, the salsa should be boiling. Press the **Cancel** button to turn off the pot and let stand for 2 minutes.

7   Transfer the salsa to an airtight container or containers and let cool to room temperature. Tightly cover the container(s) and refrigerate for up to 1 week or freeze for up to 3 months.

Notes: If your blender has a small capacity, you may have to blend the salsa in batches.

If you wish to process for longer storage, follow your preferred canning method. The salsa will keep, in a cool, dark place, for up to 1 year.

STEWED TOMATOES

PREP	0 MINUTES
COOK	40 MINUTES
PR	N/A
MAKES	6 CUPS

4 pounds Roma or
San Marzano tomatoes

5 cups water

2 tablespoons Italian
seasoning

¾ teaspoon citric acid

1   In a large saucepan over high heat, bring
2 quarts water to a boil.

2   While the water heats, use a paring knife to cut a
small X in the bottom of each tomato. Prepare an ice
bath and set it near the stove.

3   When the water reaches a boil, add half of the
tomatoes and blanch for about 1 minute, just until
the skins begin to split at the X. Using a slotted
spoon, transfer the tomatoes to the ice bath. Return
the water to a boil, then repeat with the remaining
tomatoes. Peel the skins off the tomatoes, using the
paring knife to scrape off any bits that are difficult to
remove. Cut the tomatoes lengthwise into quarters,
then cut out the cores and remove the seeds.

4   Add the tomatoes and the 5 cups water to the
Instant Pot and cover with the glass lid. Select the
high **Sauté** setting and bring the mixture to a boil;
this will take about 15 minutes. Uncover the pot and
boil for about 5 minutes more, to ensure that the
tomatoes have heated through. Press the **Cancel**
button to turn off the pot.

5   Wearing heat-resistant mitts, lift out the inner
pot. Add the Italian seasoning and citric acid to the
tomato mixture and stir to combine. Transfer to an
airtight container or containers and let cool to room
temperature. Tightly cover the container(s) and
refrigerate the stewed tomatoes for up to 1 week.

Note: If you wish to process for longer storage, follow
your preferred canning method. The stewed tomatoes
will keep, in a cool, dark place, for up to 1 year.

30-MINUTE CARAMELIZED ONIONS

PREP	0 MINUTES
COOK	30 MINUTES
PR	N/A
MAKES	ABOUT 2½ CUPS

4 tablespoons unsalted
butter or olive oil

2 pounds yellow onions,
halved and sliced ¼ inch
thick

1 teaspoon kosher salt

1   Select the high **Sauté** setting on the Instant
Pot (the timer will default to 30 minutes) and melt
the butter. Add the salt and onions and stir with a
wooden spoon, separating the onion layers and coating the slices with the butter. Cover the pot with the
glass lid and let the onions sweat, without stirring,
for 10 minutes.

2   Uncover the pot and, wearing a heat-resistant
mitt, hold the rim of the inner pot in place while
you stir the onions vigorously, using the spoon to
nudge loose any browned bits from the bottom of
the pot. Leave the pot uncovered and set a timer for
4 minutes. Stir the onions vigorously again, making
sure to nudge loose any browned bits. Set the timer
for 3 minutes, then stir the onions vigorously again
and continue to stir them at 2-minute intervals until
the 30-minute **Sauté** cooking program has ended.
Wearing heat-resistant mitts, lift out the inner pot.

3   The onions can be used right away, stored in an
airtight container in the refrigerator for up to 4 days,
or frozen for up to 3 months.

4   To freeze the onions, let cool to room temperature, then scoop ½-cup portions into the wells of a
silicone muffin pan and slip the pan into the freezer.
When the portions have frozen solid, about 4 hours,
pop them out of the muffin pan, put in ziplock plastic
freezer bags, and return to the freezer.

Note: The salt is important in this recipe, so don't omit
it! It helps the onions give up their liquid so they cook
down properly and caramelize.

GHEE

PREP	0 MINUTES
COOK	20 MINUTES
PR	N/A
MAKES	ABOUT 1½ CUPS

2 cups unsalted butter

1   Select the low **Sauté** setting on the Instant Pot and add the butter. Leave the butter to melt for 5 minutes, then give it a stir; it will be very foamy and almost fully melted. Cook the butter for about 5 minutes more; the foam will have settled down and broken up a bit. Stir once more, then cook for another 5 minutes.

2   After 15 minutes total, the simmering will have quieted down, as the water will have evaporated out of the butter. There will be a lacy/foamy layer on the surface, and you'll see a golden-brown layer of milk solids at the bottom of the pot. Stir once more, then press the **Cancel** button to turn off the pot. Wearing heat-resistant mitts, lift out the inner pot. Let the ghee cool and settle for about 5 minutes.

3   While the ghee is cooling, place a wire-mesh strainer over a bowl or 8-cup liquid measuring cup. Line the strainer with a triple layer of cheesecloth.

4   Pour the ghee through the prepared strainer, then pour into a storage container (I like to use a wide-mouthed 1-pint jar). Let cool to room temperature; the ghee will solidify.

5   Use the ghee right away, or store, covered tightly, in a cool, dark place for up to 3 months, or in the refrigerator for up to 1 year.

Note: The pot bottom will require a little scrubbing to remove the layer of caramelized milk solids. Barkeeper's Friend is my favorite nonabrasive cleaner for getting the pan shiny and spotless.

MANGO CHUTNEY

PREP	0 MINUTES
COOK	25 MINUTES
PR	N/A
MAKES	3 CUPS

1 cup firmly packed brown sugar

½ cup cider vinegar

2 medium mangoes, peeled, pitted, and cut into ¼-inch dice, or one 10-ounce bag frozen mango chunks, thawed and chopped

1 small orange, peeled and diced

2 medium limes, peeled and diced

1 small yellow onion, diced

1 large garlic clove, minced

Two 2-inch knobs fresh ginger, peeled and minced

⅓ cup golden raisins

¼ cup blackstrap molasses

2 teaspoons yellow mustard seeds

½ teaspoon red pepper flakes

½ teaspoon ground cinnamon

¼ teaspoon ground allspice

⅛ teaspoon ground cloves

1 tablespoon chopped fresh cilantro

1   Add the brown sugar, vinegar, mangoes, orange, limes, onion, garlic, ginger, raisins, molasses, mustard seeds, red pepper flakes, cinnamon, allspice, and cloves to the Instant Pot and stir to combine. Select the **Sauté** setting and cook, stirring often, for about 15 minutes, until the mixture starts to look glossy and is at a full rolling boil that can't be stirred down. Add the cilantro and continue to cook, stirring often, for about 10 minutes more, until the mango pieces turn translucent around the edges and the chutney is reduced by about 1 cup. Be careful of spattering.

2   Wearing heat-resistant mitts, lift out the inner pot. Transfer the chutney to an airtight container or containers and let cool to room temperature. Tightly cover the container(s) and refrigerate for 3 days, to allow the flavors to meld.

3   The chutney will keep, refrigerated, for up to 1 month.

Note: If you wish to process for longer storage, follow your preferred canning method. The chutney will keep, in a cool, dark place, for up to 1 year.

CRANBERRY CHUTNEY

PREP	10 MINUTES
COOK	15 MINUTES
PR	N/A
MAKES	1½ PINTS

1 large navel orange

1 pound fresh cranberries

½ cup water

1 cup sugar

1 tablespoon cider vinegar

2-inch knob fresh ginger, peeled and minced

½ teaspoon ground cinnamon

½ teaspoon freshly ground black pepper

¼ teaspoon kosher salt

¼ teaspoon ground cloves

1   Zest the orange in wide strips, leaving behind the white pith. Slice the zest strips lengthwise into thin strips and set aside. Remove the remaining white pith and chop up the orange into cranberry-size pieces and set aside.

2   Add the cranberries and water to the Instant Pot. Cover with the glass lid, select the **Sauté** setting, and cook for about 10 minutes, until the cranberries are popping and the liquid has begun to boil.

3   Uncover the pot and stir in the chopped orange, orange zest, sugar, vinegar, ginger, cinnamon, pepper, salt, and cloves. Bring to a boil, uncovered, stirring every minute or so, and cook for about 5 minutes, until thickened. Press the **Cancel** button to turn off the pot.

4   Wearing heat-resistant mitts, lift out the inner pot. Transfer the chutney to an airtight container or containers and let cool to room temperature. Tightly cover the container(s) and refrigerate.

5   The chutney will keep, refrigerated, for up to 1 week.

Note: If you wish to process for longer storage, follow your preferred canning method. The chutney will keep, in a cool, dark place, for up to 1 year.

STONE FRUIT JAM

PREP	0 MINUTES
COOK	25 MINUTES
PR	N/A
MAKES	1½ PINTS

1½ pounds assorted stone fruits (plums, nectarines, and/or apricots), pitted and chopped

2¼ cups sugar

¼ cup fresh Meyer lemon juice, or 2 tablespoons fresh lemon juice plus 2 tablespoons fresh orange juice

1   Combine the fruit, sugar, and lemon juice in the Instant Pot and stir to mix. Cover with the glass lid, select the **Sauté** setting, and cook for about 10 minutes, until the mixture begins to boil. Uncover the pot.

2   When the jam has reached a full boil, begin stirring constantly and continue to cook for about 12 minutes more, until it's thick enough to coat a spoon and registers 220°F on an instant-read thermometer. The jam will be glossy and less bubbly at this stage. Press the **Cancel** button to turn off the pot.

3   Wearing heat-resistant mitts, lift out the inner pot. Transfer the jam to an airtight container or containers and let cool to room temperature. Tightly cover the container(s) and refrigerate.

4   The jam will keep, refrigerated, for up to 1 month.

Note: If you wish to process for longer storage, follow your preferred canning method. The jam will keep, in a cool, dark place, for up to 1 year.

MIXED BERRY JAM

PREP	24 HOUR THAW
COOK	15 MINUTES
PR	N/A
MAKES	2 CUPS

1 pound fresh or frozen mixed berries (see Note)

2¼ cups sugar

¼ cup fresh lemon juice

1   In a medium bowl, toss together the berries and sugar. Cover and refrigerate for at least 12 hours or up to 24 hours. The berries will thaw (if frozen) and the sugar will soften them and draw out their juices.

2   Combine the berry mixture and lemon juice in the Instant Pot and cover with the glass lid. Select the **Sauté** setting and cook for 10 minutes. Remove the lid and boil, uncovered, for a few minutes more, stirring often, until slightly thickened. The timing will vary slightly depending on the type of berries used.

3   Wearing heat-resistant mitts, lift out the inner pot. Transfer the jam to an airtight container or containers and let cool to room temperature. Tightly cover the container(s) and refrigerate.

4   The jam will keep, refrigerated, for up to 1 month.

Notes: If using strawberries, be sure to hull and quarter them.

If you wish to process for longer storage, follow your preferred canning method. The jam will keep, in a cool, dark place, for up to 1 year.

HOT PEPPER JELLY

PREP	0 MINUTES
COOK	20 MINUTES
PR	N/A
MAKES	4 CUPS

2 large green bell peppers, seeded and diced

2 large jalapeño chiles, seeded and diced

⅔ cup apple cider vinegar (5% acidity)

3 tablespoons classic pectin (I prefer Ball brand)

3 cups sugar

1   Combine the bell peppers, jalapeños, and vinegar in the Instant Pot. Sprinkle in the pectin and stir to mix. Select the high **Sauté** setting and cook for about 10 minutes, until boiling, then cook for 1 minute. Add the sugar and stir to combine. Cook, stirring continuously, for about 6 minutes more, until the mixture has come up to a full boil, then cook for 1 minute.

2   Wearing heat-resistant mitts, lift out the inner pot. Transfer the jelly to an airtight container or containers and let cool to room temperature. Tightly cover the container(s) and refrigerate.

3   The jelly will keep, refrigerated, for up to 1 month.

Notes: As pepper jellies go, this one is pretty mild. If you want some extra kick, substitute about 4 ounces of hotter chiles (such as serranos) for the jalapeños. You may also leave the seeds in for even more heat.

If the peppers rise to the top of the jelly, don't worry. After letting the jam cool for 12 to 24 hours, give the jars a vigorous shake to distribute the peppers throughout the jelly.

If you wish to process for longer storage, follow your preferred canning method. The jelly will keep, in a cool, dark place, for up to 1 year.

BASQUE RED WINE JELLY

PREP	0 MINUTES
COOK	35 MINUTES
PR	N/A
MAKES	1 PINT

2 cups dry red wine (preferably Tempranillo, Syrah, or Zinfandel), at room temperature

1 teaspoon red pepper flakes or piment d'espelette (see Notes)

1¾ cups sugar

2 tablespoons classic pectin (I prefer Ball brand)

1   Combine the wine and red pepper flakes in the Instant Pot and cover with the glass lid. Select the **Sauté** setting and set the cooking time for 8 minutes. The wine will come to a boil after about 3 minutes. When the timer goes off, let stand covered for 10 minutes to allow the pepper to infuse the wine.

2   Place a wire-mesh strainer over a bowl or 2-cup (or larger) liquid measuring cup.

3   Wearing heat-resistant mitts, lift out the inner pot and pour the wine into the strainer. Return the inner pot to the housing, then pour the wine back into the inner pot. Stir in the sugar and pectin, then select the **Sauté** setting. Bring the mixture to a boil (this will take about 6 minutes), stirring every minute or so. Once the jelly is boiling, stir constantly for about 8 minutes more, until it's thick enough to coat a spoon and registers 220°F on an instant-read thermometer. It will be glossy and less bubbly at this stage. Press the **Cancel** button to turn off the pot.

4   Wearing heat-resistant mitts, lift out the inner pot. Transfer the jelly to an airtight container or containers and let cool to room temperature. Tightly cover the container(s) and refrigerate.

5   The jelly will keep, refrigerated, for up to 1 month.

Notes: If you wish to process for longer storage, follow your preferred canning method. The jelly will keep, in a cool, dark place, for up to 6 months.

This is a great use for leftover wine that would otherwise go to waste! The jelly is delicious spread on crackers and served with any strongly flavored cheese, such as P'tit Basque.

If you use *piment d'espelette* pepper flakes in classic Basque fashion, the jelly will be fairly mild; but if your red pepper flakes are very potent, it can really pack some heat. To tame its spiciness, you can use half the amount of pepper flakes, or if you like things really spicy, use the full amount and let the pepper flakes steep in the wine for an hour or two before adding the sugar and pectin.

DILL PICKLE SPEARS

PREP	24-HOUR SOAK
COOK	15 MINUTES
PR	N/A
MAKES	4 PINTS

2 quarts water

5 tablespoons pickling and preserving salt (I prefer Ball brand)

2 pounds pickling cucumbers, washed

Pickling Brine

2⅔ cups water

2 cups distilled white vinegar (5% acidity)

1 tablespoon sugar

2 tablespoons pickling salt (I prefer Ball brand)

2 teaspoons pickling spice

2 teaspoons dill seeds

8 fresh dill sprigs

½ teaspoon Pickle Crisp granules (optional; see Note)

1   In a large bowl, combine the 2 quarts water and pickling salt. Trim off the ends of the cucumbers so they are about 5 inches long, then cut each cucumber lengthwise into quarters. Add the cucumbers to the bowl and let stand at room temperature for 24 hours.

CONTINUED

DILL PICKLE SPEARS CONTINUED

2   To make the pickling brine: In the Instant Pot, stir together the 2⅔ cups water, vinegar, sugar, pickling salt, and pickling spice. Select the high **Sauté** setting and set the cooking time for 12 minutes. When the timer goes off, the brine should be boiling.

3   In an airtight storage container, combine dill seeds and dill sprigs, or divide ingredients equally among four 1-pint prepared canning jars. Drain the cucumbers in a colander, then pack them into container(s). Add Pickle Crisp granules, dividing equally among containers.

4   Wearing heat-resistant mitts, lift out the inner pot. Using a jam funnel and ladle, fill the container(s) with the hot brine, covering the cucumbers but leaving ½ inch of headspace if using canning jars. Lightly tap the container against the counter and rotate it gently between your hands to remove any air bubbles. Discard any extra brine. Wait 1 week before serving.

5   The pickles will keep, refrigerated, for up to 1 month.

Notes: Pickle Crisp is the Ball-branded version of calcium chloride. The white granules are added to pickling recipes to help ensure that the vegetables stay firm, even when processed in a hot water–bath canner.

If you wish to process for longer storage, follow your preferred canning method and wait at least 1 week before serving. The pickles will keep, in a cool, dark place, for up to 1 year.

BREAD-AND-BUTTER PICKLE CHIPS

PREP	5 MINUTES
COOK	10 MINUTES
PR	N/A
MAKES	2 PINTS

1 pound Kirby or Persian cucumbers, thinly sliced

½ large or 1 small yellow onion, thinly sliced

1½ tablespoons kosher salt

1 cup distilled white vinegar (5% acidity)

1 cup apple cider vinegar (5% acidity)

1 cup sugar

2 tablespoons pickling spice

1   In a medium bowl, combine the cucumbers and onion. Add the salt and toss to coat the vegetables evenly. Let stand for 5 minutes.

2   In the Instant Pot, stir together the white vinegar, cider vinegar, sugar, and pickling spice and cover with the glass lid. Select the **Sauté** setting and set the cooking time for 8 minutes.

3   In an airtight storage container or two 1-pint prepared canning jars, pack the cucumber-onion mixture, discarding any excess liquid left in the bowl.

4   When the timer goes off, stir the brine. Wearing heat-resistant mitts, lift out the inner pot. Using a jam funnel and ladle, fill the container(s) with the brine, leaving ½ inch of headspace if using canning jars. Discard any extra brine. Wait 24 hours before serving.

5   The pickles will keep, refrigerated, for up to 1 month.

Note: If you wish to process for longer storage, follow your preferred canning method and wait at least 24 hours before serving. The pickles will keep, in a cool, dark place, for up to 1 year.

PICKLED RED ONIONS

PREP	0 MINUTES
COOK	15 MINUTES
PR	N/A
MAKES	2 PINTS

3 cups distilled white vinegar (5% acidity)

1½ cups sugar

1 cinnamon stick, broken in half

4 whole cloves

6 allspice berries

½ teaspoon yellow mustard seeds

½ teaspoon black peppercorns

¼ teaspoon red pepper flakes

1 pound red onions, sliced into ¼-inch-thick rings

1   In the Instant Pot, stir together the vinegar, sugar, cinnamon, cloves, allspice, mustard seeds, peppercorns, and red pepper flakes. Cover with the glass lid and select the medium **Sauté** setting. Cook for about 10 minutes, until the mixture reaches a bare simmer. Stir in the onions, re-cover, and cook for about 2 minutes more, until the onions have softened a little bit. Press the **Cancel** button to turn off the pot.

2   Wearing heat-resistant mitts, lift out the inner pot. Using a slotted spoon, transfer the onions to an airtight storage container or two 1-pint containers, dividing them evenly. Using a jar funnel and ladle, fill the jars with the pickling liquid, leaving ½ inch of headspace if using canning jars. Gently tap the container(s) on the counter to remove any air bubbles. Wait 24 hours before serving.

3   The onions will keep, refrigerated, for up to 1 month.

Notes: You can substitute 2 teaspoons store-bought pickling spice for all of the spices used in this recipe.

If you wish to process for longer storage, follow your preferred canning method and wait at least 24 hours before serving. The pickles will keep, in a cool, dark place, for up to 1 year.

PICKLED JALAPEÑOS AND CARROTS (ESCABECHE)

PREP	5 MINUTES
COOK	15 MINUTES
PR	N/A
MAKES	2 PINTS

4 sprigs cilantro, trimmed to 4-inch lengths

½ teaspoon black peppercorns

2 bay leaves

1 tablespoon olive oil

2 garlic cloves, minced

1 pound carrots, peeled and sliced into ⅛-inch-thick rounds

½ medium white onion, sliced ⅛ inch thick

2 jalapeño chiles, sliced into thin rounds (see Notes)

1 cup cider vinegar

1 cup water

1 teaspoon kosher salt

1   In an airtight storage container, combine cilantro, peppercorns, and bay leaves, or divide ingredients equally among two 1-pint prepared canning jars.

2   Select the **Sauté** setting on the Instant Pot and heat the olive oil and garlic for 2 minutes, until the garlic is bubbling but not browned. Add the carrots, onion, and jalapeños and sauté for about 5 minutes, until the onion is slightly softened.

3   Wearing heat-resistant mitts, lift out the inner pot. Spoon the vegetables into the storage container, or divide them evenly into the same-sized containers. It's fine if some bits of garlic and vegetable remain in the pot.

4   Return the inner pot to the housing. Add the vinegar, water, and salt; stir to combine; and bring to a simmer; this will take about 5 minutes. Press the **Cancel** button to turn off the pot.

5   Ladle the vinegar mixture into the storage container or containers to cover the vegetables. You may not use all of the vinegar mixture; discard the remainder. Let cool to room temperature. Tightly cover the container(s) and refrigerate.

6 The pickles will keep, refrigerated, for up to 1 month.

Notes: If you wish to process for longer storage, follow your preferred canning method. The pickles will keep, in a cool, dark place, for up to 1 year.

If you like spicy pickles, leave the seeds in the jalapeño rounds. If you prefer milder pickles, remove the seeds.

PICKLED BEETS

PREP	0 MINUTES
COOK	35 MINUTES
PR	QPR
MAKES	3 PINTS

2 pounds beets, each about 3 inches in diameter (see Notes)

1¼ cups apple cider vinegar (5% acidity)

½ cup plus 2 tablespoons sugar

1 teaspoon pickling salt (I prefer Ball brand)

½ teaspoon black peppercorns

2 bay leaves

1 small red or yellow onion, sliced ⅛ inch thick

1 Pour 1 cup water into the Instant Pot and place the wire metal steam rack in the pot. Arrange the beets in a single layer on the steam rack.

2 Secure the lid and set the Pressure Release to **Sealing**. Select the **Steam** setting and set the cooking time for 15 minutes at high pressure. (The pot will take about 15 minutes to come up to pressure before the cooking program begins.)

3 Fill a bowl with cold water.

4 When the cooking program ends, perform a quick pressure release by moving the Pressure Release to **Venting**. Open the pot and, using tongs, transfer the beets to the bowl of water and let cool for 5 minutes. Using your fingers and a paring knife, remove the skins from the beets—they should peel off very easily. Trim and discard the ends of the beets, then slice each one into ¼-inch wedges.

5 Wearing heat-resistant mitts, lift out the inner pot from the Instant Pot housing and discard the water. Return the pot to the housing.

6 In the Instant Pot, stir together ½ cup plus 2 tablespoons water, the vinegar, sugar, pickling salt, peppercorns, and bay leaves. Press the **Cancel** button to reset the cooking program, then select the **Sauté** setting. Bring the liquid to a simmer, then stir in the beets and onions. Cook for about 5 minutes, until the beets are tender and onions are softened. Press the **Cancel** button to turn off the Instant Pot.

7 Wearing heat-resistant mitts, lift out the inner pot. Using a slotted spoon, transfer the beets and onions to an airtight storage container or three 1-pint prepared canning jars, dividing them evenly. Using a jar funnel and ladle, fill the jars with the pickling liquid, leaving ½ inch of headspace if using canning jars. Gently tap the container(s) on the counter to remove any air bubbles. Wait 2 days before serving.

8 The beets will keep, refrigerated, for up to 1 month.

Notes: If using larger beets, about 3½ inches in diameter, increase the cooking time to 20 minutes.

If you wish to process for longer storage, follow your preferred canning method and wait at least 2 days before serving. The pickles will keep, in a cool, dark place, for up to 1 year.

DILLY BEANS

PREP	10 MINUTES
COOK	10 MINUTES
PR	N/A
MAKES	3 PINTS

1 ½ pounds fresh green beans, rinsed

2 ½ cups distilled white vinegar (5% acidity)

1 cup water

3 tablespoons plus 1 teaspoon kosher salt

1 ½ teaspoons dill seeds

¾ teaspoon red pepper flakes

6 fresh dill sprigs

3 garlic cloves, peeled

1   Trim the stem ends of the green beans, cutting them so that they're 4 inches long.

2   Add the vinegar, water, and salt to the Instant Pot and stir to combine into a brine. Select the high **Sauté** setting and set the cooking time for 10 minutes. When the timer goes off, the brine should be boiling.

3   In an airtight storage container, combine the dill seeds, red pepper flakes, dill sprigs, and garlic cloves, or divide ingredients equally among three ½-pint prepared canning jars. Tightly pack the green beans into the container(s), dividing them evenly. If using canning jars, place the green beans vertically.

4   Ladle the hot pickling brine into the container(s). You may not use all of the brine; discard the remainder. Let cool to room temperature. Tightly cover the container(s) and refrigerate at least 2 days before serving the beans.

5   The beans will keep, refrigerated, for up to 1 month.

Note: If you wish to process for longer storage, follow your preferred canning method and wait at least 2 days before serving. The beans will keep, in a cool, dark place, for up to 1 year.

APPLESAUCE

PREP	0 MINUTES
COOK	20 MINUTES
PR	20 MINUTES
MAKES	ABOUT 6 CUPS

4 pounds apples, peeled, cored, and sliced into wedges

½ cup water

⅓ cup raisins

½ teaspoon ground cinnamon

1   Combine the apples, water, raisins, and cinnamon in the Instant Pot.

2   Secure the lid and set the Pressure Release to **Sealing**. Select the **Steam** setting and set the cooking time for 3 minutes at high pressure. (The pot will take about 20 minutes to come up to pressure before the cooking program begins.)

3   When the cooking program ends, let the pressure release naturally; this will take about 20 minutes. Open the pot and, wearing heat-resistant mitts, lift out the inner pot. For chunky applesauce, use a potato masher to break up the apples. For a smooth puree, use an immersion blender to blend until smooth.

4   Serve immediately, or let cool, transfer to an airtight container, and refrigerate for up to 1 week.

Notes: Applesauce freezes well, so you don't have to worry about using up the whole batch at once. Freeze 2-cup portions in 1-quart ziplock plastic freezer bags for up to 6 months. The bags stack nice and flat and take up hardly any space in the freezer.

If you like, omit the raisins and add a handful of chopped dried apples instead. The dried fruit absorbs the extra water needed for pressure cooking in the Instant Pot, so you don't end up with watery applesauce.

Using Frozen Meat

1. Thinner cuts of meat cook more evenly.

Chicken thighs or small to average-size breasts (both boneless and bone-in cuts), thin-cut pork chops, flank or skirt steak, and small fish fillets work well. Larger frozen cuts such as pot roasts, whole chickens, and pork shoulder roasts won't cook as evenly.

2. Break down larger cuts of meat and freeze them in smaller pieces in advance.

When you buy a large piece of meat, cut it into 1-inch or smaller pieces, spread them out on a baking sheet, and pop the sheet in the freezer for a couple of hours. When the meat is frozen solid, transfer the pieces to a ziplock plastic freezer bag and store for up to 6 months. It will be great for a stew or chili.

3. Freeze ground meat in a thin layer.

Transfer 1 pound of ground meat to a quart or gallon-size ziplock plastic freezer bag, then use your hands or a rolling pin to flatten it into an even layer. Seal the bag, then freeze for up to 4 months. When you are ready to use the meat, it is easy to break it up into smaller pieces. The thin pieces will thaw relatively quickly when browned.

4. Simmer, don't braise or steam.

Frozen meats cook most evenly when completely submerged in liquid. You'll have the most success with soups, stews, chilis, and chowders—recipes in which the solid ingredients are completely submerged in liquid (usually water, broth, or stock). Liquid conducts heat more efficiently than steam, so frozen meat has a better chance of cooking all the way to the center if it is completely covered.

5. Allow extra time for the pressure to build, and a little more time to cook the meat.

Frozen ingredients will lower the temperature in the pressure cooker, so it'll take a bit longer for the liquid to boil and build up pressure in the pot. As a general rule, for thin cuts of frozen meat and frozen ground meat broken into small pieces, add about 5 minutes to the cooking time indicated in the recipe.

Using Tomato Products and Dairy

Most recipes can be easily adapted to cook under pressure in the Instant Pot, but these two types of ingredients require a little bit of extra consideration and care.

TOMATO PRODUCTS

Tomato sauce is said to be a "plastic liquid," high in viscosity and with a structure that lends itself to a sputtering, spattering behavior when heated. In the pressure cooker, this makes it difficult for steam to build and bring the pot up to pressure before the contents scorch on the bottom. To avoid this problem, when you're cooking tomato products in the Instant Pot, make sure you add enough liquid. The more viscous or concentrated the tomato product, the more water is needed. Just 1 tablespoon of tomato paste requires about ¾ cup of water (a 1:12 ratio); canned tomato sauce requires about a 1:1 ratio of tomato product to water; and canned diced tomatoes with their liquid require about a 2:1 ratio of tomato product to water.

Adding tomato paste as the last ingredient and not stirring it in also helps prevent plastic liquid from forming in the pot.

DAIRY PRODUCTS

Recipes that contain lots of cheese, cream, or other dairy ingredients generally don't work in a pressure cooker because dairy, as well as coconut milk, tends to scorch or curdle when cooked under pressure. Pot-in-pot dishes like cheesecake are the exception, since the dairy never comes in contact with the surface of the pot.

The trick to making rich, creamy dishes in the Instant Pot is to stir in the dairy or coconut milk after the food is pressure cooked, like in Creamed Corn (page 241), Creamed Spinach (page 240), and Thai curries (pages 124 and 208).

Cooking Charts

Refer to these charts* to determine the cooking times for lots of foods. When converting receipes for the Instant Pot, use the longest-cooking ingredient to determine the cooking time.

Meat	Cooking Time (in minutes)	Pressure Release
Beef, stew meat	25–30	natural
Beef, meatball	15–20	natural
Beef, pot roast, steak, rump, round, chuck, blade, or brisket, large	35–40	natural
Beef, pot roast, rump, round, chuck, or brisket, small chunks	25–30	natural
Beef, pot roast, rump, round, chuck, or brisket, whole, up to 4 pounds	50–55	natural
Beef, short ribs	30–35	natural
Beef, shanks (crosscut)	30–35	natural
Beef, oxtail	50–55	natural
Chicken, breasts, with bones	10–15	quick
Chicken, breasts, boneless, skinless	8	quick
Chicken, drumsticks, legs, or thighs, with bones	15	quick
Chicken, thighs, boneless	10	quick
Chicken, whole	20–25	quick
Chicken, whole, cut up with bones	10–15	quick
Ham slice	9–12	quick
Lamb, stew meat	20–25	natural
Pork, loin roast	45–50	natural
Pork, butt roast	45–50	natural
Pork, ribs	20–25	natural
Turkey, breast, boneless	15–20	quick
Turkey, breast, whole, with bones	25–30	quick
Turkey, drumsticks (leg)	15–20	quick

Rice and Other Grains	Water Quantity (Rice/Grain: Water Ratio)	Cooking Time (in minutes)
Barley, pearl	1:1½–2	25–30
Barley, pot	1:3–4	25–30
Congee, thick	1:4–5	15–20
Congee, thin	1:6–7	15–20
Couscous (not quick-cooking)	1:2	5–8
Millet	1:1⅔	10–12
Oats, quick cooking	1:1⅔	6
Oats, steel-cut	1:3	10–12
Polenta, coarse	1:4	10–15
Polenta, quick cooking	1:4	5–8
Porridge, thin	1:6–7	15–20
Quinoa	1:1–1¼	8
Rice, basmati	1: 1–1¼	4–8
Rice, brown	1: 1–1¼	20–25
Rice, jasmine	1: 1–1¼	4–10
Rice, white	1: 1–1½	8
Rice, wild	1:1⅓–1½	25–30
Whole-grain wheat berries, spelt, farro, or kamut	1:1½–2	25–30

Beans	Soaked, Cooking Time (in minutes)	Unsoaked, Cooking Time (in minutes)
Black	10–15	20–25
Black-eyed pea	10–15	20–25
Cannellini	20–25	35–40
Chickpea (garbanzo)	20–25	35–40
Corona, giant lima, gigantes	20–25	25–30
Flageolet	10–15	20–25
Great Northern	20–25	25–30
Kidney	20–25	25–30
Lima	10–15	20–25
Navy	20–25	25–30
Pinquito	10–15	20–25
Pinto	20–25	25–30
Red	10–15	20–25

*Charts adapted from information provided by Instant Pot.

Lentils	Soaked, Cooking Time (in minutes)	Unsoaked, Cooking Time (in minutes)
Beluga (black)	n/a	15–20
Green	n/a	15–20
Puy (French)	n/a	15–20
Red (split)	n/a	15–18
Small brown (Spanish)	n/a	15–20
Yellow (split)	n/a	15–18

Vegetables	Fresh, Cooking Time (in minutes)	Frozen, Cooking Time (in minutes)
Artichokes, whole, trimmed without leaves	9–11	11–13
Artichokes, hearts	4–5	5–6
Asparagus, whole or cut	1–2	2–3
Beets, small, whole	11–13	13–15
Beets, large, whole	20–25	25–30
Broccoli, florets	2–3	3–4
Broccoli, stalks	3–4	4–5
Brussels sprouts, whole	3–4	4–5
Cabbage, red, purple, or green, shredded	2–3	3–4
Cabbage, red, purple or green, wedges	3–4	4–5
Carrots, sliced or shredded	1–2	2–3
Carrots, whole or chunks	2–3	3–4
Cauliflower florets	2–3	3–4
Celery, chunks	2–3	3–4
Corn, kernels	1–2	2–3
Corn, on the cob	3–4	4–5
Eggplant, slices or chunks	2–3	3–4
Endives, whole	1–2	2–3
Escarole, chopped	1–2	2–3
Green beans, whole	3–5	5–7
Greens (beet greens, collards, kale, spinach, Swiss chard, turnip greens), chopped	3–6	4–7
Leeks, chopped	2–4	3–5
Mixed vegetables, chopped (frozen blend)	2–3	3–4

Vegetables	Fresh, Cooking Time (in minutes)	Frozen, Cooking Time (in minutes)
Okra, sliced	2–3	3–4
Onions, sliced	2–3	3–4
Parsnips, sliced	1–2	2–3
Parsnips, chunks	2–4	4–6
Peas, sugar snap or snow, whole	1–2	2–3
Peas, green (English), shelled	1–2	2–3
Potatoes, in cubes	3–5	7–9
Potatoes, whole, baby	10–12	12–14
Potatoes, whole, large	12–15	15–19
Pumpkin, small slices or chunks	4–5	6–7
Pumpkin, large slices or chunks	8–10	10–14
Rutabagas, slices	3–5	4–6
Rutabagas, chunks	4–6	6–8
Spinach	1–2	3–4
Squash, acorn, slices or chunks	6–7	8–9
Squash, butternut, slices or chunks	8–10	10–12
Sweet peppers, slices or chunks	1–3	2–4
Sweet potatoes, cubed	3–5	5–7
Sweet potatoes, whole, small	10–12	12–14
Sweet potatoes, whole, large	12–15	15–19
Tomatoes, quartered	2–3	4–5
Tomatoes, whole	3–5	5–7
Turnips, chunks	2–4	4–6
Yams, cubed	3–5	5–7
Yams, whole, small	10–12	12–14
Yams, whole, large	12–15	15–19
Zucchini, slices or chunks	2–3	3–4

Acknowledgments

The Ultimate Instant Pot Cookbook is here! I can hardly believe it. I am so proud of this beautiful book, and I owe my thanks to many people for helping to make it happen.

To my fans and followers on the Instant Pot Recipes Facebook page, the contents of this cookbook is a reflection of the requests and questions I receive from you every day. I hope it has every recipe you need to feed your families and loved ones.

To my agent, Alison Fargis, and the rest of the team at Stonesong, thank you for your continued support and encouragement in my cookbook writing career.

To the team at Ten Speed Press, thank you for going full Instant Pot and making this book with me! Thanks to senior editor Lisa Westmoreland; director of marketing Windy Dorrestyn and publicity director Kristin Casemore; project editor Kate Bolen; art director Kara Plikaitis; production manager Jane Chinn; food stylist Robyn Valarik and assistant food stylist Kristene Loayza; prop stylist Claire Mack; and photographer Jennifer Davick and assistant Ben Manning.

To Robert Wang, Anna Di Meglio, and the rest of the team at Instant Pot, thank you for working with me and Ten Speed Press to make not just one officially authorized book, but many! Your appliances have started a home cooking revolution, and I'm happy to help spread the Instant Pot love far and wide.

To my fellow food-writing friends, thank you for your support, encouragement, and friendship. Special thanks to Emma Christensen, my friend and editor at *Simply Recipes*, for accommodating my schedule while I wrote this book, and for starting our online community of food pros. To Michelle Tam of *Nom Nom Paleo*, thanks for getting me hooked on the Instant Pot in the first place. To Andrea Nguyen, Diana Pray, and Chris Hamje for lending your delicious pho, Cincinnati chili, and Texas chili recipes to this California girl's cookbook. To Deb Perelman of *Smitten Kitchen*, Heidi Swanson of *101 Cookbooks*, and Narsai David, thank you for saying such nice things about *The Essential Instant Pot Cookbook*—I am beyond chuffed to be in your orbit.

Thanks also to my Cookbook Club ladies, Nancy Tariga, Jenny Hong, and Tania Petryszyn, for managing monthly meet-ups during this busy, busy time. I feel lucky to have met you all and formed fast friendships in our thirties—which is not easily or often done. And to my longtime friend Lizzie Paulsen, thanks for keeping me company while I cooked recipe after recipe.

To everyone on staff at Congregation Beth Am, thank you for your endless Instant Pot enthusiasm. I love how every conversation we have when I'm in the office seems to end up around food and cooking. Special thanks to Mike Mason for inviting me to chat about all things IP on your podcast, *Good Stuff Kids*. To the clergy, and to my b'nei mitzvah tutoring students and their families, I hope you don't mind the *treif*! Feel free to substitute beef or lamb in the ragu pictured on the cover of this book, and to leave off the cheese if you're so inclined.

To my mom, Cindy Harris, thanks for keeping me company, washing dishes, and helping out with countless loads of laundry. To my dad, Larry Harris, thank you for buying groceries, weighing in with your opinions on my finished dishes, and cross-testing recipes in your own Instant Pot. To my Grandma Rachel, thank you for passing on your love of gourmet cooking and entertaining. I always want to make you proud. To my brother Dave, thanks for your effusive encouragement and support.

And of course, thanks and lots of love to my husband and fellow beagle parent, Brendan. I hope you feel supported by me even half as much as I do by you.

Aaron Blumenshine

About the Author

Coco Morante is the author of the best-selling *The Essential Instant Pot Cookbook.* She is a recipe developer, facilitator of the Instant Pot Recipes Facebook page, and creator of the blog *Lefty Spoon.* Her recipes and writing are featured in numerous print and online publications, including Epicurious, Popsugar, Food Republic, TASTE, The Kitchn, Simply Recipes, and *Edible Silicon Valley.*

Coco lives on the West Coast with her husband, Brendan, and their beagle, Beagle Brendan.

Index

Published in the United States by Ten Speed Press, an imprint of the Crown
Publishing Group, a division of Penguin Random House LLC, New York.
www.crownpublishing.com
www.tenspeed.com

Ten Speed Press and the Ten Speed Press colophon are registered trademarks
of Penguin Random House LLC.

The recipe for Beef Pho from *The Pho Cookbook* by Andrea Nguyen on
page 76 is used with permission.

Library of Congress Cataloging-in-Publication Data
    Names: Morante, Coco, author.
    Title: The ultimate Instant Pot cookbook : 200 deliciously simple recipes for
        your electric pressure cooker / Coco Morante.
    Description: First edition. | California : Ten Speed Press, [2018] | Includes
        index.
    Identifiers: LCCN 2018016623
    Subjects: LCSH: Pressure cooking. | LCGFT: Cookbooks.
    Classification: LCC TX840.P7 M673 2018 | DDC 641.5/87--dc23
    LC record available at https://lccn.loc.gov/2018016623

Hardcover ISBN: 978-0-399-58205-9
eBook ISBN: 978-0-399-58206-6

Printed in China

Design by Kara Plikaitis
Food Styling by Robyn Valarik
Food Styling Assistance by Kristene Loayza
Prop Styling by Claire Mack

10 9 8 7 6 5 4 3 2 1

First Edition